LIVING ARCHAEOLOGY

*Dedicated to those anonymous
ancient people who provided the
material for my life's work*

LIVING ARCHAEOLOGY

Philip Rahtz

TEMPUS

First published 2001

PUBLISHED IN THE UNITED KINGDOM BY:

Tempus Publishing Ltd
The Mill, Brimscombe Port
Stroud, Gloucestershire GL5 2QG

PUBLISHED IN THE UNITED STATES OF AMERICA BY:

Arcadia Publishing Inc.
A division of Tempus Publishing Inc.
2 Cumberland Street
Charleston, SC 29401
1-888-313-2665

Tempus books are available in France, Germany and Belgium
from the following addresses:

Tempus Publishing Group	Tempus Publishing Group	Tempus Publishing Group
21 Avenue de la République	Gustav-Adolf-Straße 3	Place de L'Alma 4/5
37300 Joué-lès-Tours	99084 Erfurt	1200 Brussels
FRANCE	GERMANY	BELGIUM

British Library Cataloguing in Publication Data.
A catalogue record for this book is available from the British Library.

ISBN 0 7524 1925 0

Typesetting and origination by Tempus Publishing.
PRINTED AND BOUND IN GREAT BRITAIN

Contents

Foreword

Philip Rahtz has had a remarkable career. From an unlikely start and a variety of potential careers — school teacher, accountant, photographer — he has emerged as one of the foremost archaeologists in Britain today. Like so many of us who have become involved in the subject, his career development was somewhat unconventional. He did not attend university and so does not have a first degree. He began digging as an 'amateur' with no formal training. He was appointed to lecture at Birmingham University still without a degree and in a *history* department. His MA degree for research at Cheddar came a little later.

And yet his contribution so far (he is still working at 80) has been enormous, not only in terms of digging skills and contributions to knowledge of all periods and sites, but particularly to aspects of the so-called 'Dark Age' period. Archaeology in Britain has always been nurtured by enthusiasm and commitment and not by formal structuring and clear career paths. Philip is a prime example of this. It has always been to the advantage of the subject in Britain and those of us involved in archaeology here should realise that we lose this informality at our peril. If Philip was just setting out on his career in 2000 could he be expected to achieve as much as is documented here in his autobiography? I doubt it.

I first met Philip when I went to Birmingham University in 1964, not long after he had arrived there as the highly innovative lecturer in archaeology in the history department.

I began to go on excavations in the surrounding counties, organized by Philip at weekends. We worked at Warwick, Thetford, Hatton, Badby and elsewhere. We met at Philip's rented University house and were then transported to a site in his camper van, always accompanied by Radio 3.

One wet day at Warwick, Philip said I should get into archaeology, providing that timely prod that the undergraduate usually needs to get them started in a career. He provided references for jobs and was always encouraging and supportive. (When his *Festschrift* was put together, it emerged that many others had received the same encouragement from Philip.) I have worked a lot with Philip since — at Bordesley Abbey, at Deerhurst, and recently when filming in Somerset. We also share an interest in early monasteries with his recent work at Kirkdale.

Philip is a giant in British archaeology. He has been digging now for over fifty years. His work on such classic sites as Cheddar and Glastonbury changed our perceptions of the Dark Ages. The range of sites he has excavated in this country covers almost every period and type of monument — before his work at Bordesley Abbey, Philip told me that a medieval monastery was really the only type of site he had not dug. His contribution in the South West alone at Chew Valley, Cannington, Henley Wood, Beckery, Glastonbury

Tor and the Cheddar Palaces is colossal. We would know so little without these massive projects which are *all* now published and the information available to other scholars.

But Philip is much more than an excellent archaeologist and excavator. He is a superb and humorous lecturer and teacher, employing innovative ideas and themes and bringing out the best in his students. This was shown in his appointment at Birmingham and his creation of the archaeology department at York University where he was made the first professor, an appoinment which met with universal acclaim.

Well-read and thought-provoking, Philip is always good company, with the conversations ranging from science fiction through archaeology to determinism. He once said to me that everyone should write an autobiography by the age of forty and then revise it every ten years. Here is the proof of the wisdom of that approach. I'm sure, like me, you will thoroughly enjoy reading of Philip's progress through life *Living Archaeology*.

Mick Aston

List of illustrations

(see **bold** numbers in text)

The illustrations are derived from the PAR archive, except where those with other attribution (in brackets). I thank those friends who lent some photographs, and Mick Aston who made useful addenda to the captions. The illustrations include only some of the archaeological excavations or finds referred to in the text. Such will be found mainly in the site reports cited in the numbered bibliography.

Back cover: 'Antiquities of Great Britain'. This was the cover of a notebook I made in 1947; it illustrates, with its sun setting through a trilithon, and its consciously archaistic border of arrowheads, my romantic approach to archaeology in my early days

List of appendices

A   Letter to David

B   Imperator Sexualis

C   How likely is likely? *and* How to get an excavation finished

D   IFA lecture

E   Two quotations about PAR written for his *Festschrift* (Carver ed. 1993)

Preface

My autobiography is essentially an archaeological one, not a personal one. I have nevertheless included those aspects of my personal life that are relevant to my life and archaeological career; my friends (and others) will enjoy reading between the lines, and adding names where I have been discreet. Enough people have suffered from my participation in archaeology, without adding to this harm in print!

In remembering and thanking the people who have helped me over the last 80 years, I have not listed them in order of importance or in themes, but chronologically. Thus we begin with what amounts to a potted autobiography, chronicling my life by the successive influences of those who have shaped it. They also include, in some cases, those who know a lot about me that I don't, and can after my death add their own biographical detail, and perhaps contradict what I have written, where my memory is faulty or self-coloured.

This is not my first attempt at autobiography. Some aspects were covered in *Rescue Archaeology* (61); further expositions were in *Invitation to Archaeology* (107, 150) and in my Presidential Address to the Somerset Archaeological Society (89). There is inevitably repetition between these and the present book (in some cases deliberately), but even so, the passage of years colours one's memories and stances. I have written substantially all that I can remember; I have always maintained that, archivally speaking, one should write an autobiography at 40, and then reconsider it at 50, 60 and 70, not destroying the earlier versions, but constructing a new edition out of their ruins. This will be my final version: since I am approaching 80, I am over the limit, as may be clear from this book.

The numbers in brackets refer to my publications listed numerically in the bibliography at the end of this book. These will provide fuller detail on any particular excavation, place or theme.

Acknowledgements

Homo Sapiens to the early twenty-first century, ancestry and genetic influences.

Parents, Frederick and Ethel Rahtz
Ernest Greenfield
Wendy, Genny, Nicky, Diana, David and Sebastian Rahtz
Eric Brown
Dina Dobson-Hinton
Rex Hull
Bryan Hugh St J. O'Neil
John Hurst
Leo Biek
Graham Webster
Rodney Hilton
Margaret Gray
Philip Barker
Richard Tomlinson
Peter Shinnie
Susan Hirst
Rosemary Cramp
Peter Fowler
Harold Taylor
Lawrence Butler
Mick Aston
Andrew (Bone) Jones
Priscilla Roxburgh
Martin Carver
Lorna and Matthew Rahtz
All the diggers and students

This list of people provides some chronological framework to my life in archaeology; for their forebearance, help and encouragement I owe them a debt of gratitude. In many cases their names will appear again in later parts of the book, in a different or fuller context.

Like everyone else I have a long genetic debt to the numerous generations since *Homo Sapiens* can be defined as such, a point or zone in time which is still a matter of debate, and currently a theme of major intellectual interest.

Nearer to my own days four generations can be defined, but only the last two have had a direct impact on my thinking and doing. My parents, Frederick and Ethel Rahtz (née Clothier) clearly affected my predispositions heavily, while not themselves being archaeologists. They lived in the same house in Bristol from a time well before my birth in 1921 to their deaths in the 1960s and '70s. I lived there too, ultimately with my first wife and children, for over 50 years. As we shall see, that geographical location was a fundamental factor in my career.

My first archaeological mentor was Ernest Greenfield, during my time in the Royal Air Force. To him I owe an early acquaintance with method and objective description.

During the early years after the Second World War, my first wife Wendy (née Hewgill-Smith) and my first five children (Genny, Nicky, Diana, David and Sebastian) collaborated with me on digs, and bore the brunt of the disruptions in family life that archaeology generated. None of them has taken up archaeology as a career. Sebastian Patrick Quintus has, however, directed and published excavations and written several books on archaeology and computing, so that both SPQR and PAR figure in the literature, and are sometimes confused. His initials, incidentally, reflected a classical intent, and were deliberate, though he *was* the fifth child (Quintus). He feels proprietary interest in some artefacts of public services in Rome, such as manhole covers.

Eric Brown taught me to read music, and how to play the viola.

My first intellectual encouragement, in the later 1940s, came from Dina Dobson (later Dobson-Hinton). She was the *grande dame* of Somerset archaeology, writing the book on Somerset in the Methuen County Archaeological Series in 1931, and I can truly say that my professional involvement stemmed directly from her patronage.

Rex Hull of Colchester Museum also took me seriously as early as 1950, and wrote very helpfully on my work and on my first attempts at writing about Pagans Hill.

Bryan Hugh St John O'Neil gave me my first paid assignment in 1953. He was at that time Chief Inspector of Ancient Monuments in the (then) Ministry of Public Building and Works (MOPBW hereafter), and was in the position politically of being able to make or break an infant career.

His subordinate was a young Cambridge graduate, John Hurst; he became my major influence and encourager for nearly half a century and has remained a close friend to this day, from the early days of MOPBW involvement through to our collaboration at Wharram Percy in the early 1980s, and beyond.

Leo Biek, in the MOPBW laboratory, made us sensitive to science in archaeology.

Another major enabler was Graham Webster, who helped so many people to be archaeologists in the extra-mural world of the 1950s-'60s. He provided valuable external contacts and classes during my early years at Birmingham and helped me strike a balance between the relatively closed academic world and the West Midlands archaeological scene.

It was Rodney Hilton, however, who 'fixed' my transition from digger to academic. Although we did not always see eye-to-eye (our disciplines of history and archaeology were an uneasy alliance), we did manage to co-direct the DMV (deserted medieval village) dig at Upton (Glos) for ten seasons. He is also memorable for me as the first person I had met who was in a different league of intellectual brilliance, which resulted in a strong conviction of my own academic shortcomings, but also goaded me to put up a good defence.

The academic years at Birmingham were relieved by continuing fieldwork and excavation, with the collaboration of Margaret Gray, my close companion at that time, and by another of Graham Webster's *protegées*, Philip Barker. Phil and I not only had a very similar background but were also very close in the way we saw archaeology. He was one of the few really close friends I have made in adult life.

Another archaeologist at Birmingham, Richard Tomlinson, was very different — a brilliant classical archaeologist and, until recently, Director of the British School at Athens. He generously invited me to go with him to Greece to survey and excavate in Boeotia and Elis, and gave me the grand tour of the great sites of Mycenae, Perachora, etc. in the Pelopponese. This initiated a great love of the Aegean.

Peter Shinnie (an old fellow-communist of Rodney Hilton), then Professor at Legon (Accra), arranged my secondment to Ghana in 1966, which proved very fruitful; we later renewed our collaboration at his Canadian university base of Calgary.

In more recent years, Susan Hirst has been an invaluable colleague and companion, becoming, like Margaret Gray, a professional archaeologist in her own right.

A long-time supporter has been Rosemary Cramp (formerly Professor of Archaeology at Durham, now Emerita). She gave me several opportunities in the Birmingham days, and made sure that I was considered for the Chair at York in 1978; our paths have joined many times in matters Anglo-Saxon and political.

Peter Fowler (until recently Professor of Archaeology at Newcastle) I count as among my best stimulators. It was his inspiration which made me believe I had some role as a synthesiser as well as an excavator and a describer. This led to our memorable collaboration at Cadbury Congresbury, which we both rate highly among our achievements. One outcome of that was my close friendship with Ann Woodward (formerly Heard and Ellison) who has been ever since a major intellectual critic, and has collaborated with me in several publications.

The late Harold Taylor taught me much about how to look at Anglo-Saxon churches; the three volumes on this subject written by him and Joan Taylor became a bible for many of the younger generation. We joined forces with an old friend and colleague, Lawrence Butler at Deerhurst 1971-84 (172), and Mick Aston of *Time Team*, now Professor of Landscape Archaeology at Bristol, and a valued friend and hero.

In my tenure at York, and subsequently, I owe a great deal to my secretary, Priscilla Roxburgh, who saw me through some stressful periods. My successor, Martin Carver, has been more than generous in keeping me in touch with the Department at York, the archaeological world and its people; and kindly organised and edited a *Festschrift* for me (Carver ed. 1993). Andrew (Bone) Jones, has been a close friend, inspirer and collaborator through these years.

My second wife, Lorna Watts, also a professional archaeologist, helped me through the difficult years of transition to York and the problems of retirement and old age. We have collaborated in much fieldwork, many excavations, and in publications. Our work and travel has been shared by yet another Rahtz, Matthew Philip Merlin, born on the first day of January 1992.

I would also like to thank the hundreds of diggers and students who have participated in the learning process and in excavation for over 50 years; without them the long series of digs could never have been done. Their names are listed in many of my excavation reports.

Finally, I would like to thank those who have helped in the preparation of this book: Mandy Evans, who did a great job from my handwritten MS; Lorna Watts, Philip Barker and Mick Aston, who have read drafts and made constructive criticism; Colin West, who inspired me to write the book, arranged word processing, and read early drafts; and to Peter Kemmis Betty and Anne Phipps of Tempus, who masterminded the production and publication.

PART ONE

History of a life (1921-86)

1 Genes and culture: ancestry, family, home, school and accountancy (1921-41)

Ancestry and family

Every person is, in my view, a product of his/her genetic background, and the cultural and other environments one is exposed to in the nine months in the womb and after birth. After the first few weeks or months, a person's course of life is fairly predictable if the predictor keeps up with changing influences; I shall elaborate on this later.

Genetically, my ancestry is very mixed. My family cannot trace their forebears earlier than the wedding of my great-great-grandparents (on the Rahtz side). They were married in Danzig (modern Gdansk) in 1791, and their portraits survive, painted on this occasion (**1 & 2**). Apart from these, knowledge of the ancestors is firstly from the family bible, a magnificent two-volume German edition with engravings by Gustave Doré. This dates from 1873 when my grandfather married Arabella Kirk. In the bible were inscribed important family names and dates — births, marriages and deaths. These are backed up by a series of birth, marriage and death certificates which have been preserved; and my

1-2 Portraits by the artist Werner of my great-great grandmother and great-great grandfather painted on the occasion of their wedding in 1791 at Danzig (Julia Shuff)

father's boyhood diary. He was also a keen photographer, not only taking photographs, but also making up an album of all those he had inherited. He did not, unfortunately, write any account of his family, or even his own life; but some facts can be gleaned from an account of the family written by my mother late in her life (in the 1950s) 'for her grandchildren'.

The name Rahtz, she says, comes from the German root RAT = 'counsel' (cf the German Rathaus — the town hall. A rathsman is a councillor). It was said that the family originally came from a part of Germany which had been a province of Sweden — the town of Stralsund was rumoured to be where they lived. Recently my son Sebastian put his search engine on the world wide web and came up with many Rahtzs, mostly in the Hamburg area, but including some in the Americas, including Professor Don Rahtz of Illinois!

3   GWR as a young man in Odessa, c.1870

Grandfather George William Rahtz (**3**) was born in Danzig. After the death of his father, in 1858, he moved to Russia with his mother; he later set up in business in Odessa as a quarry manager, together with an Englishman, James Kirk. They lived in some style, as my mother remembered having heard. They were all paid well and living was cheap. They had their horses and carriages, one of the latter being a travelling coach in which William could sleep on long journeys. He had to report at intervals to the quarry owners — in French, of course. Also, once a year, he had to go to the great hiring fair at Nijni-Novgorod to hire labour. On one of these journeys he put up at an inn; and soon after he went to bed he became aware that someone had entered his room. He reached for the pistol which he always carried, but the man only walked quietly across the room to a corner where stood his favourite Ikon. There he knelt and said his prayers and went out as quietly as he had entered. They heard wolves sometimes on these journeys but never encountered any. One year there was a bad outbreak of cholera in the village. William was very concerned about the villagers and servants, especially his good loyal coachman, for whom he sent to England for Chlorodyne, then the only recognised specific for the complaint. Many died and many others were in danger of dying from the subsequent weakness. There were many Fast Days in the Russian Orthodox Church and it was disastrous to convalescents who needed frequent small nourishing meals. William sent for the local Bishop who came at once and blessed the wells and gave all those who had been

4 *Arabella Mary Rahtz (née Kirk) (my grandmother), in Odessa soon after her marriage to GWR, in 1873*

ill dispensation from fasting until they were strong again. No more died and the epidemic ceased.

In late 1872 (winter work not being possible at the quarry) James Kirk suggested that William came with him for a holiday to England; he was going to visit his elder brother John. He jokingly told William that John had four daughters, probably pretty, and that William might fall in love with one of them. This duly happened with Arabella Mary Kirk.

My mother later heard from her mother-in-law some stories of her earlier life before she met William, amplifying the circumstances of their marrige, and life in Russia.

Arabella (**4**) was the youngest daughter. Her father had his own school. He taught his pupils (including his daughters) their alphabet in a ring like 'Ring a ring of roses', and they sang their ABC to the tune of 'Auld Lang Syne'. His wife taught needlework and French, and subjects like history and geography were taught from books of questions and answers which were learnt by heart.

Arabella later got a job at a small boarding school at Frome, in Somerset. When she came home for the Christmas holiday she found her sisters in a state of wild excitement. Uncle James Kirk had come from Russia for a visit and brought with him his friend William, a handsome German with a beautiful curly beard and bright blue eyes. William and James called at the Kirk school and William was immediately attracted to Arabella and she to him. They never had any opportunity for private conversation, till one Sunday after Christmas. William contrived to detach Arabella from her family and walk home from Church behind the others. On the way home he proposed marriage to her and she accepted him. This was, of course, subject to her father's approval, but no doubt he was only too pleased to have one of his girls married. There was no point in waiting. The visitors would have to go back to Russia before the spring and could not come again for a year when William and Arabella would know each other no better than they did now. They were married in January 1873; and after a short honeymoon in Britain and Paris returned to Odessa.

I always wondered how William managed to persuade Arabella, from an English middle class background, to go with him to what must have been a fairly remote-sounding part of the world in 1873. In 1990, however, while on a cruise (I was paid as a lecturer), I visited Odessa, and realised what a relatively sophisticated city it had been then, built under French influence, with wide boulevards, a concert hall, a museum and of course the Steps, immortalised by Eisenstein's tumbling pram and baby.

Later in 1873 the quarry closed and my grandparents came to England, to Lowestoft, and then to London. William invested his money in a coal business in Woolwich; this collapsed when the Woolwich Free Ferry opened; any small trader could now buy cheap Midland coal. He died in 1915 of a rupture caused by carrying injured soldiers from a train.

When Frederick (my father) had been born, in 1876, something went wrong; the doctor told William that his wife would not be able to have any more children. It seems that while Arabella was in labour, the doctor sent the nurse for some brandy. William handed her the bottle, and instead of going back to the patient she went into another room to try the brandy herself, and was later found dead drunk on the floor. She was turned out and another nurse had to be found. The second one was more efficient but was nursing someone else as well, so that Arabella was not well looked after and suffered from it later in life.

She came to live with my parents after her husband died, in Bristol. She was 69 when I was born. She had her own sitting-room, a large back room which I much later used as a photographic studio (see below). She dominated my father and the household, and must have been quite a trial for my mother, and a major cause of dissension. She dressed, large and plump and German-looking, in black bombazine with hair piled up in German style. She spoilt me — when I had been in trouble I was comforted by sweets from Grandma in her dark big room with Victorian ornaments and a full-size Bechstein grand piano. Arabella clearly acted a German role with her daughter-in-law, who put up with her with fortitude. When Grandma had a cold she dried her wet handkerchiefs on the fireguard. She died in 1933 at the age of 81; I was 12 and this was the last contact I had with that generation.

My father (Frederick John) was born in 1876 in Lewisham. There are many photographs of him as a boy and a young man (**5**), very keen on travel and walking in Switzerland. He was a fine scholar, taking first class degrees in both Science and English in London and Cardiff, and (unlike me) an accomplished linguist. His first post was at the Woolwich Polytechnic; he met my mother when she was a student there. They married when she was only 18; he was 31.

Soon after, he got a job at the Merchant Venturers College in Bristol. They eventually settled in a large four-storey Victorian 17-room house in Bristol (27 Cotham Road) in 1912. He applied to join up in the First World War, but was rejected on medical grounds. He was an authority on English grammar and literature — his *Higher English* (1907) continued to earn us royalties into the 1950s, notably from Africa!

He could recognise any quotation from Shakespeare or The Bible, and was also a very successful teacher; after the Merchant Venturers he became a housemaster at Cotham Secondary School, inspiring a lot of enthusiasm. This is typified by an anecdote of a boy from 'Rahtz's House' who fell unconscious after a cross-country run, from strain. He was carried in somewhere, where in his delirium, he was heard to be muttering 'Rahtz's must win, Rahtz's must win'.

5   *Frederick John Rahtz (my father) in Bristol in c.1910*

My father was also very generous with boys. Each year he gave a big fireworks party, where there was a liberal supply of bangers and sparklers, buns and lemonade; and a few expensive set-pieces, let off in the garden, with a big bonfire. One of my rare memories of camaraderie with my father was going with him each year to collect wood shavings from the school carpenter's workshop. As the 'schoolmaster's son' I was in a slightly invidious position in relationship to the boys for whom he had parties, but I'm not aware of any problems.

He also, even more generously, took selected 'poor' boys on holidays to cheap boarding-houses or holiday camps, at Easter and in the summer, to Mortehoe, in north Devon, and to Jersey. There was a strong homosexual element here. I went on these holidays, and the boys lost no opportunity of telling me about his not-very-serious behaviour with them; I don't remember ever thinking this was odd. In retrospect I think he was lucky to get away with it, but there was a tendency for schoolmasters to be over-fond of their charges in the 1920s and 1930s. I was very cross, however, when at the age of about 15, a girl I was courting was forbidden to see me any more by her father because of my father's reputation. Whether my mother knew what was going on I never knew.

He loved travel. To pay for foreign trips to Switzerland or Italy for the family (but not me — I was too young) he organised tours for other schoolmasters, being expert at foreign timetables and hotel bookings. He had special labels printed RAHTZ'S PARTY to go on suitcases, and a crude copying device for circulating to clients.

He was a keen swimmer and walker. Musically, he was not very advanced — there were some records of popular pieces like Finlandia or Wagner's Prize Song; and he took me often to hear Gilbert and Sullivan, which I still enjoy. When I knew more about music, I was amused when he was inveighing against modern music (this was about 1937): 'can't bear all this modern music, people like . . . (and here he dredged in his memory for the name of an 'avant-garde' composer of his youthful days, and out it came) . . . DVORÂK'. But when I bought my first record he was rather proud of it in front of his schoolmaster friends, 'Tschaikovsky, you know'.

He was a respectable churchgoer and churchwarden until 1927, when his eldest son Edward was killed. He then became hostile to the Church, taking the view that God should not have taken his son.

Politically, he was very Conservative; and that is doubtless one reason for me being a life-long socialist. He lost his temper regularly over politics, especially when in my teens I had the temerity to point out that he opposed proportional representation when the Conservatives were in power, and supported it when Labour were in the ascendant! Seeing him lose his temper so often taught me how to control mine. Due to chronic catarrh, which all the family have inherited (the Rahtz Sneezing Nose), excitement and temper induced nasal congestion and a nose-clearing snorting or puffing out, punctuating his words; and also a twitching and puckering of the nostrils and facial muscles which earned him his school nickname of 'Bunny' Rahtz.

I never got on with him after my early teens, regarding him as a bad-tempered bore. He once strode into one of my sisters' parties (he was trying to get to sleep in the room above) in his pyjamas, clutching the cord to stop the trousers falling off, and rushed across the crowded room to switch off the radio.

6   *FJR in late middle age, c.1950, in Bristol*

Generosity to others was complemented by some meanness to his own family (a trait I have inherited). Typical of this was the annual event of the family grapes, grown in our greenhouse with much horse-manure and buckets of blood (from the abbatoir?) poured onto the roots. About 50 bunches grew, most of which were unripe or mildewed. These were eaten by the family, while the few that were ripe and blue were given expansively to strangers — 'Ah, do have a bunch of grapes . . . grown in our greenhouse you know'.

To be honest, he was overall a respectable and upright citizen. During the Second World War he was an Air Raid Warden; here was another rare piece of good father-son relations when I helped him put out incendiary bombs in Cotham.

In his later years (6), he took some interest in a 'country cottage' which my mother had rented at Compton Martin, about 15 miles south of Bristol (five shillings a week). There he gardened and made cider. For the latter he bought a huge apple-grinding machine, turned by a big handle; and a giant press, some 3m high, which compressed fibre mats in a pile, in which were layers of cut apple. The cider ran out from the base, firstly as 'ring cider'. This was nice and sweet, but got more sour as the weeks went by, until only Fred was able to drink it. He obtained advice from local Somerset cider-makers, but did not heed a vital ingredient that had to be put in the barrel — a dead rat.

7 *Ethel May Rahtz (née Clothier), my mother, in her early married life in Bristol, 1910*

In his last decade, he seemed to have had little in the way of intellectual interest; he read rubbishy novels, played patience, listened to the Archers and news on the radio six times a day, and went to bed every afternoon. In the end, he developed angina, and died in 1962, aged 86.

My mother (**7**) ('Mumma' to everyone, not only to her children) was a Clothier; her father had been a master baker in Woolwich. She was a very bright girl, and won a scholarship to the Woolwich Polytechnic. She had a promising academic future ahead, but gave it all up at 18 to marry Fred, a decision she later had some reservations about.

She was mostly mild and loving, though she sometimes got very cross with Fred, once (to my delight) throwing a dinner at him.

Photographs of her show a massive change from a pretty girl to a caring mother. In the 1920s I remember her playing the piano and singing songs to us such as 'Will you walk into my parlour, said the spider to the fly' (as she had?). Was this where I got my earliest appreciation of music? In later years I tried taking her to concerts, but she always fell asleep!

Fred and Ethel had five children, three boys and two girls. She seems always to have been in the basement kitchen at Cotham Road (formerly the servants' quarters in Victorian times) slaving over the stove or sink while Fred and his mother sat on the first floor. But it was to the kitchen that most visitors migrated for her company; she remained sweet-tempered and rarely spoke of Fred's unkindness.

The eldest son (Edward) was born in 1911. He was brilliant, a keen Christian and ambitious to become a minister. He was a very 'holy' lad by all accounts; much later, in the 1960s, my mother admitted he had been a 'bit of a prig'. At the age of 16 he achieved three distinctions in 'Higher' (today's A levels), a rare feat in the 1920s; he would undoubtedly have gone on to a distinguished academic career. As a reward for having done so well, my father bought him a Matchless motorcycle. A month later, in October 1927, he skidded on a dangerous bridge over the Avon at Twerton between Bath and Bristol, hit his head on the parapet, went over into the Avon and drowned. I shall say more on this below.

RAHTZ FAMILY TREE : 1790 ~ late 20th century

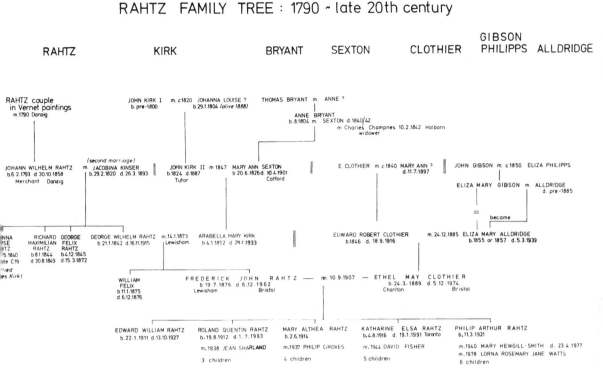

8   Family tree

My mother thereafter took us on camping holidays, rarely with Fred. Although a smallish lady, she drove a huge Sunbeam 16HP open tourer for many years; she only finally gave up driving in 1964. In later life she gradually went blind, and this demoralised her completely. She could not take to 'talking books' or tape recorders and her mind gradually went — a sad end in 1974 for a brave and buoyant mother who had been so invaluable to her family.

Their other children (**8**) all survived to maturity and gave Fred and Ethel 16 grandchildren — a big increase in Rahtzs! As the youngest by far (probably a mistake!) I was never close to my siblings. My younger sister died in 1991 of a brain tumour when she was 75; my brother in 1993, at 81. My eldest sister followed her mother in blindness and loss of mind, and died in May 2000, at 85.

Now a new generation has started, with a daughter and a son to my grandsons! It is now time to begin the real subject of this book, and turn to my own life.

My beginnings

The above introduction will have made it clear that I was born into a relatively cultured middle-class background.

I was born on 11 March 1921, the last arrival in the family. The First World War had caused the family only limited privation, which was in any case receding by 1921. The circumstances of my conception in June 1920 can only be guessed at, as I have hinted above. I was an 11lb baby (5kg), a feat equalled by Peter Ustinov, who was born in the same spring of 1921. I was indeed believed to be twins (this was in the days before the ability of doctors to find out). My mother had two small sets of baby garments ready. It's just as well I was only one baby; I was enough of a handful as I was!

The summer of 1921 was one of the best in the twentieth century. I was out in the garden in my coach-built pram for much of the first six months of my life; this is probably why I liked being exposed to the sun in later years. The following winter, however, I was ill with pneumonia; my mother decided to continue breast-feeding beyond the usual term and into my second year to make me stronger (no doubt this explains a lot!).

My parents being notionally Christian, I was baptised at St Matthew's church (the nearest to our Cotham home, though not their usual place of worship). There is a photograph of me at 4 days old, and others at 5, 17 and 26 months.

I have no memories of these early years. The earliest one is at the age of 4, when I was taken to see the school I was to attend. I was impressed on this occasion by an old lady in black who stood astride the margin of pavement and road, urinating into the gutter.

School

Kingsdown Elementary was a 'rough' school. The streets there were largely slums (ironically all now rebuilt as trendy houses and apartments) although only a quarter of a mile from our middle-class Cotham Road; in fact they were behind the houses on the other side of our road, which themselves were built later and not quite so 'respectable' as our side. My parents must have thought a rough school would do no harm, since all their five went there, and four had obtained City Junior Scholarships (the passport to a grammar school = 11+). Not surprisingly we tended to be top of the class or near it. I remember a big chart in the classroom with names on and a line of sticky gold, silver and other coloured stars for various aspects of work and conduct — I remember mine was gratifyingly long. But there was no favouritism. I was regularly caned, once I remember for making a poor job of drawing a protractor. I could never sharpen pencils or make a clean line, or be any good at art, or keep ink off everything (it was dip pens and inkwells, replenished from a huge brown stoneware jar of Stephens Blue-Black).

I was bullied in the playground as a cissy and had to play with the girls or hide in the lavatories. There was a humiliating episode of my having elastic-waisted shorts which had to be pulled down to pee — the other boys had proper shorts with flies or cut-down father's trousers. The boys were rough, smelly and dirty, and I disliked them pretty cordially and was afraid of them. I caught lice from them and had to have my head soaked in petrol to kill them (the lice!). I got on better with the girls. There was a school pantomime in which the girls dressed me up as a round Christmas pudding with lots of brown paper. I remember the headmaster, like Chalkie in Giles' cartoons, and (in the senior class) a sharp middle-aged Miss Bowen.

I can't have been all that good, as it was thought necessary for me to have some private coaching by Miss Bowen in arithmetic at her home in preparation for the scholarship exam. There was a Mr Henderson, memorable only because he committed suicide by shooting himself in the head in a garage because he had insomnia — a sensation. I remember nothing else of six years at that school.

The only other memorable incident was on an evening drive. We came upon an open tourer stopped with a woman weeping, and an older man leaning backwards over the back seat. She said they had gone out to get a new needle for the gramophone (!) and he'd dropped dead. My first corpse, but little impression except that it made a good story.

I was at Kingsdown School from 1925-32. The major family event in those years I have mentioned above: the death of my elder brother Edward, when I was six. The news came to Cotham Road at about seven in the evening, when in the dark the doorbell rang. Sister Mary answered it, and it was a policeman. She came back weeping into the dining room where we were (sister Katharine and myself) playing after tea. We became conscious of 'something up' in the hall. When Katharine and I peeped out there was the policeman near the door and my mother being supported by my father and weeping. There the memory ends. A powerful impression had been made on me at six years old, and the above minutes are particularly vivid — my siblings must have had a longer and clearer memory of what must have been the most terrible evening of their lives. I think this may still be true since none of them, since 1927, have lost a husband, wife or child in the next 50 years. Sister Mary confirmed (1997) that she did no school work for a year, and that I said to my mother that evening in the bath 'You've still got me, Mumma'. I hardly remember Edward except as a distant figure, so the impression on me was limited to those few minutes. Later I was told that Fred never spoke for six months except to say 'pass the salt'; how he went on teaching I can't imagine. I remember too seeing the motorbike brought back and lying in the 'playhouse', an annexe to the garage (next to the greenhouse where Fred grew his grapes), before it was disposed of. I must have been sent away then, I suppose, until after the funeral — Edward is buried at Portbury, near Bristol; I sometimes went to his grave with my mother in later years.

We lived at 27 Cotham Road. The ground floor comprised sitting-rooms, study, and a pantry ('for the glass'); the first floor above was for the best bedrooms and bathroom, the top floor for servants' bedrooms and a sunken basement, kitchen and scullery. Here was a big pump which got soft water from a tank under the back garden. This was large, with a garage beyond entered from a back lane; a smaller front garden gave onto the road. By the 1920s there was little of the old order left. There was a charwoman (Mrs Duckett), responsible for scrubbing, cleaning and laundry, who lived in one of the basement rooms; there may have been one or two other servants earlier on. Communication between the basement kitchen and the main dining room at ground level was by means of a lift, which could be wound up and down from the kitchen, with a cupboard door at the top. Small children could go up and down crouched in it, which was a great pleasure to all.

9 PAR as a choirboy at St Mary, Tyndalls Park, Bristol, 1931, aged 10

Sister Mary says we used to have baths by the kitchen range, and then go up to the fire in the room above. In the dining room was a large Victorian walnut table with knobbly legs and six leaves, which could be inserted by opening out the two ends on a rack worked by a handle at one end to a length of 15-20ft, to accommodate a large dinner party.

Such a big house lent itself to parties, given by my elder brothers and sisters. They were real parties with charades and elaborate games which spread all over the house — sardines, murder, etc. As a pre-adolescent I joined in only marginally as an annoying small boy, being allowed to sit up a bit later watching the proceedings.

It was possible, of course, to play practical jokes. Two favourite ones, with which I used to bait my father in later years, were to arrange strings from upstairs which rang the doorbell and brought him shambling and muttering to the front door and peering out to see who was there. The other, which could be played on anyone suitable, was to get up in the loft or boxroom above the lavatory (where its cistern was) and push down the lever normally operated by pulling the chain from below — while they were on the seat of course — so that they got a wet bottom when it flushed.

I went to two churches. The first was St Stephen's in the city, where my mother and father went — he was a churchwarden until 1927 and then renounced it all. I was afraid in the Sunday dusk of Snuggs, a reclining effigy in red (still there) on a chest tomb at the east end of the south aisle (it must have been quite a vivid image for me to be able to picture the spot so exactly!). The second was a rather higher church (Anglo-Catholic), St Mary's, Tyndalls Park, where my brothers were choirboys and servers. I became a choirboy until my voice broke (**9**), and at one time a 'boat-boy', carrying in front of the priest, an incense burner in a boat shape which I swung by chains of brass, making a marvellous Catholic smell often encountered since abroad. Sister Mary says I once slipped in a Woolworth incense cone, which made a terrible smell.

I was persecuted by other choirboys again because I was a 'cissy' (i.e. middle class, and not tough) and was severely frightened at initiation ceremonies which involved jumping over high walls. I remember once being brought home in tears by one of the men choristers who had rescued me from the pack. The vicar here was a fleshy old chap with silver hair, appropriately called Father White, whom I always thought a pillar of propriety. I was rather surprised in later years when my mother said he spent his holidays at Blankenburghe (Ostend) where he could lie around with nothing on (was this really true in the early '30s?).

The choirmaster, Mr Steer, was a music-hall-looking character with round face and waxed moustaches. Quite a humourist, he made constant jokes — his prize act was to play 'God Save the King' by blowing his nose!

Religion did not stick to me, however. I found it incompatible with my own desires (in sex especially) and with a growing rationalist outlook. I will return to the form that this took in later pages.

During these years and into the 1930s there were many family excursions and holidays. Favourite local trips (which seem retrospectively to have been easier than now) were:

1   Dundry. Here were the earthworks and cliffs of medieval quarries with lots of caves and tunnels in the oolitic limestone which were excellent places for rough games (later on I took an interest in this area as a Roman and medieval quarry).

2   Portishead, Clevedon, Severn Beach, Weston. Our nearest seaside places, but always reckoned inferior to Devon etc. because of the mud.

3   The Mendips: Burrington Combe, etc. For good picnics, occasional other places like Bath or Castle Combe; or Newent to pick daffodils. Saltford to row or bathe in the Avon.

Holidays were a memorable pleasure. Easter was often spent at a guest house at Mortehoe, in north Devon. The trip to Ilfracombe was sometimes by car, sometimes by Campbells' pleasure steamer. From there one walked four miles to Mortehoe, smelling the gorse on the high downs and the singing of the wind in the telephone wires. Once there, it was walking (only occasionally a day hot enough to venture into the freezing sea). Morning routine was down to Mortehoe village, where the square between the gold-mosaiced church and the general shop which sold *everything* (in 1991 MOR-T-EAT takeaway!). The square, barely slaty bed-rock, then down the one-in-four Chapel Hill to Barricane Shelly Beach and on to Woolacombe where Dad bought a Daily Mirror (then a respectable family newspaper) and sat in the sandhills to read it — not much to do there except look at the sea until the walk back. How long those mornings must have been, with a good hour's walk each day — we tried to get lifts back up the hill. After lunch, there were walks to the more interesting local beaches of Huscombe and Rockham. At the former I learnt the whole cycle of the tides, in their short and longer extremities, at times moving right out to expose pools never usually seen, and at high tide pounding the cliffs so that there was no foothold; pools, pebbles, shrimps, gudgeons and other darting fish, sea-anemones, and rock climbing. On a visit in 1991, there was no longer life in these pools due to sea pollution — only seaweeds. At Rockham, there was sand at low tide and a rusty wreck, and a series of beaches beyond which one could get cut off. If the tide was judged right on the fall, perilous fast climbing could get you right round seven or eight beaches to Bull Point Lighthouse. Not without real danger though — one boy did break an arm and it was surprising that there were not more accidents on those slippery rocks.

A marvellous pleasure (now alas virtually finished) was the finding of large green or white glass balls, fishermen's floats that had come ashore from their broken nets and were wedged in rocks as the tide went out sometimes, too tightly to release. But every year saw a new one or two. Once, having retrieved one and got cut off by the tide, three other boys and I tried to climb back up a frightful place. I lost a hand- and foothold and had to let go of the ball which fell down and exploded against a rock below. Looking back, this was the first of some narrow escapes from death I have had (aged 9 or perhaps 11-12). Even Dad took risks in this climbing and once got stuck on a cliff path; we boys had to get the coastguard with a rope to rescue him. There were also walks through primroses and bluebells to Lee and other places more distant, and whole day walks (which I found very exhausting) to Saunton — six miles each way at 10 years old is no joke, but nothing to Dad. The walk was via Woolacombe and its beach to Baggy Point and Croyde and Georgeham to the great panorama of six miles of Saunton Sands. Here were long waves and flotsam which included hundreds of evaporated jellyfish, and the skeletons of razor-fish and sea-urchins. I was never a keen naturalist but enjoyed the whole atmosphere. There were rough seas and an occasional seal or ship. I never left Mortehoe without regret, nor failed to like a return, though less when revisited in later years, when Mrs Chugg's camping and caravans had spread its tentacles. Repeated holidays in Mortehoe laid foundations of a love of the seaside which has been important for many years since, though less recently, as fear of the sea encroached after later death-escapes. I developed a great facility for rock-climbing, adventure, wave-dodging, and, I suppose, a good deal of fitness induced by all that walking.

In the summer it was usually a holiday with Mumma and brothers and sisters in August to Devon or Cornwall. Once or twice it was at Kilve in south-west Somerset, and once at Dawlish, but more memorably in Cornwall, the introduction to a close acquaintance with that frightening county. We stayed at St Minver in a boarding house run by a jolly widow (Mrs Harris). She ran it with her daughter (Cissie) whose young man had been killed in the first war. She served up endless chicken and vast Cornish pasties, but from there we went to all the beaches from Newquay to Tintagel, bathing, surf-riding, walking, sometimes to look at old Cornish crosses, churches, or Bodmin Moor. We never at that time penetrated beyond Perranporth.

After that there were again holidays with Dad and the boys in Jersey. Train to Weymouth, going (as it still does) through streets on its way to the harbour. Then a long sea trip on the GWR steamer, usually severe sickness as on Messrs Campbells' steamers. The steamer stopped at Guernsey where women held out nets to the ship with bunches of fat black grapes for which money was exchanged. Then a short trip to St Helier. Then bus to Portelet or was it Mr Prout's cart? He was the farmer of a filthy farm above Portelet Bay where the food was poor, but we got cheap rates. The walks over Jersey were good and here I learnt at the age of seven something that means much even in 2000 — to swim. In the warm waters of Jersey this was easy to learn, and I got very brown on those holidays.

The summers there seem always to have been sunny and warm, with occasional dramatic thunderstorms. There were excursions to Corbieres lighthouse and even to St Malo — my first visit to a foreign country.

A curious precursor was that of autumn half-term holidays (family only) to Cheddar, which was to figure twice more in my life; we went to a cottage in the Gorge, just below the Lion Rock opposite Goughs' caves. I remember misty October/November days here with smoke from the fire curling up in still air, the smell of burning wood, and the constant noise of the water; sitting outside the cottage whittling wood. A single image of memory only, but one remembered in later Cheddar (chapter 3): a place that has survived wild and beautiful in spite of all that modern tourism has been able to bring to it.

We were lucky with holidays, being away most of the school vacations. Sometimes when my parents were taking 'Rahtz's Parties' abroad, I was packed off to stay with Auntie Tottie, my mother's half-sister, who lived at Plumstead in a small house. They were quite poor — her husband ('Uncle' Scarfe) was a postman, a poor-paid and hard job, and he'd been in the first war. Their own children were by then grown up. They were very good to me. Uncle took me to his allotment (the 'plot') while he collected vegetables (he won many prizes for sweet peas and roses) and she took me to London on the open-topped red buses, to Danson Park (with a boating lake), Greenwich Observatory, Madame Tussaud's, Regents Park Zoo, Kew, Southend and Herne Bay. When I got constipated, she gave me California Syrup of Figs which induced enormous turn-outs.

I didn't grumble at going on Dad's holidays, and certainly enjoyed one in 1936 when we went to Germany and Switzerland via Paris. The first week was a 'package' in Wolfach in the Black Forest, a lovely town with a cold rushing river, canalised at one point into an open air pool, presided over by a black-bronzed hero who it was said seduced all the ladies; he, I remember, looked like the hero of 1930s films. I tried to flirt with a German girl, but we had not a word in common, although we walked by the river — she wore traditional clothes. It was all very German in the best sense with cuckoo clocks, but there were Nazi flags, German brass bands and a general 'Jugend' atmosphere. But it was cheap and splendid; food included huge cream tarts. We drove in a big fast Mercedes bus to the Rhinefalls, Schaffhausen and Donaueschingen (the Danube source); there I had the first drink of lager I ever enjoyed in a brewery which gave us lunch; also to Heidelberg and Freibourg. Then on to Gersau, a favourite spot of my parents on Lake Lucerne. The hotel was by the lake edge, and we had long swims in the deep lake, visits to other parts by paddleboat, and a memorable walk up the mountain behind (Mt Rigi, *c*.2000m); this led through flowered meadows and woods with views of the Alps from the top and a thunderstorm to send us scurrying down. How easy and cheap it all seems in retrospect and how unspoilt it was then. These are very good memories at the age of 15.

Bristol Grammar School

In 1932, I was eleventh in Bristol in the City Junior Scholarship; this enabled me to go to Bristol Grammar School, in the steps of my two brothers. After having been used to being in the top three at Kingsdown, I was now in for a nasty shock, competing with boys who had been to private schools, or state schools in 'better' areas of Bristol. I was in the bottom two or three in the class throughout my time at this school (1932-6).

I did not enjoy Bristol Grammar School, which was in a bad state at that time; the Latin master read us P.G. Wodehouse for most of his 'lessons'. At least four of the masters were mild pederasts. The French master spent his periods trying to get us to join his 'Officers' Training Corps (the OTC). A quasi-military school activity, with silly walks, the OTC had only one thing going for it: it was better than rugby, where one had to push one's head in amongst other boys' bottoms, in a scrum. The only sport I shone at was the slow bicycle race, where the aim was to cover the shortest distance in the longest time without falling off. Fungus the Bogeyman would have enjoyed this. Cricket I also hated, with hard balls being thrown at you, not to give you the chance to hit them, but to get you out (or hurt). I did however enjoy the cross-country runs in the woods around Blaise Castle, on the outskirts of Bristol. I swam a mile at 12, and won a bronze medal for life-saving at 14 (now one of my youngest son's treasured possessions); I got a year's free pass to the public baths for this.

We sang 'Let us now praise famous men' and the school motto was EX SPINIS UVAS, which was conveniently twelve letters and could therefore be round the sports field clock in place of numbers.

I was bullied again, to some extent, especially on a school camp I was foolish enough to go on at St Ives (Carbis Bay), aged 12. The worst kind of boy was there, and it was run by the PT (physical training) instructor, a vulgar man. One odd thing, however, he had his wife and another woman there, a rather brassy gypsy-looking woman, who one day appeared to let fall a shoulder strap exposing a breast and a big dark nipple. Several boys were there and she only laughed.

School really meant rather little and my life was lived outside it. I cycled to school on a splendid white drop-handled bike stopping on the way back for halfpenny Vantas red (fizzy) drink. I made few friends at school. But now a short digression, jumping over half a century.

In 1986, one of my schoolfellows, Frank Palmer, organised a reunion of the 'class of 1936'. He found and contacted most. Three of the original eighteen had been killed in the war; one was too ill; one was in Nairobi; one couldn't be found; but 12 assembled for lunch at Frank's house in Reading. Of these there were two professors (Frank and myself); one Foreign Office high-up (Geoffrey Green — always top at school); and others in various good jobs. One, André Heintz, was a French boy, who had some contact with Bristol, and was at school with us. He came from Caen in 1986 with bottles of champagne; he had been very much a leader in the Resistance, in the Battle for Caen in 1944. He welcomed me very enthusiastically because (it seems) I taught him all the sex words, which gave a great advantage in welcoming British troops into Caen. I have no memory of this, or of other things they said: that I often went to sleep in class (of which they were envious, in view of what it implied I'd been up to); and that I was a great joker; I didn't really remember them as much as they did me.

Since 1986, two have died, and most have aged rather; they had reunions every year to which I didn't go, but attended in May 1991, when seven of us met again at Frank's (with wives): Allsop, Green, Bruce, Thompson, Rahtz, Palmer, Heintz. In between we also stayed with André in Normandy. We met again in 1995 and 1998.

To return to my narrative. In my secondary school years I must have had some feeling for the world of the past, however, since I took the classical option — Greek, Latin and

Ancient History as special studies. I cannot remember that I was pushed into these, but it may have been simply that two elder brothers had taken this course, with university classics in view. Another major stimulus which stays in my mind was the then headmaster, the famous (though by that time less effective) J.E. Barton. He lectured on the monuments of Greece and the Roman world, and I remember sitting up and taking notice of his slide of the Lion Gate at Mycenae, as well as being impressed by his sonorous reading of Milton's *Lycidas*. In the event, rather to my parents' and schoolmasters' surprise, I did get enough credits to matriculate, including the classical languages and culture, which has stood me in good stead. Hardly surprisingly, I failed in French.

There was nothing here that would presage my later interest in Dark Age studies; but I was told by my girlfriend (Bobbie; **10**) of that time (fortunately re-met after 50 years; **11**) that I was always interested in things Arthurian as a teenager — Arthur was, after all, my second name.

10 My first girlfriend, 'Bobbie' (Laura Brooks, now Laura Cella) in 1936

In these years of adolescence before the Second World War, there was one activity which had some archaeological strings attached. I was a caver (**12**), penetrating deep into the famous Mendip Caves as a member of the Wessex Cave Club. This was a purely sporting organisation — its only link with scholarship was that its members not only explored known caves but found new ones by digging in likely places — and this involved some knowledge of geology. Another caving organisation (of which more later in this book) was the University of Bristol Spelaeological Society (UBSS) which not only treated caves and their formation in a more learned way, but also published a very respectable *Proceedings*. Their members also got involved in the archaeology of caves, those on Mendip being especially important as places of dwelling and burial. Some of their senior members went further and wrote papers on the barrows of Mendip, and also excavated them. So I was marginally exposed in the 1930s to some kind of archaeology, and was introduced to the archaeology of cave collections in Bristol and Wells Museums, and in that of the UBSS itself.

11   Meeting Bobbie again after 50 years, 1987

Accountancy

I disliked grammar school, and had no desire in 1936 to prolong my studies into the sixth form, or aim at a university course. I had no clear idea at that time, however, of what I did want to do. Barton thought that accountancy would be a good career for me because he thought I was good at figures. I became an articled clerk to C.J. Ryland & Co. of Clare Street in Bristol — an odd idea. This opening, however, did appear to offer some independence, even of money; I was to get five shillings a week as an articled clerk rising to 15 shillings after five years — this was no big deal, especially as my father paid £250 (cash in a suitcase) for the articles. I am appalled now at his spending this — the equivalent of thousands today — to start me on a career, and indeed how could he afford it, *and* keep me as well?

I really can have had no imagination or guts then to submit tamely to what was patently a disastrous situation. But 'business' seemed quite glamorous, accountancy did seem a cut above other office work like banking, it was in the city, and promised ultimate financial rewards. In fact it wasn't too bad, and I learnt a lot that was useful to me (and may even have saved my life in the war — see later). The three partners were Henry Keeler, 60ish, grumbly, nose picking; Jarrett, a withered 45; and Charles Maggs, a dapper 45; but I never got on with any of them. The other clerks were quite kind to me, such as old Mr Court, Mr Stibbs (a small-time racketeer, his brother Norman was much nicer), and fellow

12 Caving on Mendip (Wessex Cave Club group), 1938; PAR second from right

articled clerks Flook, Newman and White (where are they now?). We had longish hours and few holidays, but not all work was in the office. It consisted of endless adding-up and checking vouchers, invoices and ledgers, but was at least half in other firms' offices. They included the University, Hosegoods Grain, Caperns Bird Seed, Hales Cakes, and others in Clevedon, Portishead and Weston; and the best of all the University's Agricultural Research Station at Long Ashton where strawberries, perry and cider were all to be had freely. Even the clerks were well-received at these places, as we were the outside auditors: rather like financial police, to catch out wrongdoers from the office boy who faked the postage book to the big crook. Before I joined the firm, the presence of our clerks, and their subsequent probing, had driven a cashier to suicide and we were warned to immediately disclose any irregularities.

To qualify as a chartered accountant I had to take correspondence courses in bookkeeping, accounts, executorship law, accountancy and other frightful subjects.

Four years of this career did, however, teach me about the 'real' world of trade, business, law, and accounts, which has also been of great use since. I soon realised, however, that my developing left-wing leanings did not match up with a career devoted to putting more money into peoples' hands who had too much already.

Like many adolescents in the 1930s, I read books and articles emanating from the Left Wing Book Club; I also became aware of anarchist literature such as the writings of

Kropotkin. More importantly, and more relevant to archaeology, I read an early Pelican, Susan Stebbing's *Philosophy and the Physicists*. This collection of essays influenced me very considerably, not only to the attractions of philosophy as a discipline (I later took evening classes in the Royal Air Force), but in particular I was taken with her determinist rejection of the concept of free will. The latter has recently apparently been supported by the revolutionary and baffling world of quantum theory and the 'uncertainty principle' of Heisenberg, still echoing down through the decades in the pages of *New Scientist*.

Stebbing's exposition of the essential 'truth' of determinism totally convinced me, as it has ever since. My conviction has been reinforced in recent years by the major current exponent of determinism, Professor Ted Honderich, of University College, London. This is no place for a detailed exposition of determinism or of its radical implications with relation to reward and punishment, crime and society, etc. (but see Appendix A). Suffice to say that it confirmed any incipient left wing ideas I had, and went, in my view, a long way towards explaining the many social improvements that have been made in British society in the twentieth century.

More importantly, I have since always been convinced that nothing happens or has ever happened without a cause, which a super-computer could theoretically identify before the moment of choice in the actions or thoughts of any individual. The factors that determine the cause of events may be cosmic, climatic, environmental, cultural or genetic, with a strong dose of natural selection.

The belief that we are all creatures of our own environment and genes has coloured my interpretation of human behaviour and settlement patterns. It is their material residues which are the stuff of archaeology. I shall consider this again in relation to the changes in archaeological theory, notably the unfashionableness of such beliefs in the latter decades of the twentieth century.

One of my sons, David, emigrated to Australia; he became a born-again Christian, and a minister in an American Evangelist Church, which believed in the literal truth of the Bible (God personally supervises all translations) and that the cosmos is 6,000 years old. I wrote to him in 1986, elucidating my own beliefs; I include this as Appendix A.

In contrast to such heady matters, my adolescent thoughts, like most other boys, were principally on sex. If only we'd known then the hidden truth — that girls thought about it as well!

I have mentioned my girlfriend Bobbie, in my later schooldays — as beautiful today in 2000 as she was then at 15. There were a series of later affairs when I was in accountancy (**13**): such as Iris, from Hales Home Bakery, who used to take me punting on a river near her home, very slowly (or stationary) under bridges.

There were continuing holidays. One in particular in 1939, just before the war, was to Italy; this may have influenced my future career more than I was aware of at the time. I remember that 21 days all-in — hotels, all excursions, meals, etc. — cost £21; it would cost many times that today, but exchange was in our favour. The trip was good and I was impressed and this doubtless helped in my appreciation of classical antiquities. We visited Turin, Milan, Pisa, Venice, Florence, Rome, Naples, Pompeii, Vesuvius, Sorrento, Capri and Assisi. Venice was predictable, Pisa startling, Florence I remember the millifiori, at Rome all was good — the Forum less cleared than now and more beggars and lots of

13 At Clifton open-air pool, 1939; the girls were office girls

Mussolini posters with SPQR and *fasces*. The beggars included middle-aged ladies who wanted to guide you, and compliment parents on children, etc., and stacks of stray cats. Assisi was impressive for its atmosphere as if St Francis and St Clare had been nineteenth-century saints — so many of their things were to be seen — and it was clear that Assisi brought out my parents' feeling for religion more than anywhere.

One strong memory of this place was the mummified body of St Clare, rather ragged in 1939, lying on a pedestal, with a sunken area around it. Into this pilgrims threw money. When we went to Assisi again in 1975, St Clare's body had been defleshed and put in a glass-sided 'coffin' for pilgrims to see. She was now a skeleton, neatly wired together and 'dressed' in white muslin, holding a holy text between her skeletal hands.

I remember many places well (but perhaps more through my photographs than memory). At Capri we went in the Blue Grotto and the boatmen sang a song. At Vesuvius one walked through snow and hissing fissures in the ground which burnt your feet by the crater; but even here, on rounding the corner of a mountain path, there was a band playing 'Santa Lucia'. At Pompeii the ladies were sent on ahead while the guide beckoned to us males. 'Genelmen — plis zis way', and led us into a building of the brothel frescoes. Dad said 'Ah, yes, mmm' and laughed embarrassingly. I didn't know where to look, though I'd like to have studied them in detail, as I have since in books. There was also a shutter over a street fresco of a giant weighing his phallus — all made big impressions on me at 18.

Other holidays continued, though not long ones. I went to Alderney by myself in 1939 to chase up a girl called Nola whom I'd met there before and enjoyed myself in that non-tourist island with its racing seas.

I developed some musical interest. I was a compulsive Radio Luxembourg listener and can still remember all the words of Ballito Silk Stockings and the Ovaltine Jingle:

'We are the Ovalteenies, happy girls and boys,
Make more requests, we'll not refuse you,
We are here just to amuse you,
Would you like a song or story?
Will you share our joys?
At games and sports, we're more than keen,
No happier children could be seen,
Because we all drink Ovaltine,
We're happy girls and boys'.

On the BBC was Henry Hall, Arthur Askey, and Much-Binding-in-the-Marsh; all much appreciated.

But I can trace my interest in serious music quite precisely. It must have been 1937 or '38 when I saw a film of Dutch bulb fields in which Tschaikovsky's Flower Waltz was played and I thought it was rather nice. Noting it in the *Radio Times*, I listened to it and the rest of the Nutcracker Suite, thence to other Tchaikovsky and on to Beethoven's Fifth, Grieg's Piano Concerto, etc. etc., and bought records; now the family had an electric (as distinct from a hand-wind) gramophone. First was the Flower Waltz and the Barber of Seville overture, Beethoven's Fifth (which I conducted in my bedroom), and I began to go to concerts. By the time war started, I was, therefore, able to appreciate the fact that the BBC evacuated their symphony orchestra to Bristol and one could go to concerts for a shilling, lunchtime and evening. I saw Henry Wood conduct Bach's Brandenburg One, and Beethoven's Fifth in the first half of a concert, and a sprightly 40-ish Walton conduct his First Symphony, probably the first performance in Bristol. Never having had in the family more than Gilbert and Sullivan and the like, I was not prejudiced against modern music and could and can take most things with an open mind. I bought my first modern record in 1940 of the then recent Walton Violin Concerto, and by then liked Stravinsky, Bartok, etc. There was hardly any music that I did not like; and if I didn't, I wanted to know *why*. There was not much chance to hear music during the war. When I was demobbed, I listened to a lot, and was much educated by the Pelican edition of *You and Music*, by Christian Darnton.

There was also naturism (then called nudism). Originally this was for me closely linked with sex, with surreptitious buying of soft porn in Paris, and nudist magazines. But from this grew a genuine liking for nudism which has been with me ever since (see chapter 15).

In 1939, however, life took a more serious turn, and not specifically because of the war. Wendy Hewgill-Smith came to stay with us in Bristol after taking a London degree in English. She was a college friend of my sister, Katharine. She had been living with Dorian

Cooke, a poet of the 'New Apocalypse' group, on the fringe of which was Dylan Thomas. On the outbreak of war, Cooke was offered a job in Zagreb in Yugoslavia (then a remote place) with the British Council. He wanted her to go with him, but she had second thoughts, and retreated to Bristol. She would have probably had a better life if she had stayed with him, and gone to Zagreb.

However, we 'fell in love at first sight', and were soon intimate. In 1940 we were married, and by 1941 we had a daughter, Genny. My life had changed; but since this takes us into wartime, we now turn to the war itself, and another major end to my boyish laughter.

2 War; life in the RAF;
beginning in archaeology;
Studio Rahtz and school teaching
(1941-53)

War

Any idea about futures or careers became increasingly uncertain with the imminence of war; it saved me from having to make decisions. It wasn't clear how soon one was going to be called up or when the bombs would start. I remember going out from the city accountant's office at 11am for coffee and seeing the posters on the declaration of war on 3 September; we waited for bombs the same day or night but none came. I was just due for a holiday but it was difficult to make proper plans, so Wendy and I went to my mother's cottage at Compton Martin. The summer was hot and we cycled over Mendip day after day, swimming in Minories Pool, and picking blackberries in Ebbor Gorge.

On our return to Bristol, it was clear that there was to be no imminent call-up into the armed forces. I continued to study for the intermediate examination of the Institute of Chartered Accountants (which I did eventually pass in 1941 at the third attempt).

Wendy gave up a temporary secretarial job she had been doing since coming to Bristol. We were then what are nowadays called partners, and my life had fundamentally changed; I had enough money left (from a legacy from my grandmother) to support us for the time being, and I was now earning some fees from selling nude pictures of Wendy (emasculated in those days) to the nudist magazines *Sun Bathing Review* and *Health and Efficiency*. Oddly enough, my father was quite proud of these, and showed them off to his friends.

We went to live for a while at Compton Martin. We had a lot in common, especially music and such literature as I had become aware of.

We were in this rather idyllic state through the autumn of 1939, and in time for the great ice storm in the winter of 1939-40 when rain froze on the trees and coated everything with ice; trees crashed everywhere and telephone lines and all buses stopped for several days because the roads were blocked. We were stuck there but didn't mind. We walked over the frozen Mendip top to Cheddar and saw huge icicles in the Gorge.

In 1940 I purchased my first motorcycle for £5 — a 150cc Triumph (14). I had to keep it secret from my father, because of my elder brother Edward's death. It took us on many trips during the uneasy days of 1940. It was strangely in the spring at Compton Martin that we experienced our first bomb. A German raider unloaded over the woods, hit a cottage and killed the family in it. The bang in the middle of the night was tremendous. And then the next morning we were in the garden and a delayed action bomb went off with a frightful 'crump'.

14 My first motorbike (Triumph 150cc), bought for £5, 1940 (note headlamp war-time shield)

During 1940 Wendy became pregnant, and I had to face up to real responsibility for the first time in my life. After initial feelings of doom and disaster I resigned myself to a ruined life, not altogether unmixed with some pride at the prospect of having a family of my own, and pleasure at shaking off the shackles of accountancy. Wendy went through all the chemical changes that accompany pregnancy and remembered little of the war, or bombs or anything, and took to impending motherhood quite calmly. We were married in November 1940, not from any personal wish, but to please both families.

We were at Compton Martin when labour began; we had arranged with Mr Gough's taxi at Cheddar to take Wendy to Southmead Hospital in Bristol; he grumblingly arrived and took us there in the middle of the night. She had a difficult labour of some 27 hours. In those days fathers weren't encouraged to be present; I went back to Cotham Road and had a stiff drink. I remember still feeling rather reckless and irresponsible.

My sister Mary, who lived at Cheddar, agreed to have Wendy and the new baby, and teach Wendy the skills of being a young mother. Daughter Philippa Gentian (Genny) was a splendid baby, and won a baby show at Cheddar in June 1941. I went back and forth from Bristol to Cheddar, putting in rather irregular appearances at the office in the city.

We spent some time at Compton Martin as well; by being in the country Wendy missed the blitzes on Bristol, and I was also out of the city at weekends when the bombs came down.

We did, however, witness the big daylight raid on Filton aircraft factory, north of Bristol, which killed hundreds of people. There was a tremendous roaring in the air and over the Channel we saw 50 or so bombers and as many fighters in dense formation heading for Bristol. They got back to Germany without loss, the Spitfires being elsewhere or too few. They tried the same thing the next day but never got beyond the south coast.

I returned to Bristol some Monday mornings to disaster. Once I found the city in flames and all the firemen's hoses frozen into ice which was all over the burning buildings round Bristol Bridge; it must have been a cold night.

Once I made my way up towards Cotham Road finding house after house in ruins and wondering if the family house at No. 27 would still be there; it was, but it had been a near thing. The house behind the back garden was gone and another up the road — a microsecond on the bomb-aimer's push-button. The family (**15**) were in a state of shock, Father white-faced, Mumma strained and Katharine weeping; and this several hours later. Another night, when we were there, there was a fire-bomb raid. Incendiaries fell with a terrible clatter and some six or seven were in the house and garden. We rushed out to put them out with sand, the whole sky was light and there was shrapnel flying; Father was at his best as an air raid warden. The people next door were away and a fire-bomb was burning in the top flat. We had to break down the door with an axe. Sometimes on other occasions I'd

15 Wartime family group in 1941; back row, Roland, PAR, Roland's wife Jean, my first wife Wendy, sister Mary, and cousin Morris; lower row, sister Katharine and Morris's wife; and my mother with her first three grandchildren; Gentian is on her left side on her lap

been on the top floor when a few bombs whined and I shot down to the basement — four flights down in as many seconds. I also did a rota of fire-watching in the city.

1941 was an uneasy year, not only because of our rather mixed living and travelling, and the general gloom at the way the war was going, but also because of the increasing likelihood that I should soon be drafted.

There was in those days some social disgrace at being a conscientious objector, and apart from a general feeling of dreading service, I did not attempt to avoid it. It was increasingly clear that this war at least had to be fought; the issue was clear-cut — it was either to win the war or become part of the Third Reich. Hitler was the very embodiment of evil for my generation, and remains so today; though there have been many horrors in the meantime. Having become a husband and a father, I was also depressed at the prospect of not seeing my family, perhaps not for a long time. I was 'called up' in October 1941. I chose to go into the Royal Air Force (RAF) as less unpleasant than being a soldier or going to sea. I could doubtless have got a commission if I'd passed aircrew requirements (as Philip Barker did) but would have been unlikely to survive (he was lucky!).

I went to Penarth for 'kitting out' and came 'up against it' for the first time in my life, the horror of having to be on intimate living terms with what my mother would have called 'awful working-class men', and being bawled at by even worse sergeants and corporals, having to wear rough blue clothing, woollen coarse underwear and boots (which took some getting used to); and brass and other webbing which had to be polished, blancoed, and cleaned; and hard beds with hair mattresses and awful food. I loathed it all.

Everybody had to be assigned a 'trade'; I was put down to be an electrician; this was not a choice, but an order. My 'intake of airmen' was due (after two weeks) to go somewhere else to learn drill, etc, but they asked for volunteers to stay behind for fire-watching and then to go on to the drill station with the next intake. I decided, anything to delay that; so I volunteered — a fateful and successful decision. For once I did the right thing; the intake I was now in went to Weston-Super-Mare for drill and then onto Melksham for electrical training while the original intake went to Morecambe in Lancashire, and then to Henlow in Middlesex. So I was near home for over six months, and could get back to Wendy and Genny at regular intervals. Four others of my intake had similar ideas. It should be said here that a considerable proportion of the men were far more depressed than I was — the men of 34 or so who'd been torn away from home and family and job. It was a miserable gathering at Penarth. But of course the five of us who stayed behind were immediately an experienced élite, and soon experts in avoiding all work; we struck up quite a friendship. What an unlikely quintet we were! Young fresh-faced Sussex bicycle repairer from the country, short, innocent and how appropriately-named Frank Butters — sounds like someone out of a Benjamin Britten opera. Why did *he* volunteer to stay in Penarth?

Then Ron Haslam — a clerk from Torquay, *c*.28, absolutely sour and cynical, but with some sick humour. Tony Davis, a wild and excitable schoolmaster, tall and thin and very Welsh. And lastly Edgar Jackson, a shy, reserved slightly effeminate dark chap who missed his pretty wife terribly. He'd started off as a cigarette-boy in a Warminster cinema, had risen to be manager of it and also played the piano at the cinema. What did we have in common that made us volunteer? Like those on the River Quai Bridge? Or did we — and

16 Aircraftman Rahtz: studio portrait, Bridlington, 1942

here a thin memory pokes — actually find ourselves in a group, perhaps at a canteen table or in a queue, or in a dormitory. We decided to go it together; perhaps none of us singly would have dared to take such a chance — there was after all the well-known service rule 'never volunteer for anything'!

After this two weeks respite, we were now all fitted out in our scratchy uniforms, we were aircraftmen second class (AC II) (**16**) and proceeded to Weston-Super-Mare. Weston was ghastly: we slept in some terrible boarding house on 'biscuits' — square hair mattresses on wooden floors and blankets with no sheets — and this was in November. Then up at 6.30 to walk into town for an awful breakfast. This was followed by a parade on the front which had a certain grim majesty in winter with seagulls in the early morning light, muddy waves breaking over the yellow-grey sands, but always in the background the glorious mass — unspoilt then as now — of Brean Down. Here we would march, halt, turn round shoulder rifles (SHOULDER ARMS they shouted, and then ORDER-R-R ARMS), and how to stick bayonets into horrible Germans screaming at them in a frenzy of blood-lust. Very difficult to feel blood-lust when faced with a sand-bag; it was all pretty ridiculous. A further torture was teeth. I'd had continuing fast decay and neglect in adolescence because I was afraid of pain, but now there was no escape, I had to be dentally fit. So here was a fast, ruthless but efficient RAF dentist who did a dozen fillings at a time — all amalgam, which lasted for years. One wasn't a success; he filled on a nerve and when the anaesthetic wore off, the nerve jumped as if a red-hot needle was stuck in it; this jumping went on for days — very demoralising. It was cold out on that seafront in the early morning. Every Saturday a tall booming flight-sergeant (F/S) told us we'd all have to be on Sunday church-parade and every Saturday night I'd sneak off to see Wendy and baby Genny and have Kelloggs cornflakes and cream instead of porridge, and every Sunday evening I'd sneak back trembling in case I'd been noticed — I never was, luckily.

There were lighter moments, as when on frosty mornings, with ice on the front, the F/S would shout SHOULDER-R-R-R AR-R-RMS and a lot of men fell down — big laugh, temporarily discipline breaks down — even F/S smiles. Even better when a grim Warrant Officer (the worst kind — risen from the ranks — the real officers did at least speak English) got up on top of the pavilion of the swimming pool on the front to survey us at drill; he put his gloved hands on the rail in front then took them off and with a bellow that echoed over to Brean Down and back again: JESUS BLOODY WEPT!! — his gloves were all covered with fresh red paint — a great moment.

However after six weeks the horror ended to be supplanted by a new one — Melksham. This was a dreary camp where we went through the Grade II electricians course, and learnt the basic elements of electric wiring and motors that kept an aeroplane in the air. The winter of 1941/42 was bitter and ice and snow stopped us from getting out much. The cooped-up conditions led to trouble (even fighting) with so many men living together. The five of us had moved on to this course together and we moved through quite easily. I found the theoretical side easy but when I tried to take electric motors to pieces they flew in all directions. However, we all passed and Butters and I (in June 1942) were posted together to RAF Acklington, a long way from home in Northumberland, where I hardly understood the way they talked. Here I was put in the battery charging shed, keeping aeroplane batteries charged and ready for use. My lack of practical sense let me down here and I always let the batteries get too fizzy. On one memorable occasion I accidentally siphoned a whole carboy of sulphuric acid all over the floor and spent some hours mopping it up with sawdust.

Life on the station wasn't too bad in that summer. It did at least have some point. There was a hero-élite of dashing young men who periodically took off to harry Germans and who never expected to return, so lived it up as best they could in Ashington or Morpeth. Many didn't return. But the ground crews were devoted to them and didn't grudge the toil and sweat of keeping those machines fit. But the pilots had all the best WAAFS (the Womens Auxiliary Air Force).

A romantic episode took place by the banks of the River Coquet close to the magnificent ruin of Warkworth Castle. I trespassed through a riverside garden in search of an upstream hermitage cut in the rock about which I'd heard, and here met the owner, one Elizabeth, a beautiful woman of *c.*25-30 with two young children and a husband away in the Navy. She invited me to have tea two or three times and we got on well, if politely. Then one evening I called when she was alone and we sat quietly by oil lamps, and eventually we were holding hands. I was beginning to entertain high hopes, when the phone rang — it was 'Charles', whose ship had just docked somewhere and he was on the way, so I was hustled out. I was invited to meet him the following Saturday afternoon and there was a polite tea-party to welcome him home; he didn't seem to suspect anything, and I wondered if there was anything to suspect after all; but when Elizabeth came out to bid me goodbye on my autocycle she gave me a passionate kiss. I never saw her again. (I returned to the spot in 1997; the house was still there, but an old lady living there was *not* Elizabeth, though she was a relation of the family.)

Summer ended and I was posted back to Melksham for a Grade 1 electricians course, thus being near home yet again (September 1942). I left Butters to his fate. (I did, however, see him again. In 1974 he decided he'd tour the country searching for his old pals. He'd found Tony Davis dead long since, Edgar still in the cinema, Ron not traced, but he found me after a lot of trouble, in a university seminar at Birmingham; he came with his wife and two children in a car-caravan.)

Now, back at Melksham, the hand of 'Fate' stepped in — the first in a series of long fortuitous events that have punctuated my life and career. A minor illness in 1942 set me back from my initial draft of fellow-trainees being taught the mysteries of electrical systems. On returning I fell in with the next draft; in the next bed to that allocated to me was Ernest Greenfield. I was rather untidy, but he was quite the opposite. He looked at me as though I were something that crawled out of a hole as I unpacked my books, marmalade, etc. and spread them around. I was obviously the epitome of what he disliked most. I nevertheless tried to be friendly — I was learning a lot by then about how to get on with people — and tried to engage him in conversation. He tried ignoring me and being rude, but when I asked him what he did before joining the RAF he thought 'Ah now, I can really snub this horror', and so he drew himself up to his full height and said 'I was a student of archaeology', hoping that would really finish me and put me in my place. However, I was interested enough to ask him more about it and in the end won his confidence — he showed me maps of his part of Kent and sites he'd like to dig when he got out, where he knew for various reasons there was something to be found, and one of them was called Lullingstone!

I made another friend at Melksham: Derek Helps, a six or seven footer from Daventry (where is he now?). We competed for top place in the exams; he was first and I was second of our class, though I still couldn't take a motor to pieces. We were both kept on nominally to be instructors. He went away finally on an instructor's course but mine never came through, I suspect because I'd fallen foul in the waiting period of one of the most unpleasant men I've ever met, Warrant Officer Baxter. I was kept on as a maintenance man at Melksham falling even fouler of W/O Baxter, especially when I was rewiring his room light and put my foot through the ceiling. I was got rid of by transferring me in early 1943 to a small group on the station who put aircraft together for instruction or something — I never quite gathered what it was about. Just before I joined there had been a fatal accident: an aircraftman was crushed when an undercarriage folded up when he was doing something to a wheel. The same thing happened again when one of our corporals was trapped by the neck; he screamed like mad — he'd seen the previous accident — and we lifted the wing off and pulled him out; his neck was bruised and cut a bit, but he remained in extreme shock for weeks and wouldn't go near an aeroplane for months.

But things seemed fairly quiet at this time (1943) so I got Wendy and Genny into a rented room at Lacock and cycled in every day. That was a happy time: the weather was good, it was a nice room, and now I was living out. I could get food to take home and we had a good summer of maybe 10 weeks. In the later summer of 1943 I was posted; W/O Baxter had got rid of me at last — the signal said 'Centaurus Flight' which meant nothing to anybody. But it turned out it was a new unit being formed to test the new Centaurus engine in service conditions, and there was a rumour that it would travel around — an awful prospect. There was nothing worse that not having a permanent home on a station.

Melksham hadn't been too bad — I remember Wendy and I went to a concert in Melksham by a new young singer who sang delightful folk songs; his name was Peter Pears.

I was delighted when I was told where to go to report to this new unit — RAF Locking, on the Compton Martin side of Weston! So I now lived with Wendy and got a lift each day into Locking, where we did absolutely nothing except sign on, since no one was ready to do anything with this Centaurus engine. So weeks went by, living in some fear that someone would start the thing; several other people had arrived by now; there was still the rumour that the unit was mobile. When orders came at last it was to go to RAF Filton at Bristol; this was really getting ridiculous! Meanwhile the war went on, and Genny was growing up. At Filton in late 1943 we were put with the 'civvies' (civilian aircraft workers) in the factory, ostensibly to be trained by them, but nothing happened — I saw for the first time what factory life was like. The heroes of the civvies here were the test-pilots, and one was killed when I was there, when a propellor came off and went through the fuselage.

Again I was living at home, this time at 27 Cotham Road and going back and forth on an autocycle, signing on at 8am and going up the road to have a bacon sandwich until 10 — a real 'scrounge' as we said in those days.   After a few months we moved over to the RAF side and the unit got going. It was not a happy group and seemed doomed from the start. I was supposed to check the aircraft electrics every day but I can't now remember actually doing anything. After a while one of our test aircraft crashed in Wales killing one of our pilots, but luckily it wasn't due to any negligence of mine. I wasn't really thought much of; I had not been popular either with the officers who would prefer the mechanics to be subservient, or the other men who thought I was peculiar. However, I stuck it out (as I was at home) until I was posted again, this time in 1944 to 'Azon' (whatever that might be) and this time significantly to Salisbury Plain.

Now the Air Force, after nearly three years, began to get tolerable. Firstly, Boscombe Down, the new station, was near Amesbury and Stonehenge; secondly, it was entirely a research establishment and there were a lot of eggheads there and, therefore, a lot of 'culture' going on; and thirdly, it was only a few hitching miles to Salisbury. Because there were thousands of troops all round, of the Army and RAF, it was full of entertainment, education, chamber music and more culture of all kinds. And, oddly enough, there again was Ernest Greenfield, who'd been having a miserable time with Lancaster bombers in the meantime. He now began to take me round Salisbury Plain to see lots of barrow groups, then intact except for tanks, and Stonehenge. I was now beginning to realise I was really interested in archaeology; I was impressed by the beauties and monuments of the Plain, over which I now regularly hitched to Bristol, returning free on the train on Sunday nights by some ruse which involved hiding in the lavatory at some point and then getting out through the goods yard at Salisbury.

My new unit was a nice one. Azon turned out to be an American radio-controlled bomb tail. They arrived in great crates — we fixed them up on bombers which then tested them in the New Forest ranges. As the bomb dropped, a flare started on its tail, and the bomb-aimer could then guide it by radio control onto its target. I found myself deputed to understand the electrics of it which were fairly straightforward; there were two other instrument people, Richardson and Tidy, with whom I got on well and tried to set on the road to culture, and Sgt Breward who was a bit of a flashy bully, but sufficiently intelligent to get on with. There was a poor underprivileged GD (general duties) man to clean up; he was a broad Liverpudlian whose only retort to anything was 'Ar — git away and fook'. We set up a nice cosy little racket on the bomb tail. The testing officers were very nice and I photographed the Squadron Leader's children. This may have saved my life, because when I was later (in 1944) posted to south-east Asia Command (SEAC) — which as it turned out, at that time, meant Japanese concentration camps and death or worse — he cancelled it (after I'd had embarkation leave and all the innoculations) on the pretext that this bomb tail was important and it would take months to train anyone else in my place, which was quite untrue — I could have trained someone in a week.

I had in all these three years been fighting a losing battle to have proper music instead of pop, but it was impossible to avoid the latter. All the time in our little unit hut we had the American Forces network on. I fixed a switch on the door so that when anyone came in, it switched off automatically. I can still hear that tune which introduced the big band noise: 'This is Sergeant Ray McKinley saying "how-de-do", and all the boys in the band saying "Howdy" too'. I went regularly to Salisbury, however, and heard a lot of music, plays and other cultural events.

In 1945, about April, another break came; a notice went up asking for volunteers who had matriculation to become EVT instructors, educational and vocational training, for personnel wishing to get in some education before returning to civilian life; now it looked as though the war with Germany was going our way. I put my name in and was sent on a splendid crash course at RAF Snitterfield just outside Stratford, my first visit to the Midlands. It was only a mile from where, 30 years later, I was to locate the palace of Hatton Rock (52). Here at last we met as an 'educated' group and were treated as such by skilled instructors. They made us into teachers in three weeks — we were taken to the Stratford theatre, to Warwick Castle and (to make sure we could speak) were asked to arrive with a 10-minute talk prepared. I had been reading Winbolt's *Britain BC* and I gave mine on the Mesolithic Tardenoisian and Azilian cultures — my first archaeological talk. It all went very well and thus began my third career, that of teacher. I returned to my home station of Boscombe Down with immediate promotion to sergeant, with all the benefits and higher standards of living of the sergeants' mess, and began teaching bookkeeping, English and Current Affairs — we were given hand-outs on the latter each week. Particularly interesting was the period of the 1945 Labour landslide; I had a mixed class of officers and men; the officers thought the end of the world had come.

We (**17**) had what seems, in retrospect, a good programme of some 45 subjects covered by about 16 teachers, under the control of the education officer; he was an ex-grammar school master from Stockton-on-Tees. Again I was posted to SEAC and (again after embarkation leave and innoculations) was reprieved because I was the only person in the station who could teach bookkeeping, which was much in demand. That's how accountancy may have saved my life!

The summer of 1945 was a fine one; the war in Europe was now over, and, although we still had to deal with the Far East, England was more relaxed. My life was divided into two parts, Boscome Down and Compton Martin. In Salisbury, I met in one of the forces canteens (a sort of club where volunteers did meals and which organised some cultural events) a very healthy, sporty private school teacher named Kay who introduced me to delightful places in which to swim nude — the river behind Salisbury Cathedral, and an even better place, now destroyed, at Great Durnford in the mill pool; the ruined mill was of several floors with wood and grain boxes, and these made excellent places in which to retire after swimming. On one occasion we had an assignment in her landlady's house in

17 Group at Stonehenge at dawn on the Summer Solstice of 1945; with some of my fellow-teachers on the EVT courses at nearby Boscombe Down; PAR on right

Salisbury. The landlady was due to go away one weekend but she didn't; so I was smuggled in and had to take my boots off and creep up the stairs while Kay engaged the landlady in conversation.

Wendy was again pregnant during this year, and our first son was born on 14 September, Nicholas Dominic (Nicky). We could better afford the extra expense now that I was getting a sergeant's pay.

I had been able in that final summer of 1946 to get to Bristol a good deal, having now acquired a car — a 1931 Austin 7. This not only meant that with a little machination, I could get away for three nights a week, but also made Wendy, Genny, Nicky and I more mobile. We began to drive around the area south of Bristol, looking especially now at ancient monuments, like Stanton Drew stone circles and churches, but also searching for new sites, with newly acquired 6" O.S. maps, on which we plotted our observations in the traditional manner.

My sojourn on Salisbury Plain had been educational; not only in meeting Ernest Greenfield again and being introduced to all the barrows and other monuments, but in realising that archaeology was not just about finding things; a belief encouraged by the popular knowledge of such figures as Howard Carter and Tutankhamun. I did not understand yet that it was an academic subject (and I hardly knew what that implied); nor exactly why there was any special point in knowing about the past or understanding the processes of history. But it had given me an appetite for the prehistoric landscape, and the great potential of fieldwork.

I was finally demobilised at the end of 1946, at the age of 25, after over five years in the RAF: not wholly a wasted time, and far better than those of most of my fellow-airmen. At Lytham St Annes I was checked out and given a new set of civilian clothes in which to return home to a new life.

Beginning in Archaeology

That new life had in a sense already begun, with our tentative beginnings of fieldwork while still in the RAF. In our search for new sites in the Compton Martin area, we had noticed a splendid mound by a farm at Butcome (4), about three miles away. Here was another turning point. Had I been a responsible sort of person I would have done more non-excavational fieldwork, putting entries on ordnance maps, etc. I found, however, that my curiosity was too great. What was the point of finding an earthwork or a mound and not knowing what was inside it?

So Wendy and I took the bold step in 1946 of asking the farmer if we could dig the Butcombe mound. He readily agreed: the die was cast. I was to be an excavator not a fieldworker. Greenfield had given us a copy of that excellent do-it-yourself textbook, *Field Archaeology*, by the late Richard Atkinson, still a young man in 1946. With this, and some hints picked up from Greenfield, we began a trench across the mound, 5ft wide (*c*.1.5m); armed with a spade, a shovel, two trowels, a prismatic compass, a measuring tape, string and a notebook. Such a proceeding sounds incredible in retrospect, almost criminal. I had no training, nor had I even seen an excavation. There was however no law against it, and no one to point out the folly, though Greenfield was rather alarmed, at a distance.

My motive was largely egotistical; I felt rather important doing archaeology. We soon found pottery beneath the topsoil on the edge of the mound, and a stone 'pavement' sloping up to the centre. Being still stationed at Boscombe Down, I took the pottery to Salisbury Museum. I explained to the late Hugh Shortt that I'd found this in a barrow at Butcombe and assumed it to be Bronze Age. After a pregnant pause he informed me 'Ah, well, no, not really, you see it's green-glazed, and that means it's medieval — probably thirteenth-century . . .'. Clearly, here was a problem; and this I would rate as another turning point, both as regards the pottery and the stone paving. I realised with a rare feeling of humility that I hadn't the slightest idea what I was doing, and sought some help.

By this time I'd got hold of a copy of the Methuen *County Archaeology* series on Somerset, by one Dina P. Dobson. Quite fortunately she lived near Butcombe, at Wrington, as I found out from the telephone directory. I called her and explained what I'd been doing, and my problem. Her reply on the phone was 'How very interesting: do come to tea'. I can only now imagine her horror, but she hid it well. It turned out that the mound was well-known and had a catalogue number (T40 in the UBSS Series) and was believed to be a barrow, and a prized one at that. Had she been hostile I might well have been completely put off, and become the worst kind of self-opinionated amateur.

It has to be remembered here that there had been very little archaeology done at all in Britain during the War, and almost none in Somerset. It was thus probably politic on her part to encourage someone who at least showed some interest. She came to visit and so did Greenfield (by that time back in Kent). He noticed some millstone fragments among the spoil we'd thrown out. This was the clue: it was not a barrow, but the mound of a medieval windmill. We subsequently found the cross-shaped trenches for the post-mill (4). The fact that it was medieval and not, after all, Bronze Age, may be seen as another harbinger of my future destiny as primarily a medieval archaeologist.

Demobilisation brought freedom from the ghastliness of being ordered about by unpleasant people, but also its own problems, the principal being what was one to do? School teaching was in the family and, as I had acquired a little experience in my last years in the RAF, I applied for the Emergency Teachers Training Course, a scheme designed to provide the numerous teachers now needed in British schools. There was however a waiting list, so I had to think of something else for at least three years. With my gratuity from the RAF I bought a suitable camera and other equipment and set up Studio Rahtz in a back room of the large family house in Bristol. This kept the wolf from the door. Again it was learning by doing. I also had a certain facility in getting babies to smile, dogs to look alert, being the awkward but necessary interloper at weddings, and I also developed a skill for hand-colouring. I also made roll films out of second-hand backing papers and ex-RAF film. These sold well in a time of scarcity and came back for developing and printing as they had my address to give them credibility. I had an outlet in Cheddar Gorge, but little knew how important Cheddar was to be in my later archaeological life.

As with accountancy, the photographic experience was useful for my future as an archaeologist. We continued digging at Butcombe, also getting to know more about the archaeology of the North Somerset area.

A crucial visitor brought to Butcombe by Dina Dobson was Bryan Hugh St John O'Neil, then the Chief Inspector of Ancient Monuments for the MOPBW, a powerful and influential man. His visit to our small dig was I thought very flattering, and did much to boost an inflated ego. Had I made it so soon into the ranks of British archaeologists? He was polite but non-committal. It was only years later that I learnt he had been asked to come to see if I should be stopped. He had the power to do this. His comment, as I later learnt was 'Well, Dina, he's making a mess of it, but he seems to have some flair for it, so let him go on and see what happens'. I would have been severely deflated had I known!

On the Ordnance Survey map we saw the name Pagans Hill, near Chew Stoke: a romantic-sounding name. This led us to view some earthworks on a hill with a panoramic view to the east over the Chew Valley. There was a prominent mound and other odd banks and hollows. What it all was I didn't know, but was determined to find out.

O'Neil came to see the site and thought the mound might be a building ('I get a square feeling') and other earthworks. We soon found out it was in fact Roman: material had been found here in the early nineteenth century by the indefatigable Reverend J. Skinner. He kept a major *Diary* in 90 volumes recording his tours on horseback, and the antiquities he encountered. The diary was mostly not about archaeology, but also people, especially his own parishioners at Camerton; so unflattering was he that his will stipulated that his diary was not to be published until 60 years after his death (by suicide in 1840). So it was never seen until this century, and proved to be a goldmine for north Somerset archaeology. It has still not been fully transcribed or indexed a century later.

Having gone as far as needed at Butcombe in 1949 and filled it in by hand (I had by now found that archaeology was hard graft), we were ready to start on Pagans Hill in the summer of 1949. By this time I realised that archaeology was a major intellectual challenge; and its purposes far deeper than finding things in romantic contexts.

We began work by excavating one quadrant of the prominent mound: a method used for barrow excavation, and (as it turned out) appropriate to any concentric mound, giving a radial section on two axes. Patches of a stone flagged floor appeared; it was clear that the mound was the site of a very substantial building. Advice came from all sides that its hilltop position made it very likely that it was a temple. A Roman temple was romantic and exotic beyond our imagination.

Either side of the floor patches were deep trenches full of masonry debris, with large stones at the base. A kindly visitor (Mr Priestley, who discovered the Roman temple of Apollo at Nettleton Scrub) explained to me that these were robbed-out *wall-trenches*, where the temple walls had stood, and had later been dug out to re-use the stone. Not only did Priestley refrain from asking me what I was doing excavating a Roman temple if I didn't know what a wall-trench was, but even put 10s (50p) in our collecting box, then a substantial contribution.

The temple excavation was completed (**18**) between 1949 and 1953 with the help of friends, and proved to be a double octagon in plan, of late third-century date, possibly dedicated to Apollo (1, 2, 6, 7, 143). Finds were numerous: a good example of learning by doing was the finding of a Roman coin (the first of many) of the Emperor Tetricus II. The obverse inscription was clear: TETRICVS/IUN. I got a copy of Seaby's Coin Catalogue and was quickly into Roman numismatics, reinforcing my scanty school ancient history. All this was of course done on a shoestring with the same minimal equipment.

In 1950 I was admitted to the one-year teaching course at Redland Training College at Bristol. I nearly failed this. My first 'teaching practice' (sending one out in real schools) was rather a disaster. I did well on the academic side, however, including among other things a thesis on John Donne. The History tutor, Miss Saywell, commented that my whole manner was too laid-back for the rough and tumble of state schools; that I had the style to suit a grammar school, but not the material. She told the Principal, however, that I would be a good person to have on a school staff; so a final teaching practice was arranged, in which I was given a class of 11-year-old children at Ashton Gate School. They had a real horror of a martinet teacher, and were so relieved to see me that they ate out of my hand; clearly Miss Saywell had done a fix.

One interlude was that a group of us were sent to Denmark for a week to observe the 'Folk High School' system there, a means of stimulating what is now called continuing education, and as a kind of cultural exchange. The voyage out in the *Krön-Prinz Frederich*

18 Pagans Hill c.1950; 'Porthos' (Herbert) Taylor and his wife are at top left; he was the most experienced archaeologist in the University of Bristol Spelaeological Society. Ernest Greenfield is in the trench

(via Harwich) was traumatic. We ran into a great storm, which that night sunk many ships, and drove more scurrying into harbour. Most of the ship's passengers were sick, and no one was allowed on deck. In our cabin after a noisy night we heard the engines stop, and thought with relief that we must have arrived at Esbjerg, where we were due at 8am. I staggered up on deck to find some coffee, and discovered that we had indeed stopped, but in the middle of the North Sea, hove-to facing into the waves, which were the highest I have ever seen — they looked to be rising 15m or more above the deck. All the saloons were flooded, and many windows broken.

We eventually limped into Esbjerg about 3pm; several of the crew were taken off on stretchers, with broken limbs. The captain was reported in the paper the next day as saying that the crossing had been the worst he had known in 50 years at sea. We travelled through the rest of the day by train and ferry to Elsinore, where we were to stay in a college.

Denmark was in a poor state after the German occupation, but we were well looked after and taken to see a number of places, such as the Tivoli Gardens and Elsinore Castle; and were given a memorable lecture on the great Danish philosopher and theologian, Kierkegaard.

We were also taken on the short ferry across to Sweden. Here, at Halsingborg, was a different world — all clean, smart and prosperous, as Sweden had managed to stay neutral. The contrast with Denmark (and England to a lesser extent) was dramatic: bright lights and shops full of food and goods (the rationing system was still in force in post-war England). I was able to bring back a nice jacket for daughter Genny, and butter! We were also taken to the great cathedral city of Lund, where we saw a little of the half-century of archaeological work in the city — my first glimpse of archaeology in a north European country.

Sweden was a reminder of pre-war England, and a promise of the hoped-for economic revival of the later decades. I was disappointed to find that the Swedes (contrary to popular belief) did not have mixed nudist swimming in the public sauna plus swimming pool complex at Halsingborg; but it was a stimulating break in our Redland course.

I was duly appointed to the staff of Baptist Mills Primary School, where I didn't do too badly. One of the staff, Leslie Harris, took an interest in Pagans Hill, and joined with me in later excavation (2). After only a term, I was shifted to Greenbank Secondary Modern School, then ruled with wisdom and the cane by the famous Herbert Mizen, who had achieved good results in terms of school discipline and post-school careers. He glared at me, clearly gaining an unfavourable first impression: 'we don't have any passengers here, Mr Rahtz'.

Greenbank brought out, in the two years I was there, homicidal tendencies; I often went home and cried from the stress. I did, however, win through from my 'new boy' state, by organising a successful 'inter-house' drama competition. But had I stayed in teaching, I would have specialised in the intellectually-backward children — who had hardly learnt to read or write properly by the age of 12. With them I had some sympathy, unlike the (slightly) smarter horrors. It is odd that my career eventually took me to the other end of the spectrum, to teaching undergraduates.

Some relief was afforded by being allowed to take selected boys to Pagans Hill for an afternoon's 'digging'; this made some impression on them, as I learnt from 'thank you letters' gratefully received many years later, when the boys had grown up.

Another major event was making a new friend in Eric Brown, the only member of staff with any cultural aspiration. He was the music-master; he not only taught boys individual instruments, but even ran a school orchestra, writing several 'musical comedies' for them himself, with written-out parts for each and every boy according to his

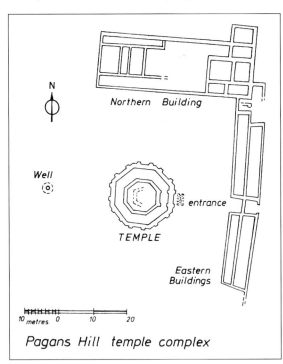

Pagans Hill temple complex

19 Plan of Pagans Hill

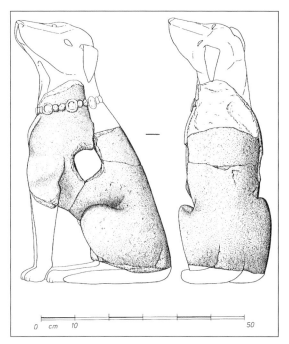

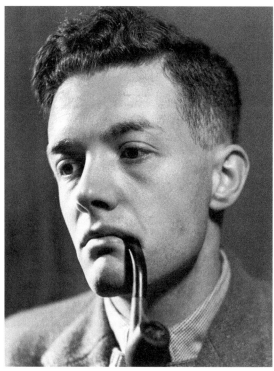

20 Stone statue of a dog; this was published in 1958 as having surmounted a Tudor gate post; but after 30 years it was shown by George Boon that it was in fact Roman; he suggested it was part of a temple sculpture group, centred on a statue of Apollo

21 The late George Boon as a young man c.1950; he helped a great deal with Pagans Hill, and we continued to collaborate until his death in 1994

ability. In this way he taught me to play the viola, and enlisted me in the orchestra. He came back to our house, and we played sonatas by Bach and Handel: a great stimulus to my increasing love of music, though I never learnt to play well (see chapter 15).

Unpleasant though school-teaching was (quite the worst two years of my life), there were weekends and longish holidays, when the family could go camping in Cornwall and digging at Pagans Hill.

1951 saw the completion not only of the temple plan, but also of its ancillary buildings (**19**) (by selective trenching: much remains to be dug there), and the temple well. This was 17m deep (56ft) and 87cm wide (2ft 4in), its emptying was a deep and dangerous exploit. We did, however, have the help of an experienced caver (the late Leslie Millward) who organised steel flexible ladders and baling gear: water came in fast at 10m (32ft); Millward became our crucial safety officer.

The stratification of the well was complex, and this is no place to describe the sequence of finds in detail (2, 7, 143). Two finds may however be selected, as being of special interest in a wider context. The first was the stone torso of a dog, rather larger than life size (**20**). It was only *c*.6m (20ft) from the surface. The great scholar Ralegh Radford (who died aged 98, in 1998) pronounced it to be post-medieval, the kind of dog that sits on gate-posts at the

22 Seventh- to eighth-century glass jar from the well

ends of drives leading to great houses, bearing an escutcheon; and it was published as such (7). A quarter of a century later, the late George Boon (**21**) had second thoughts, and thought it was Roman after all. He supported this by scholarly research and was able to convince Radford. It is now seen as part of the temple statuary — an attribute of the god (143).

The second find was the only really valuable thing (in cash and academic terms) I have ever found — a blue glass jar, nearly complete (**22**). It was in the well at a depth of 11m (36ft), with the remains of an iron bucket. At the time of its recovery we assumed it to be Roman, though admittedly a classy piece. I sent a photograph of it in 1952 to the late Donald Harden, then the principal authority on glass in Britain. To our great surprise, he pronounced it to be seventh century, of Anglo-Saxon manufacture, as also was the bucket (7). Re-examining the excavation diary, I realised it had indeed been found above the main mass of Roman debris.

Here was a harbinger indeed, my first introduction to the late and post-Roman centuries in the west (the 'Dark Ages') which was to be my major pre-occupation in research for the next 40 years. Even at that inexperienced time, it was obvious to me that something important had been going on in the temple some three centuries after the 'end of Roman Britain' (88), though the full implications have only more recently been realised (143). A curious fact here, possibly no more than a coincidence (though I don't think so) is that the glass has eight panels in its decorative strips, the same number as the temple walls (**23**)! I shall discuss the wider ramifications of the post-Roman evidence in chapter 9.

We realised that the temple, having been a very substantial building over 20m (60ft) in diameter and of at least this height, would not have been easily demolished. Indeed that it

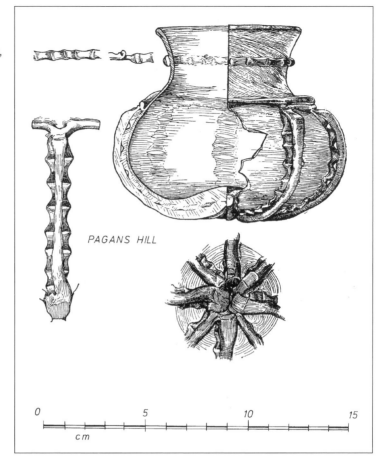

*23 Drawing of the
glass jar; it has
eight vertical strips,
echoing the eight
sides of the
octagonal temple*

PAGANS HILL

```
0           5          10          15
├──┼──┼──┼──┼──┼──┼──┼──┼──┼──┼──┼──┼──┤
      cm
```

was still standing in medieval times was shown by numerous finds of medieval pottery on its floor below fallen Roman roofing tiles (1): again difficult to interpret.

Another curious find from the temple ruins was a small blackish figurine. Ralegh Radford identified this as a votive offering, a little figure of a priest by an altar. A photograph was sent to a great art-historian, the late Jocelyn Toynbee; it reminded her, she replied, 'of the provincial sculpture of north-west Gaul'. I sent it to Rex Hull for a Festival of Britain exhibition he was organising in 1951; alas, he told me, it was not Roman, but from a black basalt Wedgwood teapot, the decorative knob from the lid, of the widow and her cruse (a Biblical motif used by Wedgwood)! But where was the rest of the teapot? Was this a modern votive offering, cast upon a site known locally as 'numinous'? The name Pagans Hill, incidentally, proved to be a modern one, derived from the name Payne (143). Under all these Roman and later levels was important Earlier Iron Age material (6) — my first introduction to prehistoric excavation.

Pagans Hill had made me well-known and relatively respectable both as a local archaeologist (**24**), and more widely. Having my picture in the paper did a lot for my ego, offsetting my dismal failure as a schoolmaster. But more importantly, as we shall see in the next chapter, it paved the way for my whole subsequent career and life. Apart from such

24 Poster for my first lecture at Chew Stoke, near Pagans Hill

a direct link, I often thought of the site in later years, not least because of its post-Roman aspects, which became more and more relevant as other Dark Age sites were excavated (see chapter 9). I wondered whether, in my inexperience, I had missed more subtle finds of Dark Age evidence than that of the finds in the well? I remembered the 1949-53 excavation as being relatively straightforward, with few complications, such as stratigraphic complexities. Was it all so simple as I'd remembered?

I therefore determined that at some suitable time I would return to Pagans Hill. Here we jump forward over thirty years. I decided that as a last act as Professor at York (see chapter 7), and to celebrate my impending retirement, I would use the resources of the department (and the students' fieldwork allowances) to go back at last to Pagans Hill. Thus in spring 1986 we approached the present farmer for permission to dig again; to our delight he not only agreed, but he and his wife contracted to put us up and give us all meals. In the bitter Easter period of that year, we re-opened and enlarged the area around the well, and opened a new trench between the temple and the well; and another on the south side of the temple itself (**25**). We found little new: the site was as straightforward as I'd remembered, but the gnawing doubt I had was settled. The new work was able to put

25   Back to Pagans Hill after 35 years; the well area uncovered, in the very cold Easter of 1986

the old into a better perspective; the subsequent publication (143) was used to discuss other relevant finds in the area, and to elaborate on the wider significance of the site.

It has sometimes seemed that the sites I have encountered got more and more difficult, ranging from the simplicity of Pagans Hill to the severely challenging problems of Cheddar in the 1960s and Cadbury Congresbury in the 1970s. I have had the rather uncharacteristic feeling that my sequence of digs had all been arranged for me by the 'Great Archaeologist in the Sky'; but that way madness lies, and we will now turn to the events that led from Pagans Hill to my professional involvement in archaeology.

3 Escape from school; being paid; rescue and research archaeology (1953-63)

Bryan O'Neil now comes into the picture again. Near Pagans Hill, the Bristol Waterworks Company (BWC) were beginning the construction of a large (485 ha/1200 acres) new reservoir in the Chew Valley (the Chew Valley Lake — CVL). O'Neil asked me to section the only antiquity then known in the area to be flooded — a minor Roman road at Moreton (**26**). I was flattered, especially when I realised I would have *workmen*, a *hut* and would be *paid*. I agreed to do this in the Easter school holiday of 1953.

Ernest Greenfield had spent the years since the war excavating at Lullingstone, which proved to be one of the most interesting Roman villas in England, with a wealth of important structures, including a Roman Christian room with wall-paintings. But his personal and financial affairs had gone disastrously wrong, so he was looking for work. He came to visit me in the Chew Valley to see our road excavation. While he was there, some BWC men came to visit. They informed us that we should really be over at an area being stripped by machines by the River Chew (Herriotts Bridge, 79); here, they said, there was much black pottery and dark marks in the clay. We were taken aback to find that an entire Roman settlement was being uncovered, over several hectares — masses of pottery, hearths, a few human skeletons, and dozens of ditches for drainage of the low-lying area; quite unsuspected, not being visible on air photographs of pasture. O'Neil arranged for Greenfield to deal with this site. In the evenings we walked over the area of the proposed reservoir and found more sites, including a villa (Chew Park, 79) indicated by building debris and pottery kicked up by moles. I applied to the Bristol Education authorities for leave of absence, which was granted for the next term. When the scale of the work needed became clear, I applied for a further year's leave which was refused. I resigned.

Thus I burnt my boats and became a professional archaeologist. I knew I had to succeed in this, or it was back to the schoolmaster's desk — the strongest of incentives. In the event, Greenfield and I dug continuously through two summers and two winters, excavating an astonishing variety of sites, revolutionising the archaeology of that part of North Somerset. This had hitherto been confined mainly to the Mendip Hills, though the presence of the Stanton Drew stone circles, further downstream, should have warned everybody what lay in the fertile valley bottom of the River Chew. Here major timber circles have recently (1997) been located beneath the stones.

Our earliest finds were hundreds of flint flakes and tools, extending back into several thousand years BC. The earliest structure was Neolithic (*c*.3000 BC), a small house based on timber uprights, the first habitation of this period found in the area. Another unusual

26 Group at Moreton, in the Chew Valley, 1953. Left to right: Ernest Greenfield, George Boon, Robert Hurdle (a Bristol artist), Bryan Hugh St J O'Neil, and Mrs D.P. Dobson-Hinton; before the Chew Valley Lake excavations

find was a circular cremation burial of the Early Bronze Age, with pieces of eight Beakers (a distinctive pottery type of this period; *c.*1800 BC), a barbed and tanged flint arrowhead, with male cremated bone fragments, and a flat stone quern, for corn grinding. The last was of especial interest, as the earliest evidence of cereal cultivation in the valley. Another 'ritual' pit of this period (but with no cremation) yielded an archer's wrist guard and sherds of Grooved Ware, another special kind of pottery of this time, often found in the neighbourhood of great ceremonial sites like Stanton Drew.

Clearly the valley had been widely used in the pre-Roman millennia. There would in the marshy valley have been rich resources not only of arable soil but of fish and wild-fowl, now of course both famous features of the new reservoir.

There were many structures of the immediately pre-Roman centuries; these were contemporary with an Iron Age hillfort (Burledge) on higher ground south of the Chew Valley; in the hillfort we did some small excavations as an 'extra' to the rescue work in the valley (79).

The most extensive exploitation of the whole reservoir area came, however, in the Roman period. In the first century AD the Roman military and administrative machine had gained control of North Somerset. The Romans were especially interested in the extraction of lead and silver from the mines at Charterhouse-on-Mendip. The forced labour here would need feeding; it would not have been easy to grow enough on the rather poor soils of Mendip. The Chew Valley provided the nearest good arable soils linked to Mendip by the Roman road. To achieve this, the whole valley was extensively drained for the first (and last!) time in its history. A great network of ditches, large and small, was dug over wide areas. These we were able to map, by the use of large machines — the first time I had used mechanical excavation. The big scrapers were available from

BWC at a nominal cost, when not being used for the stripping of clay for the reservoir dams. In an hour, at a cost to us of £1.50, the great machines could cut a trench 30m x 3m to depth of a metre. The ditches could be seen as darker fillings in the red clay subsoil, and sampled at intervals for dating by pottery. Herriott's Bridge was, we suggested, a peasant or forced labour settlement for all this work and for the growing of cereals on the large scale that followed.

We also watched all the machine stripping carried out by the BWC themselves. We used to ride on the backs of the machines (strictly against regulations) and watch the clay subsoil being exposed behind them. When we saw a feature (a ditch, pit or grave) we jumped off, quickly excavated it, gave it a record number, described it in a notebook, put the finds in a bag, took magnetic bearings with a prismatic compass on two telegraph poles so we could map it later, and jumped back on the next passing machine. Exhilarating archaeology!

With this and hand excavation we were able to chart the course of the Roman development of the valley over the first three centuries AD, with extensive arable cultivation, burial enclosures, humble settlement sites, and a great barn-like building, presumably to store produce.

But now at the end of the third century AD, there was a big change, from state to private enterprise. A villa was built at Chew Park, a slightly raised area in the centre of the valley. A big square lime kiln, using limestone from the nearby hills, provided the mortar for a stone-built residence. This had several rooms, two wings and a front corridor. One room had very deep foundations; this we interpreted as a grain-storing 'tower'; but there was also ample evidence for other forms of farming, notably stock-raising, in the form of numerous animal bones.

As a villa, Chew Park, while well built, with iron grilles across the windows and painted plaster on the walls, was not luxurious. There were no underfloor heating systems (hypocausts), no mosaic or tessellated floors, and no baths. We were sure that there was no bathhouse, as we were able to strip a large area around by machine.

The inhabitants did, however, enjoy a relatively high standard of living, with hundreds of coins, and iron, bronze, silver, wood, bone and jet objects; the latter included a nice little lion figurine, which I had the pleasure of finding on my birthday in 1954.

The most remarkable finds came, however, from the well (**27**), only 10m deep, but larger in diameter and easier than that at Pagans Hill, which had given me such useful experience in this dangerous form of excavation. The permanent waterlogging, in the damp valley environment around the River Chew, had ensured a high degree of preservation: all the coins and other metalwork were uncorroded. There was much other material rarely found in 'normal' conditions: wooden buckets, rope and other organic objects, mosses and even fruit, such as cherries with the flesh round the stones still recognisable, if not eatable; thousands of animal bones, and sherds of hundreds of pots, including whole ones.

Outstanding among this very rich haul of material were a complete pewter jug, a copper jug, and some flat pieces of wood. The latter proved to be pieces of writing tablet. Greenfield was down the well when he felt the first piece with his fingers among the cold mud and water. Fortunately, he recognised it for what it was. He shouted up to us at the surface 'I think this is a writing tablet. I'm putting it on a piece of mud in the top of the bucket — needs very careful handling' (all finds were being sent up in a bucket attached to a rope).

Normally, Roman writing tablets have a recessed area filled with wax; the sender incises a message with the pointed end of a metal instrument (a stylus). The recipient reads this, erases the message with the flat end of his or her instrument and writes back a new missive. Sometimes tablets have been found (such as those at *Vindolanda*, on Hadrians Wall) in which the writer has pressed too hard and gone through the wax to the wood behind, leaving a faint impression, which can sometimes be deciphered.

At the top of the well we were, however, startled to see several lines of writing in ink, clearly visible in the bright sun. The chances of this remaining visible in bright light after sixteen centuries in a stable environment seemed to us slim; we hastily repacked it in mud in an airtight box, and sent it off by special messenger to the Ancient Monuments Laboratory in London.

27 The well at Chew Park; baling out the well with a ten-gallon oil drum

It was there carefully washed in distilled water, and the writing was fortunately still visible. It was in a cursive (running) script, with no obvious spaces between words, or even clear letters. Indeed, Bryan O'Neil, who happened to be in the laboratory when it arrived, thought it might be in Greek — a not very unusual language in Roman Britain.

After two years of sporadic study by Professor Eric Turner (Turner 1956), it was however deciphered as a Latin text. Certain words and phrases indicated that it was part of a legal document concerned with the transfer of land, probably the very deed of privatisation when the villa was built, thereafter a redundant document. Alas, the names of the parties involved, or that of the land, were not on the piece of tablet recovered.

Work on the very wide variety of material in the well involved over 72 specialists. Their efforts were masterminded by one of the most under-valued archaeologists (or rather archaeo-scientists) in Britain, Leo Biek (**28**), who was head of the AM Lab at that time. He visited Greenfield and myself and Chew many times, and became our lifelong friend and adviser in all the decades and digs that were to follow.

28   *Leo Biek and the late Vivien Russell in her last years, on a camp-site at Treen in Cornwall in 1989, with PAR*

One specialist he brought to see the well residues was one Dr Metcalf, an eminent botanist. His only baggage was a japanned metal box on a strap round his body. We imagined that this would have an impressive array of botanist's implements and watched curiously as he unslung it from his shoulder and opened it. From its interior he carefully drew a razor-blade.

The villa did not have a long life; it was flourishing in the Constantinian period (earlier to mid-fourth century AD) but hardly outlasted the 360s, certainly not going on to the 'end of Roman Britain'.

In the light of what I have written so far in this book, and that which will follow in later chapters, it is anticlimactic to have to report that in all our two years of intensive archaeology in the Chew Valley we found absolutely no evidence of Dark Age use of the area, even though Pagans Hill, overlooking the valley from its eminence, exhibited such positive material.

We were, in 1953-4, in the earlier stages of our work, much taken up with the prehistoric and Roman settlements. It is doubtful whether, left to ourselves, we would have paid much attention to the medieval sites in the valley, in which neither Greenfield or myself were at that time substantially interested. The Inspector sent down by O'Neil to oversee our work was, however, a young man who had recently completed his education at Cambridge — John Hurst. He had become extremely interested in medieval archaeology, and will figure prominently in later aspects of my life. He urged us to continue, and to excavate everything we could find of Norman and later date; and we needed employment!

I would have excavated the backyard of Woolworths rather than return to being a schoolmaster.

There was a medieval moated nunnery (St Cross) which we stripped completely, recovering a complex plan, including a chapel; and a shrunken medieval village (Moreton). Of this only a few farms survived into modern times. In between these were earthworks of older sites, going back to the eleventh and twelfth centuries AD. They included a chapel of St James, where John and Alice de Morton worshipped in 1345; we also excavated what we think may have been their manor house; and a mill-house, which was also a bakery. All of these we examined, either by trenching or machine; parts of this village still survive on the edge of the reservoir.

The medieval period also provided an interesting tailpiece to the story of Chew Park. Two circular lime-kilns were constructed in the twelfth century just by the villa: not now to provide the mortar for the building of the villa, but using the ruins of the villa as limestone to burn to make mortar; probably for the building of one of the local churches. By a curious coincidence, the medieval lime-burners had dug their flues (to provide the necessary through-draught) into the hollow left by the Roman lime-kiln which was a thousand years earlier. They must, we felt, have recognised the earlier limey residues of their forebears, and put two and two together, as we did in our interpretation of this sequence.

Apart from the reservoir, we also watched pipelines, trenches dug by machine to take the water to distant pumping stations. This was an early example of 'linear' archaeology, transects across landscapes, revealing many sites; or in some areas, none at all. These were a foretaste of the later massive motorway transects, but those from Chew were rather more of a 'random sample', since the motorways were often on ancient routes.

All this work was done by organising summer digs for volunteers, and by a few devoted local helpers who worked all the year round (notably Dorothy Crampton and Mollie James). We also had four workmen, provided and paid for by the MOPBW (now English Heritage).

As the work progressed, other professional assistants were appointed for limited periods; they included Anthony Paget-Baggs, then a rolled-umbrella-carrying undergraduate, Arthur ApSimon, a prehistorian (both now distinguished academics), and the late Gill Duckett (subsequently to be John Hurst's wife).

We did some very uncomfortable digging during the severe winter of 1953-4; by the next spring the water was beginning to rise, and Chew Park (by then the principal site) gradually became an island. At first we made a causeway of planks and oil drums, but the water rose higher. We then pulled everyone across on an inflatable ex-RAF dinghy on a line. One night in a gale this broke loose, sailed down the lake, sailed over the half-built dam, and landed on the lawn by the night-watchman's hut. We then brought a boat for £18; a rotten old boat it was, but it served its purpose all through the summer of 1954 taking everybody across (including ultimately all BBC TV men and scientists, Leo Biek, etc.) and also gave my family much pleasure in rowing it about, and observing the developing wildlife.

The Chew Valley may be seen in retrospect to have been one of the first major pieces of landscape archaeology in Britain; but we were sadly ill-equipped to deal with it in those terms, lacking basic on-site environmental expertise or help. We had no equipment to excavate below the water table, or even to carry out extensive augering.

Greenfield and I had, however, learnt a great deal. It would not be possible nowadays to get such wide or intensive experience. Apart from the excavation and recording we were also exposed to the specialist disciplines I have described above. The scale of the work left a mass of data, which took more than two decades to bring to publication (79).

Greenfield and I were, in 1953-5, among the first 'rescue archaeologists' of the post-war decades, appointed on a slender daily fee basis (as 'consultants' (61)). The 'supervisor' was paid two guineas a day, his assistant one. Greenfield and I took it in turns to be supervisor. This would not have been enough to live on; the idea was still current in the 1950s that to be a 'consultant' in this way was not to be a professional excavator, one was supposed to be a 'gentleman'. Others in this 'consultant' category included the late Margaret Jones, the late Faith Vatcher, the late Charles Green, Brian Philp, John Wacher, Brian Hope-Taylor and Stanley West; all later well-known archaeologists.

The only way we could survive was by being paid additionally 'subsistence'; one was supposed initially to stay in a hotel and then find lodgings, so this payment was on a down-sliding scale. Needless to say, one was not supposed to camp, which is what Greenfield and I did in the Chew Valley, in tents; or in farms or cottages, abandoned as the reservoir progressed.

Receipts for lodgings had to be produced. We had special notepaper printed with the address of my mother's house in that area (at Compton Martin, see chapter 2); we wondered whether the Civil Service clerks who processed our claims would decide that it would be a good place for a holiday!

Most of us 'few' were untrained in any formal way. Our employment on sites, which included some of considerable importance, was somewhat frowned upon by what was left after the war of a senior generation of archaeologists. While we might be good at excavating, it was argued, we were unable to put our data into the wider academic context needed for archaeology to prosper as a discipline. We were referred to by Paul Ashbee as 'itinerant *soi-disant* archaeologists, rather like archaeological tramps, ignorant of all but the outlines of European prehistory'.

In 1955, John Hurst assured me that there was no problem of future employment if I was prepared to dig medieval sites; I was, but as it turned out my future digs were to cover all periods of archaeology (**29**).

This is a good point at which to sum up my approach to archaeology in 1955. My main justification for it was that if something ancient was buried beneath the ground, it was worth uncovering; in doing so one inevitably learnt more about the past, if only by the recovery of artefacts, structures and graves as witness to what had happened in that place. This was also taken for granted in all rescue archaeology, by MOPBW. Their resources could not investigate all sites in Britain threatened by nature or man (61), but they did their best. This necessitated giving priority to some sites which were 'more important' than others — or seemed so at the time; but there was no question of setting up what is nowadays called a research design, based on selected themes and problems.

29 Map of all PAR's excavations 1946-96

There *was* research on a small scale by the few senior people in the universities. They were asking wider questions about European prehistory and the development of man; and an even smaller number went out to investigate the problems in other countries — the Middle East, Africa or Australia. There was a sharp division in Britain between prehistory and the archaeology of the classical world (including Roman Britain). There was some interest in the Anglo-Saxons, notably their graves (especially since the heady finds in 1939 of Sutton Hoo) and to a lesser extent of their churches. Medieval archaeology proper did not take off until the foundation of the Society for Medieval Archaeology in the late 1950s; up to that point the subject had been dominated by art and architectural specialists. There was also still a wide gulf between history and archaeology, the latter still being regarded as a useful means of illustrating the former; and certainly not of challenging its basic conclusions.

It is against this background in England that my own career was developing, by the fortuitous combination of a successful start in local archaeology, the construction of a nearby reservoir, and an accelerating pace of destruction of sites. It was, it must be remembered, largely an accident that the MOPBW, through its Inspectorate of Ancient Monuments (IAM), took on the 'rescue' responsibility, rather than some other department of government. Monuments, their conservation and display, was their business, not excavation (especially of sites where there was nothing to be seen, where a site was discovered only in the process of destruction, as at Chew).

Some work was done by the Inspectors themselves, but with poor resources; for instance John Hurst, digging at Norwich, had to use his hotel bedroom as a place to wash and mark finds. Among these were some well-preserved leather shoes. To stop them from drying out, they were put in water in a bedroom receptacle. They were, alas, thrown away by the chambermaid as something nasty.

Pagans Hill and the Chew Valley had been an intensive experience. I derived great satisfaction from recovering long-lost artefacts and enriching the collections of Bristol Museum; and increasingly from recovering the plans and constructional details of buildings and other structures; and the history of their beginnings, flourishings and decline. I remember feeling some sense of achievement in restoring to human knowledge the work of past master-builders; of delineating their plans, which must have borne more than a slight resemblance to my own; bringing them some immortality as in the discovery of a lost piece of music in the binding of a book: pleasures which remain with me half a century later.

I had at this time little consciousness of contributing to major themes of the understanding of the past: the *studies* of temples and villas, the development of the peasant house, the sequence of Somerset pottery styles, the history of technology. But I was becoming aware that such things existed, and that our sites north of Mendip were making major contributions to knowledge, and not just that of the local area.

Of much greater import, however, was the realisation that knowledge gained by excavating was only useful if it could be put into the public domain by publication. This was a skill I had to learn; not only the ordering of recorded data into text and tables, but also how to draw — plans, sections, elevations and finds. I had no natural talent in either.

My early writings were no more than adequate, and had to be put into shape by kind editors. My early drawings were rather dreadful, especially their crude lettering (eg. 1-2), but were a good way of learning, and a prelude to the thousands I have done since.

My first effort, on the Butcombe post-mill, was rejected; the second, on the Pagans Hill temple, was submitted to the Somerset Archaeological and Natural History Society's *Proceedings*. Oddly enough, their then editor tried to make me deposit the finds at Taunton, rather than Bristol, as a condition of publication. I made a fuss about this as unethical, and he was overruled by his committee; it was duly published (1), the finds going to Bristol.

This publication was obviously a major factor in being asked to do more work for MOPBW: *c*.200 papers and books later I can look back on this first effort with some nostalgia. It did, incidentally, have glimmerings of real research in it since I included some discussion on other octagonal temples in Europe, using the famous article by Koethe (see 1) translated for me from the German by my father.

It was with some trepidation that I entered on a career which took me away from home in 1955. I had sworn after demobilisation never to stir from hearth and home again, but the lure of archaeology (and the horror of school teaching) caused me to renounce this declaration, to the detriment of wife and family.

At Butcombe, Pagans Hill and Chew they had joined in the digging and holidays spent camping in the Chew Valley (there were now three children to support, and another on the way). Now I had to go where the work was, often at short notice; to dig sites of which little was known, and sometimes not even their period. They were in counties I hardly knew existed, let alone their archaeology, sometimes in very difficult conditions. MOPBW arranged a team of local workmen (or occasionally their own workforce), a hut and tools. I would arrive a day or two before the work was to start, and would be faced at 7am on Monday morning with a fairly recalcitrant group of men, under a foreman; they often considered archaeology a waste of time and money and their labour (as compared for instance with digging drains). I had to put on a good show of pretending to know what I was doing, and why; and did my best to train them to excavate stratigraphically ('you see, sir, we always like to keep a flat bottom to the trench, and straighten it up afterwards'). It was, however, usually possible to stir their curiosity ('you never know what you might find') and try to explain about finds and the work of their ancestors.

A series of such digs went on through the summer (with occasional winter urgencies), and the winters were devoted to writing up the results. We itinerant diggers were, however, only paid for digging; there was no question in those days of one's being paid for writing up or publishing (unless one was an Inspector!); we were again expected to do that as 'gentlemen consultants'. In my case, income was eked out by keeping Studio Rahtz going, and being paid for the odd lecture to the local Women's Institute (at two guineas a go). This was another skill I had to learn; not only of site exposition, but also lecturing, and of these I was by now getting plenty of experience; a skill begun in the RAF.

It was also important to talk to visitors, local people and societies. One had to dispel suspicions about 'Ministry' archaeologists muscling in on what had been the preserve of local archaeologists. It also led to recruitment of local volunteers, to work at weekends,

30 At Downton Roman Villa, Wiltshire, 1955; PAR (age 34) is holding a complete New Forest beaker

sorting out what had been destroyed by the workmen during the week; and to washing, marking and bagging up finds. How, under these circumstances, we ever did get sites written up, I can only now wonder. Pagans Hill did finally get fully published in 1957 and 1958 (2 and 6, 7), and Butcombe (after revision) also in 1958 (4).

Surprisingly, as if the active summer digging was not enough, I found the energy to do some personal small trial hole digging in the winter from Bristol with friends — part of a scheme to test the date and ceramic sequence of local Iron Age hillforts, with some success (Kings Weston Down in 1956, (3); Blaise Castle in 1957 (11); Maes Knoll in 1961 (26).

Although John Hurst had implied that it was in *medieval* archaeology that there was a shortage of archaeologists, the first site I was given in the summer of 1955 was a Roman villa at Downton (Wiltshire) which turned up in a newly-built council housing estate. One of the new tenants came on a tessellated floor while digging a hole for a clothes-line post ('What are all these funny little square stones?'). I had the embarrassing job of moving into each garden in turn (which had been newly laid out) until I had excavated the whole villa and a nearby corn-drying furnace (24).

The Downton Villa (**30**) was surprising in that there didn't seem to be any living quarters. All the rooms and linking corridors were tessellated, mostly plain patterns, but with one grand picture-mosaic in the central room (this was lifted and is now in Salisbury Museum). There was, nearby, a nice little bath suite. The whole thing seemed more like a governor's palace. Yet the large corn-drying furnace was not far away, which suggested that this was a grain processing centre — perhaps a state-run estate nucleus, gathering in tribute in corn from surrounding farms; the whole grandeur of the 'villa' being to impress local people with the sophistication of the Roman way of life.

A large field between this and the River Avon was in 1955 due for similar development. I rather enjoyed the swimming here, so I persuaded MOPBW to let me trench this field in 1956 by long transects. Apart from the finding of peripheral Roman roads and other features, there was also a Mesolithic site with thousands of flints and some structural detail, Neolithic and Beaker settlements, and a Saxon gravel pit.

This led to further work in 1957. The late Eric Higgs of the University of Cambridge (a very remarkable man) came with his wife and students to dig the Mesolithic site. His two chief assistants have both since become very famous: Professor Brian Fagan in the USA, and Dr Ian Longworth (British Museum). While they were engaged on this very productive site, Lawrence Butler and I excavated the Neolithic and Beaker areas of the field (**21**) and we later returned to do the rest (**29**). Downton also provided a good summer camp for the family (now five) though my then youngest son Sebastian had a narrow escape from drowning in the River Avon.

I here leave archaeology a little, to examine a few personal relationships. Generally speaking I got on well with paid workmen, but there was a notable exception; and since this was at Downton, this is a suitable place for an interpolation.

The MOPBW had given me a regular team of men drawn from their permanent staff, for the work in this field. They had recently taken on a new man who must remain anonymous. He made it clear to me at once that he thought he was a cut above the others — he 'listened to chamber music in his lodgings' he said. Not surprisingly he got on badly with the other workmen, the more especially as he preached doctrinaire communism to them. Their only retaliation was swearing at him, about which he complained to me. I told him I wasn't surprised, and tried to give him jobs apart from them. He then went above my head and complained to the District Superintendent. The latter sent the letter back to me and instructed me to tell him not to be such a bloody fool! Copies were sent of another vituperative letter, vilifying me, personally and archaeologically, to the MOPBW in London, the Chief Constables of Norfolk and Wiltshire, the Archbishop of Canterbury and Mr Kruschev! The latter gentleman did not reply. .

The letter to the MOPBW had, however, being written to the Civil Service, to be 'dealt with'. The Chief Inspector passed it down the line to John Hurst who assured the CI that it was all nonsense.

This was, however, not all. Our man in Downton also complained that I was incompetent. He'd read some archaic book on geology which told him (or so he understood) that the surface of the land is going down several centimetres every 1000 years and yet I was telling him that a flinty surface he'd found 20cm down was a Roman road. He was, sadly, a good and intelligent digger and it was he who first located the very dense mesolithic flint assemblage — he had the hundreds of blades laid out in rows! But he got more and more awkward and I had to get rid of him.

The MOPBW gave him another chance and sent him to Old Sarum to help with a proposed timber bridge across to the Keep and he told them the design was all wrong. He then went to work with Charles Green at Caistor. Green interpreted certain rooms in an inn of Roman date as the cubicles of a brothel. Our man took exception to this 'obscene' interpretation, saying the rooms were a dairy.

The MOPBW finally gave him the boot. He later worked in a factory and got beaten up, ending in hospital. Then came his most remarkable act — he, with the knowledge he'd acquired (and he was quite personable) went to Maryport in Cumbria, and posing as an MOPBW supervisor, hired labour and tools to dig the Roman fort. He signed for it all on behalf of the MOPBW and this landed him in prison.

Many years later, Peter Fowler mentioned Downton in a broadcast and our man wrote to him asking if it were published. Peter replied politely giving him the reference — he must have gone to the library and looked it up, for he wrote to Peter again, another long great letter about capitalist-consultant Rahtz, pointing out how wrong all my report was; and that it was in fact he who had discovered the whole shebang.

In fairness to my detractor, not all of his letter was fantasy. One of his accusations was about my sexual immorality, of which our man strongly disapproved. In rather Chaucerian terms, he found out that I was having an affair with 'the tanner's wife'. This is perhaps a good point to enlarge on this more personal aspect of my life. I have acquired a reputation of being a 'womaniser', and, in that I prefer women to men, this is true. Since I was a boy going to see every available foreign film in the hope of seeing a bare breast, I have to some extent lived up to the title of my *Festschrift* (Carver ed. 1993), with just one letter altered. I don't think I am unusual in this, but perhaps less discreet and less sensitive to other peoples' feeings. As I have said, my decision to follow archaeology as a career (or an obsession?) after 1955 was not good for my family. One pays a high price for marital infidelity, notably the loss of trust and respect by wife and growing children. Digging away from home not surprisingly led to extra-marital affairs, but I do not intend to recite a Leporello-type catalogue of them, even to ensure massive sales of this book!

There is something about digs that is conducive to sexual (and alcoholic) licence. This is part of the social history of archaeology, about which little has yet been written. This is true, I believe, especially of British digs, in which a number of young and older people are thrown together in an intellectually interesting situation, often in some discomfort and intimacy. Opportunities are numerous and restraints few.

It may be that this facet of archaeological behaviour is due to the wide perspective of time and human affairs that one is dealing with, generating a morality that is independent of one's own culture and time; being Christians, teachers and parents told us that sex was naughty and dirty. We may also, as archaeologists, be influenced here by our mental pictures of what life may have been like in former times, backed up by the more lurid accounts of sexual freedom in selected parts of the recent world, as retailed by imaginative social anthropologists. This is a subject that needs more study.

I do not believe my genes are more selfish than anyone else's; and it may be said that mine have had more than their fair share of passing themselves on; but I have not perhaps had the religious or moral restraints that some others have had. I recognise the great power that sex has over us all, hardly surprising in a long process of natural selection. I have written a piece on this long history of the evolving power of the sexual imperative, which I have included as Appendix B.

But as to being a monster — or a man and monster, as Humbert Humbert was to himself — reports, like those related to Mark Twain about his death, have been greatly exaggerated. Nevertheless, our man in Downton was right. I entered at Downton on a deep and lasting relationship with the wife of the manager of the Downton Tannery, Margaret Gray. She was, in 1955, President of the Downton's Womens' Institute. Having heard of the dig, and looked up 'archaeology' in the dictionary, she came to ask me to give a talk to the ladies. Margaret played an important role in my life in subsequent digs and years; she became an archaeologist in her own right, a Fellow of the Society of Antiquaries (FSA), and still a close friend.

To return to archaeology and my career, in this work and others I realised another important thing — one had to *sell* the site. This is what I had done at Downton (fortunately successfully) by *talking* about it and writing rather glowing interim reports to persuade MOPBW to put more money in (and secure employment for me). This ploy stood me in good stead in later decades in persuading people to finance my archaeology.

At Chew and Downton, I had also demonstrated that I was *lucky*; that I had green fingers; that wherever I put my trowel, there was something important (with very few exceptions), or if it was of minor interest, I made it *sound* important, 'crucial to the future of British Archaeology'.

So it went on: in the later 1950s Downton was succeeded by further rescue excavations. A very uncomfortable winter dig at Dover (5) was memorable for sheer horror. I was sent there to collate data that had been carefully recorded (together with many Roman finds) by the quantity surveyor for a major building construction. The finds were over 6m deep and associated with Roman harbour construction. The surveyor had recorded everything so well that there was little for me to do except collect the data from him; I did, however, take the opportunity of looking around the centre of the town. It was very cold, in January, below freezing, and occasionally snowing. I idly looked into a very large hole being dug for the basement of the new Lloyds Bank, in Market Square. It was some 6m deep, and the sides were virtually all comprised of archaeological layers and structures. If I'd had any sense I would have quickly looked the other way and expunged the whole site from my memory, but my archaeological conscience was by now well developed; it was clear that if I didn't do something about it, no one else would in that weather. I rang up the MOPBW and they authorised me to do what I could. I took a deep breath, and borrowed a ladder. Setting it up at intervals all around the pit, I drew all four sections, and recovered finds from most levels. I couldn't stand on the bottom of the pit, which was half-frozen mud and slush; I soon found out where this had come from. Further up the hill, someone's lavatory had formerly emptied into a large sewer crossing the pit area. The sewer had been destroyed, but no one had informed the user of the lavatory. Periodically there was a noise like subdued thunder, and then a liquid rumbling and a large SPLAT! as the effluent discharged into the open side of the pit, and trickled to the base, freezing as it made its way down.

The sequence was a major one: the natural brick-earth levels of the estuary of the River Dour were used in Neolithic times; then followed huge constructions of the series of Roman forts of DUBRIS; and, in the upper levels, the foundations of the large church of St Martin-Le-Grand. All this was to be fully understood long after I had published my report (5) as the result of the heroic efforts of Brian Philp, another of the post-war rescue diggers.

From the lowest levels I recovered not only Neolithic flints, but also soil samples, from which Leo Biek subsequently recovered environmental data. Forty years later, in the 1990s, they were still the only such data available from Dover, in which I was again involved, but now in a very different context (see chapter 14).

There followed, in the later 1950s, more rescue digs: a late medieval moated site at Leicester (8); mechanical cuttings across the Ermine Street in Lincolnshire (10) (where I managed to cut right through the whole network of telephone cables to the north: big panic, but not my fault); two odd mounds at Row Down, in Berkshire (14); Roman town defences at Caistor, Lincs (16) (where I doubled the previously-known extent of the town); a medieval village near Bath (18, 78); and a fine Bronze Age barrow at Lambourn, Berks (22).

Shearplace Hill, Dorset (20) was a good example of the unknown quantity. It was a small earthwork, which the farmer wanted to level. No one knew what date it was, but the Royal Commission on Historical Monuments (RCHM) at Salisbury suggested it might be linked to the neighbouring field systems and droveways, still earthworks in those days in that wonderful chalk landscape. The first find was a Roman brooch, so I thought 'Ah — its a Roman period farmstead'. The second find was a large chunk of very coarse pottery, the like of which I had never seen before. When the workmen had gone home, I hot-footed it to Dorchester Museum and compared the pottery to that in the cases there. With a slight pricking sensation in the back of my neck I found that the pottery was middle Bronze Age, of the second millennium BC. We subsequently found two very well-defined roundhouses inside the earthwork. Shearplace Hill, in which I was assisted by Peter Addyman (now Director of the York Archaeological Trust) and the late Vivien Russell (*see* **28**), became one of the classic sites of British prehistory.

Another harbinger of my current interests was a small dig in 1958 at Whitby, North Yorkshire (23, 43, 70, 161). The local council wanted to level some earthworks outside the known area of the great Abbey. These were quickly shown to be of quite recent origin, but at deeper levels I found Anglo-Saxon features and pottery. These showed that the famous Anglo-Saxon monastery extended much further than had been realised. I was to get involved in Whitby again, in a very different way, many years later.

I was sent in the same year to excavate part of the late/post-Roman linear earthwork on the Wiltshire/Hampshire county boundary, known as Bokerly Dyke. The alignments of a major Roman road approaching the principal entrance through this Dyke were on a dog-leg angle. This had for centuries been the cause of an awkward bend in the main road from Salisbury to Dorchester; a dangerous spot which the local road department wished to straighten out, involving the destruction of a small part of the Dyke.

Now there had been an earlier excavation across the Dyke in the nineteenth century, by no less an archaeologist than General Pitt-Rivers. He is often thought of as the founder of modern scientific archaeology. He was the first to declare that common finds, like pottery and boot-nails, were more important than exotic finds in efforts to understand the past. By their very nature, he insisted that the unusual finds are unrepresentative. He published very full details of all his digs, including Bokerly Dyke, in enormous blue and gold volumes. I had to understand exactly what he had done in order to make the most of my opportunity.

I cut a few new trenches across the bank and ditch which comprised the Dyke, and found that my interpretation differed from that of the General; notably the depth of the ditch system at a crucial point. To resolve the problem, I found and emptied the backfill of one of his trenches; to my surprise his record was inaccurate in important respects; I was able to make a revised hypothesis on the Dyke sequence (see also p197). When I came to publish this (27), I was able to sign my drawings P R, after P R. I was the first person ever to re-excavate one of his cuttings in this way. Our paths were to cross again later in life (182).

Rather to my pleasure, in these first years of my professional career, the work that came my way was by no means all rescue archaeology. MOPBW was asked to recommend a suitable person to answer some problems that had arisen in the great compilation known as *The History of the King's Works*, being written by Dr Howard Colvin, one of the most eminent of medieval architectural historians.

In this work I investigated a crumbling ruin known as King John's Hunting Lodge at Clipstone, Nottinghamshire (12); a moated site of the same name at Writtle, Essex (40), and the hillfort at Old Sarum (just outside Salisbury) (13). The sequence here extended from the Iron Age, through Roman and Saxon, to a great Norman castle and cathedral and later features (30). Colvin was particularly interested in the royal works here, especially in a tunnel cut through the earthwork defences in Norman times. This had not been seen since its discovery was reported in the *Gentleman's Magazine* in 1795. On that occasion the entrance collapsed, a hole appeared, and local explorers entered the rock-cut tunnel for a hundred metres or more. Colvin wondered if all this was true. We accordingly dug a trench into a likely looking hollow. At a depth of about two metres we were having doubts, but a clay pipe appeared — we were clearly on the right track. A hole appeared; from it came a draught of warm air (our dig was in November 1957, so the air in the tunnel was warmer than that outside). Enlarging the hole, we found ourselves in the tunnel, beautifully cut with fresh Norman tool-marks in the chalk. We were only able to get in about 50m, where the tunnel was choked. The walls were literally 'disfigured' by graffiti, some very rude; they were in pencil and candle-smoke, of the years 1801-22 when visitors had last been able to get in.

An anecdote here serves to illustrate contemporary attitudes (in 1957) to 'alternative archaeology'. Local volunteers recruited for the dig included members of the local Salisbury field work group, led by John Musty. Their President, Ralph Whitlock (then well-known as a radio personality) fancied his skills as a dowser, using rods to find the tunnel (before we had dug); he used empty lemonade bottles on his rods on the principle of 'space finding space'. This was harmless enough, and he was in fact successful. Unfortunately, however, the local press photographer snapped him doing his divining. He included the picture, with others, in a batch which he sent to *The Times*, who spread them over its back page. Trouble ensued: Beatrice de Cardi, the Secretary and really the founding mother of the Council for British Archaeology (CBA) wrote a letter of strong protest to MOPBW on 'the use of non-scientific devices on Ministry excavations'. I had to make a full report in triplicate on how I had allowed such a heinous thing to happen and be photographed. I had to explain that when support is given by a local society, one should not be obstructive or rude to its President.

Other opportunities of a non-rescue kind also came. In 1958 I was asked to dig a house-site on the deserted medieval village (DMV) site of Holworth, Dorset. A local wealthy patron had offered £1000 to finance a dig here, to be done under the aegis of the Dorset Natural History and Archaeological Society (DNHAS); to be done entirely by members of the Society, with one paid assistant (Lawrence Butler, a lifelong friend). In a very wet August, we made a significant contribution to DMV studies of peasant houses, and to the study of medieval pottery of Dorset (9).

Some of the volunteers were quite elderly, having dug with Sir Mortimer Wheeler at the famous dig at nearby Maiden Castle in the 1930s. Others were younger men and women anxious to learn the techniques of modern archaeology, and have since (such as Ron Lucas and John Bailey) made their own reputations in Dorset. Indeed the dig marked a renaissance in the DNHAS as an active field Society. It was also the first occasion on which I had run a training dig, but not the last!

The same circumstance arose at Pleshey in Essex (15, 83) where the sponsoring body was the Essex Archaeological Society; again a number of younger people were trained, this time cutting a major section through the Norman defences and excavating the castle chapel of this great site.

Through these two digs, and similar ones at Weoley Castle, Birmingham (with Philip Barker and Peter Addyman) I laid the ground for my future career; not as an excavator, but as an academic teacher.

To return to rescue archaeology, however; while all the above took me far from home, one enabled me to work from home, with obvious advantages: an excavation on the medieval walls of Bristol (17) necessitated by redevelopment of the bombed city. Here we found a surprisingly high number of sherds of French imported pottery of the thirteenth/fourteenth centuries. Rescue work in Bristol went on for several years. I returned there to dig the church of St Mary-le-Port, described in chapter 10 (112).

Apart from some skeletons and cremations in the Chew Valley, and a big urn (**31**) with a cremation in a Wiltshire barrow (47), I had encountered few human remains in the excavations so far described. In the spring of 1959 I was, however, despatched to Sewerby on the East Yorkshire coast to excavate an Anglo-Saxon pagan cemetery of the fifth to seventh centuries AD. A few skeletons had turned up in a farm extension; they had been dealt with not by archaeologists but by the police, suspecting recent murder.

31 Margaret Gray holding a large complete burial urn from the Bronze Age barrow at Knighton Hill, Wiltshire, 1959

Our job was to clear the area of any further graves, and put the whole episode into perspective. I had as assistants Andrew Selkirk, the founder of *Current Archaeology*, and Peter Addyman; and my family (**32**). We dug some fifty graves with a wide range of grave-goods of fairly standard types, familiar from other cemeteries of this period in East Yorkshire. More graves were excavated by Susan Hirst in 1974; she subsequently published an exemplary monograph on the whole cemetery (111).

One grave in this cemetery was outstanding. Under a large spread of chalk rubble was the outline of a large grave. Not far down in the fill was a contorted female skeleton buried face down, with the arms and legs at odd angles. This was interpreted as a live burial — a ritual killing. This skeleton was drawn, photographed and lifted on what was to have been the last day of the excavation. We were rather surprised that such a large grave had been made for a very odd burial. I investigated the base of the grave and there was *another* female skeleton; I had to go elsewhere to do another dig, so I left it to Peter Addyman to finish. It turned out to be the richest burial of all: such a complicated assemblage (including a 256-bead necklace) that it took him another two weeks to complete. The first intimation I had of what he had found was on the back of a comic squeaking postcard purchased at

32 Family at Knighton Hill, 1959 (Gentian, Diana, Sebastian, David, Nicholas; aged 18, 11, 4, 7 and 14)

nearby Bridlington; the picture on it was of a comic character with eyes rolling behind plastic (see p129).

A further Yorkshire dig in those early years was at Little Ouseburn, where I had the invaluable help of Tony Pacitto, a Yorkshire-born-and-bred archaeologist. He was then a young man. Thirty-five years later I find myself working with him again (p222). This was a big barrow being destroyed by ploughing. We failed to find any primary burial or grave goods (142). There was however an oak-tree coffin, which had left a complex stain. I applied what was to me at that time an advanced method of recording by *planum* (167). The Early Bronze Age grave-diggers, who lowered the massive coffin into a pit, had left their (shod) footprints in the surrounding clay as they scrambled out. These were preserved by a turf stack they then piled over the grave, capped by a magnificent boulder cairn and a further turf mound.

This takes me into 1960, the end of an action-packed five years as a fully-fledged professional, following on work in the Chew Valley. Ernest Greenfield and I had gone our separate ways after Chew, he too going on to do some remarkable digs before giving up archaeology for wood-cutting in Cornwall, where he died in 1993 at the age of 80 (157).

This is also a good point to stop and cover another field of work, which as noted above led to my future career. I had done one or two lectures to local societies and other bodies; the University of Bristol was however unwilling to give me extra-mural classes in the winter to eke out my income, because I had no degree. Thanks, however, to Graham Webster who had heard of my work, I was given one or two lectures to give to his students in the Birmingham area. This led to a major involvement in the winter of 1958-9, based at Nottingham. The late Maurice Barley (*see* **82**), then Archaeology Tutor for the extra-mural archaeology there, had to have a winter off for an operation. He assigned me all four of his regular classes (admittedly with some trepidation, in view of my rather unacademic background). Margaret Gray and I drove up to Nottingham on Monday afternoons to take a class in that city, then Stamford on Tuesday, Grantham on Wednesday and Mansfield on Thursday; with a few extra ones, I gave 104 classes that winter, earning me a very useful £500 or so.

All went well: the students were stimulated by a new face, and by being regaled by my dense field experiences. Maurice later told someone 'Rahtz lectured entirely on his own excavations!'. This was not strictly true; I had built up some background and slides, and had the use of the Nottingham slide collection and library.

Margaret and I lived for three nights each week in a caravan, driving back late on Thursday night after the Mansfield class, to get back to some report-writing at the weekend. This was really being thrown in at the deep end, but laid the foundations of a long lecturing career in subsequent years.

I was slightly dubious about the value of evening classes in archaeology. Certainly, they gave a good stimulating evening out (or even a good sleep) for the members, but it was very difficult to get them to make class contributions, or to do the 'required' follow-up reading. There were however rewards. Several students have said I changed their lives; a few actually took up archaeology. I remember, with great satisfaction, an elderly member of my Stamford class, who was so impressed with an evening on Sutton Hoo, that he went to London the next week to see the finds in the British Museum.

After Nottingham, Bristol did give me some classes. These were more practical, dealing with a topic that was beginning to cause concern — how to teach amateurs the skills of report writing — in which I now had wide experience (see chapter 12).

In 1960 I excavated for the second time in an actual ancient monument (the first being Old Sarum) this time at the famous Kenilworth Castle. The Inspectorate wanted to know what the former ground level had been in the Outer Court there — a simple enough question, it seemed. I was provided with four members of the permanent staff of the castle, who had access to a wide range of equipment. We dug a trench 1.5m wide right across the area from wall to wall. It reached a depth of over 5m. The whole sequence of use of the Castle was revealed for the first time: the great defensive ditches of the times of the Normans and King John; the thick burnt levels when Kenilworth was under siege in 1266, complete with stone ballista balls; the Tudor buildings of the great period of the entertainment of Queen Elizabeth I; and the huge amounts of rubble resulting from the Civil War destruction. The original question was thus meaningless, so the grass level over all this was left as it was; but a fine sample of the Castle's history had been sampled (35).

There were further rescue excavations as well: more prehistoric earthworks and settlements on the chalk in Wiltshire and Dorset (116, 117). The big one, however, came at the end of this year, the excavations at Cheddar, which deserve a more extended discussion.

The agent of impending destruction here was a new school, to be built over an area where there were the ruins of a chapel; this was dedicated to an early saint, Columbanus. The late C.A. Ralegh Radford, who had already given me useful advice at Pagans Hill on temple architecture (see 1 for his contribution) was asked his opinion of the chance of the chapel being important. He pointed out to MOPBW that in 1321 there had been a bishop's enquiry at Wells as to whether St Columbanus' chapel had been a 'royal free chapel', i.e. exempt from certain dues.

It was well-known from historical sources that there had been a great royal palace at Cheddar, in Anglo-Saxon and medieval times. The royal estate was listed in King Alfred's will, and there were meetings of the King's Council (known as the *Witenagemot*) in 941, 956 and 968, in the reigns of King Edmund, King Edwy and King Edgar. On each occasion there would have been a great concourse of the principal men of the kingdom: the King, his family and his councillors (the *Witan*, or wise men); archbishops, bishops and abbots; the secular aristocracy (dukes and earls); foreign visitors; and other important people. With their retinues, such an assembly would have been hundreds strong. They had to be housed and fed, as well as their horses.

Such meetings took place at many centres in England, including country places (where the hunting was good, like Cheddar) and towns like Oxford, Gloucester or London. Preparation had to be made months in advance by the local reeve (the agent of the King); and there had to be great halls where everybody could meet and talk; and a church or chapel for Christian worship. Matters to be discussed included the assigning of land rights, foreign policy, and local justice. An important adjunct to all was feasting and especially hunting.

The first meeting at Cheddar of which we have a written record, that of 941, was the occasion of a rather dramatic episode. At the court was a rather serious cleric named Dunstan. The young King Edmund resented his attempts to curtail youthful excesses, and there was a good deal of persecution. Edmund was hunting on Mendip and the stag he was chasing went over the edge of Cheddar Gorge. His horse was about to follow, and Edmund felt himself to be in mortal peril. It flashed into his mind that he had treated Dunstan unfairly, and vowed to make amends if his life was spared. As usually happens in these cases, the horse pulled up sharp, and Dunstan was appointed Abbot of Glastonbury; later he became Archbishop of Canterbury.

Apart from the Anglo-Saxon Kings, Henry I had a palace here, so did King John; and finally the Bishop of Wells. Cheddar, south of the Gorge and caves, is a large area, and the site of these great meetings was quite unknown; but Radford's 1321 clue suggested that it may have been in the area now threatened by the new school. It was a long shot and the Ministry were somewhat reluctant to act on such a slender clue without further evidence. I was given £100 to see what I could find around the chapel in the Christmas of 1960; with a few friends I dug some holes, and found enough to enable me to persuade the Ministry to invest some more money.

I realised that this site was the most important that I had so far been entrusted with; if it was the site of the palaces covering a period of several centuries, it was going to be a big job. I knew nothing about Saxon or medieval palaces, but luckily nor did anyone else (that is to say archaeologically), however well-documented the history was. I got the promise of a further £1000,and read all I could on pre-conquest royal sites.

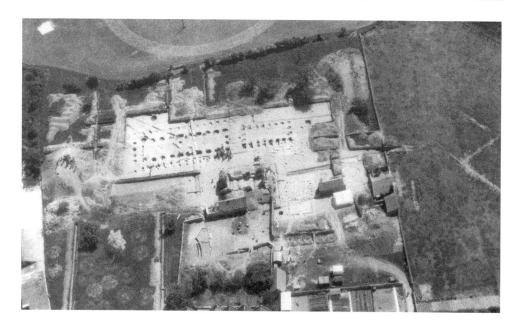

33 Air photograph of Saxon and medieval palaces at Cheddar, in final stage of excavation, 1963; some of the post-pits of the great timber hall are 2m deep (copyright Cambridge University Collection, no. AFC 42, Dr J.K. St Joseph)

It was indeed the right place, and the excavations were long, arduous and taxed all my energy and acquired skills. There were problems (see below) and by 1963 I was in a poor state — the nearest I have ever been to a breakdown.

I was able to define a great series of buildings, principally of timber (**33**), some small (for domestic use) and mostly very large, among the greatest halls of their day (**34**), up to 35m long and 17m in width, based on huge timber posts, of which the settings survived as construction pits up to 2m deep.

With the evidence of coins, metal objects, pottery and structural sequences, it was possible to reconstruct the history of the site, in a material sense, in seven periods, broadly matching the historical dates. The ruin of the chapel of St Columbanus was indeed on the site of a royal chapel of the palace in the tenth and later centuries, but was itself built over an earlier hall of the ninth century.

Apart from the problems of excavating the site, including a session in the severe winter of 1962-3, local political difficulties began to arise. The school was badly needed, and there were suggestions that it was us who were holding up the work of construction. This was in 1963, with about a month of digging and some crucial contexts to examine: a site of European importance.

We had not been very successful in explaining the archaeology to visitors. One local councillor is reported as saying 'they say they have found a palace — all I saw was a lot of holes'. Another said 'they say that this was a palace of King Alfred — now he was a great believer in education — he'd say "get on with the school"' (in this he was undoubtedly

34 Cheddar palace in the winter (copyright executors of Alan Sorrell)

correct). The vicar saved the day at a local meeting by proposing that we be allowed to continue: 'you never know', he said, 'they might find something interesting'. Moral: take more trouble with site tours.

In the final week, the architect of the school came to look — he was impressed; so much so that he decided to alter the plans, and not to build on the site of the great halls, but on ground we hadn't dug. It's not often that I am speechless! The school (the 'Kings of Wessex') flourishes but few people seem to understand now what all the little concrete posts are for (they mark the position of the postholes); and I have never been asked to talk to the school, though I have offered more than once.

There were of course the problems of bringing all this to publication, but this was eventually achieved (25, 119 and especially 87).

Cheddar was the second such royal site to be excavated. That at Yeavering, in Northumberland, had been brilliantly excavated by Brian Hope-Taylor in the 1950s, but that was in the very different context of the far north (93), in the sixth to seventh centuries AD. Cheddar now provided an example of a palace of the Kings of Wessex and of medieval England. Even historians were interested to see the reality which lay behind the sparse documentary references. The excavation had led to a major new understanding of the highest level of timber building, and something on the economy, trading connections and industry of such a complex.

Although the whole work was expensive and demanding, it was not an excavation of the highest quality. In order to get at least the ground plans of these great buildings, we had to use mechanical help (earth-moving machines) extensively, which led to some loss of finds and other data. We had some professional assistance, notably Christine Mahany, Vivien Russell (*see* **28**) and Ronald Lampert; but most of the work had to be done by local volunteers and a few untrained workmen, and technical resources were few. I was not even supplied by the Ministry with a theodolite!

I have, not surprisingly, often wondered whether another excavator, give the same time and resources, would have arrived at the same 'story', the basic phasing and chronology. There would obviously have been a broad similarity, but there would have been differences. I shall have more to say on the uncritical attitude of scholars towards such reports as the Cheddar volume, in a later chapter.

Cheddar, nevertheless, has become one of the classic sites of Anglo-Saxon archaeology, and should merit at least a few lines in any later textbook! It also made me (relatively) well-known. It led to a grant of £250 from the Society for Medieval Archaeology to enable me to do the grand tour of NW Europe (Germany, Holland, Denmark, Sweden) to meet continental medieval colleagues, find parallels for the Cheddar structures, and to investigate all the great contemporary excavations such as Feddersen Wierde, Wijster and Hedeby. It also led to close contact with the archaeologists of Holland, notably Wim Van Es, later Director of the Dutch State Archaeological Service (*see* **106**). He later came to Upton (see below) with his wife to study English excavation method.

Another great opportunity for research at state expense came in the 1960s at Cannington (37, 181), near Bridgwater. In our final weeks at Cheddar Palace, we had been visited by two brothers, John and Anthony Locke. Their father was the foreman of a large quarry. They had watched the work and (in spite of parental disapproval) noticed human remains. They excavated graves in the area immediately threatened and recorded them with commendable skill. They realised that further graves lay in the path of the quarry and sought our help.

We soon found that these were not the first skeletons to be found at Cannington. There were records going back to the early years of the century; in Dina Dobson's *Archaeology of Somerset* (see p52) she noted that it was estimated that over 1000 graves had been destroyed by then. They were locally believed to be those of Danes, killed in the famous 'Raven' battle with the Saxons in 878. The Chronicle records that 1000 died in this fight, so obviously this was who they were! Indeed on this slender basis, the place is marked on the Ordnance Survey maps with the crossed-sword symbol and 'Site of Battle 878' — thus do legends arise.

It was clear that we were dealing only with the residue of a very large cemetery; but fortunately probably the most important part of it, spreading up towards the summit of the hill.

We dug here for several seasons in the 1960s, excavating over 500 graves. Finds indicated that the cemetery was not of the Viking period, but much earlier. To cut a long story short, radiocarbon determinations eventually indicated a date range of *c*.AD 350-700+: late Roman and Dark Age (see chapter 9).

This was a stroke of luck indeed for my growing interest in the post-Roman centuries in Somerset, which began so auspiciously at Pagans Hill. Cemeteries of this period in this area are rare, and few are large. Cannington soon became, and still is, the type-site for a Western British cemetery of this period. As an added bonus, the contiguous hill was a

35 Don Brothwell reconstructing skulls at Cannington (1963)

hillfort with major earthworks. Trial digging here showed that this, although primarily Iron Age, also had late Roman and later levels (42). So we had a complex here of the greatest importance.

It is not easy to determine the date of settlement sites of the Dark Ages, nor how long they were used. Cemeteries paradoxically provide the key evidence for settlement. People live in an area, they die, and get buried. We guess that here was a settlement of village size (*c*.200 people) probably living in and around the hillfort, over a dozen generations; here was the best evidence of continuity from late Roman times into the Anglo-Saxon period. We do not know how or why the settlement of this period began in the fourth century, but it is likely that it was abandoned when the Anglo-Saxon village of Cannington (a few miles away) was founded in a reorganisation of the landscape by the incoming English.

The excavations yielded a mass of evidence and finds, of Neolithic, Bronze Age, Iron Age, Roman and post-Roman date, evidence of a much longer period of settlement than that of the cemetery itself. The finds were mostly not grave-goods; indeed we had dug over 300 graves, finding only a few knives before two infant graves were located with some highly interesting and dateable (late seventh- or early eighth-century) grave-goods.

Here lay a problem. In the 1960s the principal incentive to dig cemeteries was to recover grave-goods, notably the rich cemeteries of the pagan Anglo-Saxons. This was before the days of the large excavation of Christian churchyard cemeteries, which are now undertaken; graves were not regarded primarily, as they are now, as a source of valuable demographic and biological data.

In the light of these 1960s attitudes, the Ministry, when we told them that grave-goods were extremely rare, wanted to call the whole thing off. It was entirely due to one person that the work went on. This was Don Brothwell (**35**), now an Emeritus professor at York, with whom we are still collaborating in the 2000s. He was then at the British Museum, and on his way to becoming one of Britain's leading physical anthropologists. He persuaded the Ministry that a large sample of a Western British skeletal population would be valuable to his research, so the threat was averted. I was however strictly ordered to work fast, and to give up drawing the skeletons at 1:6 scale (1 inch to 6 inches) as I had been doing, but to record them only at 1:48 (1 inch to 4 feet) — a decision which has caused us many problems since.

The cemetery was of males, females and children — a typical 'normal' community — but with a rather surprising minority of males. The graves were dug in rows in the limestone bedrock; the skeletons were on their backs, mostly extended, and all orientated within the solar arc, i.e. their feet all pointed to the place of sunrise at different periods of the year (see 84).

On the summit of the hill was a stone-based circular and polygonal structure which we interpret as a late Roman (fourth- to fifth-century) rural temple or shrine (see 88), rather separate from the main grave concentrations. Among the latter was another nucleus of later date (sixth- to seventh-century), a low mound marked with a setting of non-local stone slabs and a decorated stone. A path led to this from the west. We had high hopes that this was an important person, such as a local 'chief' or 'saint'. Surprisingly, in a grave beneath the mound was the skeleton of an adolescent, with no grave goods or identification whatever. Later graves had crowded around the mound and cut into it and the path. There was clearly a story here. Who was this young person who had been dealt with so carefully at death, and whose grave had been much visited and revered; and by whom it was so desirable to be buried?

So often one has a local legend of some person who had special gifts, or around whom there were strange occurrences; or whose death was accompanied by portents or miracles; but with no supporting evidence beyond folklore. Here we have the evidence, but not the story.

The ambiguity of a scientific approach to the Cannington cemetery was not however shared by the then incumbent of Cannington Church, Canon A.R. Moss. He claimed the skeleton as that of the earliest Christian of his parish, and succeeded in retrieving it from the British Museum. The bones are now interred in a small grave inside the church (with the slab setting around them) and with a rather evocative (sexually ambiguous) wooden statue above. The stone slab marking the grave has a Chi-Rho symbol, and the inscription 'The name is known to God' — so it may be, but not alas to us!

A local girl, aged 12, came to help us; she proved to be very skilful at excavating graves and showed a keen understanding of the whole process. Her name was Lorna Watts; she is now my wife, and mother of my son Matthew. Another visitor asked if he could examine the graves; he spent some time gazing at the skeletons; as he left, he thanked us, and concluded 'that was very helpful; you see, my wife died last week'.

I should also include a note here on one of our most faithful volunteers, Joan Tanner. She had been a gardener at Chalice Well (see below) and had helped in the digging there. She subsequently came on all our digs right up to the 1980s; she sadly died recently (2000) in a nursing home in Glastonbury.

She had originally been a helper at the Chalice Well for rather mystic reasons; and brought these with her. She once straightened up from excavating a skeleton at Cannington, and gazed north-eastwards to Glastonbury, where the Tor could just be glimpsed on a clear day. 'Have you noticed, Philip', she said, 'that this hill and Glastonbury Tor are exactly in line with each other'. 'Yes, Joan, and if one took a compass bearing from each to the other, the two readings would be exactly 180° different; and that if one looks across north-westwards to Brent Knoll (by the coast) the three sites form a triangle'. She took such teasing in a very good-humoured way.

The whole of the Cannington hill is now quarried away. We estimate there to have been originally about 2000 graves there, so any conclusions we have drawn can be only partial. Susan Hirst, Susan Wright and myself have however constructed a major monograph on this cemetery (181).

Finally in this round-up of my pre-academic career, I still, in the early 1960s, found time and energy to do a few 'personal' digs. For instance, the late George Boon and I excavated a Roman coin-counterfeiting site at Whitchurch, near Bristol in 1961 (34).

Fate also led me to another major involvement — the hot-bed of Glastonbury, where myth and fact had become inextricably entangled. Ralegh Radford was asked to do some excavation to establish the basis of Early Christian associations in the area of Glastonbury Tor and Chalice Well. The work was to be financed by the Russell Trust, who support much 'Christian' archaeology. Radford refused; having dug in the Abbey himself, he was wary of getting involved with the Chalice Well Trust, who were rather a 'fringe' organisation. He suggested me as a substitute to do the first dig, at Chalice Well itself; I agreed, little knowing what I was letting myself in for. The Chairman of the Trust at that time (really my employer) was a remarkable man, the late Major W. Tudor Pole. He was a highly intelligent person, who believed in transubstantiation (the living of successive lives). His own earlier lives, it transpired, had been in the first century AD, in Jerusalem; then as an assistant in the great library at Alexandria in the Justinianic period; then as a cardinal in the fourteenth century; and finally in his twentieth-century role as ecumenical mystic: a cycle it seems of some seven century intervals. In talking to him, I had the uncomfortable feeling that he knew exactly what I was thinking. He had become well-known for his 'contact' with a soldier killed in the First World War; and for his collaboration with the great novelist, Rosamund Lehmann, in publishing her similar contact with her daughter, Sally, who died tragically young. I went with them both, at his invitation, to Devenish Island in County Fermanagh, where he was to deliver an ecumenical address for the celebrations of the 1600th anniversary of the death of the Devenish-based Irish saint Molaise.

Chalice Well is the site of a major spring, now rising within a structure displayed as a 'well'. It was locally believed that it had been an important feature of Early Christian settlement, and was, it was claimed, the place where the Vessels of the Passion had been washed. I was engaged to see if there was any archaeological evidence to support such a Christian antiquity. Trenches in the area did indeed reveal evidence of ancient use of the spring area in Mesolithic and Roman times (flints and pottery), but the 'well' was shown to be a medieval well-house, built in the late twelfth or early thirteenth century, to safeguard the water supply for use in the Abbey. Subsequently the well-house had become buried in silt washing down from higher levels, and a hole made in its roof, hence its present appearance; still, however, claimed locally as a 'well'.

Tudor Pole was not disappointed by my report (31). Although I was a sceptic (and he was well aware of this!), he was pleased with the results, and this led to the more extensive excavations on the Tor and Beckery which figure in later pages.

I had by 1963 realised that I could not continue being a freelance archaeologist indefinitely. The pressures of digging and writing were building up, and Cheddar had created considerable stress. Relief, or at least change, was, however, now imminent, as the next chapter will show.

4 Entry into academia: the University of Birmingham, teaching and research in the West Midlands and beyond (1963-9)

Rodney Hilton is one of the most eminent medieval historians of our day. He was in the Medieval Department of the School of History of the University of Birmingham. Principally due to his influence, teaching and research were heavily Marxist-based. Rodney has been a life-long left-winger, and was especially interested in peasants, and their aspirations to overthrow their oppressive masters. He realised that to get behind the written sources to the material culture it was necessary to recover archaeological evidence of their houses and possessions. He decided, therefore, in the late 1950s, to embark on the excavation of the deserted medieval village of Upton, in the Cotswolds, as part of his study of West Midlands' society.

He also believed that to participate in a dig would be socially and intellectually stimulating for undergraduates reading medieval history. He was personally in no position to direct an excavation, so he secured the services in 1960 of one of the itinerant freelancers, listed in earlier pages. This was to be a great coming together of the disciplines of history and archaeology.

The first season went well, initiating the excavation of a peasant house. The students responded well to being on a dig. The only problem was that although the archaeologist concerned handled everything very efficiently, he was very reluctant to talk about what he thought it all 'meant'; they waited expectantly while he examined the dig, puffing on his pipe, and then — just walked away!

Students do not like being treated and frustrated like this, they want to be involved, especially having done the hard work. Rodney, while pleased with the definition of material culture that was appearing, sought a different director. Graham Webster recommended me as someone who would talk and discuss the dig, and I accordingly met him and his student Jean Birrell (later to be his third wife) at Upton in the spring of 1961.

I was very impressed by his powerful personality and intellect, though more than a little awed — he was the first *really* clever person I'd ever met. My first season went well; I established that I could explain to undergraduates what archaeology was all about, the methods used, and how data was used to reconstruct the sequence of events on the site, and the quality of peasant life.

I did not approve of the 1960 system (a grid excavation), and explained how a peasant farmstead needs to be dug by the open area method (see chapter 8). This created a

36 Upton, peasant house in early stage of open area excavation, 1962, with the turf and topsoil removed, exposing the collapsed remains of the house, 1964

problem in that in my first and second seasons the work consisted of stripping large areas of turf and topsoil and cleaning the latest stage of the final dereliction of the farmstead (**36**). There was thus straight away a conflict between the needs of archaeology and those of students wishing to do more interesting archaeology; this led to some mutterings, and (especially in bad weather) near-mutiny (**37**).

Rodney, although interested in certain aspects of the results, such as the high quality of the building, its fittings and the peasants' personal possessions, found the detailed work rather tedious. For instance, in vain did I explain that to establish a type-series of medieval pottery was crucial to both the understanding of the village's external contacts and markets, and to its chronology of foundation, floruit and decline; apart from being a first step in the understanding of all Cotswold medieval sites.

Fortunately, however, it appeared not only that I ran a student training excavation successfully, but that it would be a good move to incorporate medieval archaeology within the department on a permanent basis. So, in the rapid expansion of university posts in the 1960s a job was 'fixed' for me; I was appointed to the post of assistant lecturer in the autumn term of 1963 (**38**).

To restrict my experience for the moment to the work at Upton, we continued with a summer dig each year until 1968. In nine seasons, one peasant farmstead in one village had been fully excavated, and this work led to two major publications (33 and 41). While this was wholly satisfactory in the then-developing theme of medieval village studies, it failed

37 Rodney Hilton (middle right) and the students at Upton

to answer the major problems that a medieval historian would ask: the origins, growth and decline of upland rural settlements over a wide geographical area. The excavation was however illuminating in finding at least some evidence of continuity of settlement and land-use through Roman and Saxon times, the establishment of a well-built stone-founded farmstead, and something on the functions of its various components.

Upton, together with the courses that developed within the university from 1963 onwards, also helped in the production of graduates who were familiar with the disciplines of both history and archaeology; some of our Upton diggers went on to distinguished academic careers, such as Jean Birrell, Sally Harvey, Chris Dyer, Howard Clarke and (in post-Upton days) Grenville Astill, Susan Wright and Terry Barry.

While I was encouraged to develop special subject teaching, and to give general lectures, seminars and tutorials, it was all seen as rather subservient to what was regarded as the major subject of written history. I struggled to build up a one-man archaeological empire in the School of History. This was assisted by my external contacts, and my increasing involvement in West Midland archaeology and politics.

I was rather horrified to find that I was also expected to do some first-year teaching of Medieval European History, in which I was largely ignorant. I remember how it gradually dawned on me that Charlemagne, Charles the Great, Karl der Grosse, and Carolus Magnus were all the same chap! I found, however, that the students I tutored did rather better than the others. Realising they would learn little from me, they were driven in the last resort to reading books, an activity not greatly to their taste. My special subject students were more successfully dealt with; I remember Chris Dyer (now Professor) at the end of his degree course handing me a reading list he had compiled. 'I think you might find this rather useful for next year's students, Philip.' So does one learn the complexities of university teaching.

My past and continuing output of publications, and my non-university excavations stood me in good stead, and with the help of certain colleagues, I achieved promotion to Lecturer, Senior Lecturer and Reader in the 1960s and earlier 1970s.

I was surprised to find that the Department of Archaeology and Ancient History at Birmingham were rather annoyed by the coup of getting archaeology into the School of History, especially when some of their students (including Raymond Lamb, Alan Saville and David Miles) enrolled on my special courses. With the exception of Lawrence Barfield, who worked at Roman Droitwich as well as Northern Italy, the staff had little involvement in the West Midlands, either in excavations or in politics: this was something, in their view, better left to the extra-mural world and the CBA. They tended to get as far

38 Assistant Lecturer, School of History, University of Birmingham, 1964 (passport photograph)

away from Birmingham as possible — to Peru, Greece, or Orkney. During my tenure, the Roman fort on the University campus was progressively destroyed by university expansion and car-parking, with no efforts by university archaeologists to do anything about it.

I exacerbated such matters by writing a paper for the University magazine (45) which listed all the archaeological work being done from the University, locally and in distant areas.

Nevertheless, Richard Tomlinson, later head of that department, invited me to join him in Greece to survey and excavate, in 1967 and 1969, in Boetia and Elis. This was a splendid new opening for me into the archaeology of the eastern Mediterranean, and also a chance to see the great classical sites of the Peloponnese. We drove there on each occasion in a Land Rover: five days each way, a gruelling journey, but a fine transect through Europe. On the outward journeys it was a great relief to arrive at the luxury of the British School at Athens, where afternoon tea was still served.

The challenge of university life and teaching was, however, very beneficial to me intellectually, broadening my horizon above the edge of a trench, and encouraging me to go beyond description and site reports to synthesis. In 1964 I wrote my first book review (of Graham Webster's *Practical Archaeology*). In 1967 I gave my first short conference paper at Nottingham, on sub-Roman cemeteries (of which more later), subsequently published (37); and a paper on monasteries as settlements, at Edinburgh (53).

All the talk on Dark Age Somerset (see chapter 9) that had been accumulating led to the first exposition on the problems by Peter Fowler (then extra-mural tutor in Bristol) and myself (39), and to a fuller exposition on 'Somerset 400-700' in Leslie Grinsell's *Festschrift* (51). I tackled the pottery in Somerset of this period in a seminal paper (62); and an even wider synthesis on the then state of medieval and later archaeology in England and Wales in a Polish Marxist journal (44).

In gaining confidence, I began to think more clearly about the relationship of archaeology to history. To me, with such a wide spectrum of experience in the field of millennia of human development, the study of written sources seemed rather limited: to those aspects of human settlement which were thought to be worth committing to writing, and then processed through a human mind; and finally only for relatively recent times, an arrogant view which I developed more fully in later years. Marxism, as an explanatory mode of interpretation, seemed even more limited in its concentration on the control of the means of production, and on an 'inevitable' sequence of change.

My West Midlands involvement in the later 1960s extended also to politics. At that time, there was widespread concern about the acceleration of destruction of sites by very diverse human and natural threats; this was relatively minor in the earlier years of our itinerant rescue digging, but came to a head with the runaway success of a new organisation: RESCUE, with its dramatic poster of Stonehenge being removed by mechanical excavator.

The 'think-tank' which gave rise to this was significantly in the West Midlands, a memorable four-day mid-week session at Barford, near Warwick. The leading protagonist was Philip Barker with his paper 'Not Waving, Just Drowning'!

I was involved to a lesser degree, serving on the RESCUE Committee, and editing and contributing to a successful book on the magnitude of the threat (61). Locally, I wrote on the crisis as it affected churches (55), the ideal local organisation that would be needed to cope with the problem (57) and the particular case of gravestones (58), a topic to which I was to return.

During the years at Birmingham, I was fortunate to be able to go on digging. The duties of an academic were much less onerous and competitive than they are today; and I was really fairly peripheral in a large School of History, where even medieval history was regarded as a curious digression by the modernists, at least partly because it did not seem to them to be 'socially relevant', especially to twentieth-century historians such as John Grenville, the then Director of the School. Vacations were long, and there was also the occasional term of study leave. The excavations I did elsewhere were now under the aegis of the University, and I could now enrol a considerable body of student help; and also I was still able to acquire funds to dig from the Ministry of Works, as well as some finance from university research grants.

Firstly there was a return to Cheddar; this time because of a threat from housing development. The new work was not on the palace site, but near the Church of St Andrew and its vicarage (36, 54) where there was a Roman site, presumed to be a major villa. We had found a good deal of Roman material in our palace excavations; not surprisingly as the palace area would have been part of the environs of the villa. To understand something of the Roman complex was clearly highly relevant to an appreciation of the later palace. Any Roman estate here probably retained some identity in the Dark Ages; it may have been a unit of land ownership or management taken over by the Kings of Wessex and later used as an administrative centre and palace.

This was not its only relevance. The contiguity of the Church of St Andrew and the Roman site was no coincidence. The area where they both lie is closer to the River Yeo than the palace, giving ready access to water for domestic and animal uses, and for power (the swift Yeo drove several mills in later centuries); and at the key point where the river debouched from a dry gravel terrace into the rich alluvial land to the south, often flooded. Coupled with a favourable micro-climate and hunting on Mendip, the topographic circumstances made Cheddar a very desirable property: Cheddar was and is a pleasant place and rich in agricultural and horticultural potential (hence the strawberries and cheese!). In Roman times a road (still traceable) led up the steep southern slopes of Mendip to Charterhouse-on-Mendip. Here lead was mined as early as the reign of the Emperor Claudius, in the 40s of the first century AD (see chapter 3). Mendip lead has been shown to have been used at Pompeii. It was conjectured that Cheddar might have been one of the points from which it was shipped abroad by river and sea.

The Gorge also leads up into Mendip, and in it are impressive caves. They were known at least as early as the twelfth century, and it is very likely that they had been a local attraction in centuries before this, to add to the other desirable attributes of the place.

It was hoped that there might be some direct connection between the Roman villa and the religious site of the Minster that followed — for instance if there had been some Roman Christian nucleus here; or if early Christian evangelists had found a welcome on the estate (Glastonbury is only a dozen miles away!).

Parch marks had been seen in dry summers in the vicarage lawn; one or two holes here (where trees had decayed) located typical villa evidence (hypocaust ash, tesserae, etc), so clearly this was the nucleus of what must have been an extensive range of buildings. But it was the periphery we were also interested in, where evidence might be found to bridge the gap between the villa and the Minster. There were some areas of worn gravel and possible light foundations but the areas available were too small to make any sense of it. It is sad that this important area is now largely built on; but there remains much of the vicarage lawn.

I have described above how I became involved in Glastonbury and Chalice Well, and the ethical problems involved. This led on to bigger things, this time not a state-supported enterprise, but privately financed. This was no less than an invitation to excavate on the summit of one of the most famous land-marks in Britain — Glastonbury Tor.

There were dark hints that it was hoped that I would find 'something' (as at Chalice Well) that would support the long-held idea that Glastonbury was the cradle of

Christianity in Britain, in the first century AD. Indeed as I have often recounted, there were some at Glastonbury who believed that Christianity was invented there by the Druids, and were only waiting for Christ to be born to give the new religion a name.

I have described elsewhere (158) the whole apparatus of myth and legend that encircles Glastonbury like a fog, obscuring whatever elements of truth can be gleaned from history or archaeology. The archaeology (38, 49) is however sound, and of the greatest interest in illuminating the history of the Tor. We had no preconceived ideas of what might have taken place at such a dramatic place. The only starting point was the standing tower of the medieval church of St Michael; one obvious target was to find the plan of the body of the church to which this tower belonged; that was achieved, but with many difficulties and doubts. There was the burial of John Rawls, who asked in his will (1741) to be buried on the Tor; his grave was found but he was left in peace. There were one or two post holes that could have supported the gibbet on which Abbot Whiting of the Abbey was hanged by order of Henry VIII's Commissioners in 1539. These were events known from written history, as were the use of the Tor as a beacon, and an earthquake in 1275 that fissured the whole bedrock and made the archaeology very difficult. More sinister things too: the use of the Tor for witchcraft for which there was slight (and rather unpleasant) evidence; and by pilgrims: archaeology recovered a gold millefiori cross of Italian origin, and a silver ring bearing the emblem of the Bahai faith. But was there anything earlier?

We were lucky: all the things described above were on the flat summit, but around the edges were, very fortunately, accumulations of soil which had resisted erosion; and here we did find evidence of earlier occupation. There were Neolithic flints and a stone axe; Bronze Age flints; and many Roman finds including tile fragments and pottery. Clearly this had been a place which people came to far back in prehistory. I have often wondered if there had been a Roman temple, or even a beacon structure, on this splendid viewpoint, which had been totally removed by the levelling associated with the church.

The most interesting evidence, from my point of view, was the Dark Age material found around the edges of the summit. It seemed, yet again, to be falling into my hands. There were a few bones of two human burials of young males, thousands of meat bones, and evidence of metal working: hearths and crucible fragments. There were postholes and slots of timber structures too. All this was dated by the finding of 14 sherds of sixth-century amphorae from the Mediterranean. I had heard of these as having been found on other sites, notably Tintagel; and it later transpired that there were a few at Cannington.

They are the key finds in identifying sites of this period in the West of Britain and Ireland, and witness remarkable trade contacts with distant lands. But what was the nature of this Dark Age outpost? Such finds are usually associated with people of high status, either secular or monastic. This is no place to argue all this yet again (see 49 and the rather different view in 151; see also chapter 9). Without any more positive evidence, but a gut-feeling (something which has no place in archaeology?), I leant in the direction of its being a small Christian eremetic monastery, principally because there was later evidence on the shoulder of the hill for an Anglo-Saxon monastic complex — small cells cut in the rock.

The importance of the work on the Tor cannot be overemphasised in the Glastonbury context. Extensive excavations in the Abbey had not found anything as early as the sixth century. So we had perhaps shown that Christianity arrived at Glastonbury not at the

Abbey, as all previous commentators had assumed, but on the Tor; though not as early as many people hoped for!

All this took three seasons (1964-6) which were on the whole enjoyable, with a splendid mix of Birmingham students and other volunteers — one of the best teams I've ever had. We lived in a school, which in term-time was for Millfield boys; all food was laid on and there was a swimming pool; altogether it was an ideal framework for archaeology — plenty of room for finds processing, and discussions on the day's results. One remarkable feature was a communal bathroom, with a row of unisex tubs. This afforded great pleasure to the male diggers.

The only problem was logistic. Little could be left on the Tor overnight — tools, drawing equipment, cameras: all had to be carried up each day, up what is still a steep and difficult ascent. On the exposed summit of the Tor we were very much at the mercy of the weather; rainstorms drove us into the slight shelter the tower could offer; in hot weather it was baking; but the worst thing was the wind. When it was strong, the soil that we had moved out of the dig blew back in again; several times we had to give up for the day. But it was always a great experience to have the distant views and the clouds, looking back towards Mendip, or down into the sometimes flooded wetlands of the Somerset Levels.

My religiously-orientated employers were well-satisfied with the substantial results, though some of their followers were disappointed. To repeat one 'accusation' (yet again): 'there are three reasons, Mr Rahtz, why you haven't found anything (sic); you are digging in the wrong place' (well, yes this charge could be levelled); 'you are digging at the wrong time' (I couldn't help this, not at this time having mastered the art of time travel); and 'you're the wrong person' (I couldn't win on this one).

It is disappointing that when one has put a lot of effort into major enterprises like this, so little gets out into public consciousness. Often have I read in the years since 'Why doesn't someone excavate on the Tor?'. This was obviously our fault. The publications we did put out were not popular ones; and although I gave lectures locally, they clearly were not enough. When I did make an attempt to write a popular book on Glastonbury in the early 1990s (158) it reached a wider public; but had short shrift in the Glastonbury bookshops amongst the welter of mystic rubbish about Avalon, Arthur, Atlantis and Anti-Christ; even though I had played into their hands by giving some credence to Geoffrey Russell's concept that the upper terraces on the Tor were not merely agricultural or geological features, but part of a three-dimensional maze (see 158); an idea that I am pursuing again in 2000 (188).

The Tor dig was followed in the later 1960s by two seasons at Beckery (60, 158), one of several satellite monasteries of the Abbey. This was associated with another set of legends concerning no less a person than the Irish St Bridget, but Arthur came into it as well. We did not here succeed in taking the history of the site back before the eighth century, but we did find a predominantly adult male cemetery, a 'founder's' grave, and a small timber shrine enclosed inside Norman and later churches, a satisfactory archaeological expansion of a sparse background.

The work at Chalice Well, the Tor and Beckery laid a good foundation to the important digs in the 1970s, to which I shall return in chapter 6; but I take a break now into a very different world from that of Somerset and the West Midlands, that of West Africa.

5 A term in Ghana

As an interlude in my British academic career, I spent a term in Ghana, in the autumn of 1966. I was 45, and in a time of personal crisis, so it was a good opportunity for a complete change, and to take stock of my life. The visit was arranged by Peter Shinnie, who had been Professor of Archaeology at the University of Legon (Accra). The idea was that I should go as a visiting lecturer, and help David Calvocoressi (a member of the Legon staff) to set up an urban research project at the ancient site of Begho. The importance of this medieval town was that it was a meeting place of the Arab traders from the maritime areas of North Africa and the local Africans: a great trading-station where Mediterranean material of high value and exotic interest would be exchanged for gold, and possibly other resources such as slaves. The gold would have been gathered from many sources by panning or mining, and its location kept secret. A big town, with all its services, divided up into 'quarters', would have been needed for the necessarily lengthy trading, and for the 'northerners' to replenish their supplies and energy after the long camel trek across the Sahara. Gold was much sought after by the merchants of Europe, the Middle East and North Africa. It continued to be an important source of wealth for the area known after independence as Ghana (previously the Gold Coast). In the war between the British and Ashanti at the end of the nineteenth century, gold was a target. When the chief of the Ashanti, the Asantehene, was exiled, the British demanded huge fines in gold; but there is still plenty to be seen in Ghana, adorning people and forming an important element in museum collections.

In the 1960s, one could still take what amounted to a luxury cruise of two weeks on a ship out of Liverpool; to travel slowly was to become easily accustomed to the radically different atmosphere of the tropics. It was a great pleasure to leave the darkening autumn skies of England and arrive first at a sunny Gran Canaria. The next intimation of what was to come was the highly distinctive smell and feel of the wind blowing out from the coast of West Africa, and arriving first at Freetown (Sierra Leone). As the ship slowed down on entering harbour, the breeze of its motion, which had kept us relatively comfortable, stopped. Now I experienced my first taste of heat and humidity, which I knew I had to cope with for a few months. After a walk round the amazing scenes of African life near the harbour area, I also found that I had never known what thirst was before! I was relieved to find that I could stand the hot and humid atmosphere.

Here in Freetown was my first taste of African archaeology, of relatively recent date. There were visible and evocative structural remains of the buildings and steps of the slave trade: millions left here for the Americas. There was plenty of ethnographic material to record and photograph. Especially relevant was a tin church near the harbour, with graves either side of the altar of murdered early Christian missionaries: a situation reminiscent of the problems faced by the Church in early Christian Europe, and the graves of the early martyrs to the faith.

The ship resumed its progress after a few hours, and came finally into Accra. I was welcomed to the Archaeology Department at Legon almost as a visitor from outer space. Archaeologists with news from England were a rare treat. I was, however, greeted with the news that Calvocoressi was very ill, with several of the endemic diseases to which non-Africans fall prey. Although he eventually recovered, there was no chance of him being fit enough to embark on an expedition to Begho.

I knew virtually nothing about West Africa. Urban excavation theory is one thing, understanding the nature of the sites in the flesh (or dirt) is another. When I found later that Begho was not (as I'd imagined) a ruined town in the savannah, but a quite amorphous collection of mounds and hollows with no visible pattern, extending over many hectares, I was rather relieved not to have had to pontificate on it. Some years later, in the 1970s, excavations did take place there; this proved that it was extremely difficult to find even walls, let alone buildings or quarters; so it was just as well that our plan fell through.

The problem in 1966 was what I should do for a term at Legon. I gave a few lectures and seminars to the staff and students on British archaeology, but they were hardly more than politely received, evoking nostalgia at best.

I found the social life of Legon rather unsatisfactory. Europeans and Africans had 'palm wine' parties, mixing rather stiffly; but there was little social intercourse with the Ghanaians. Not because they didn't wish it, but because firstly the food they ate in their homes was unpalatable to the Europeans, and secondly because their homes were lived in by many people. When a Ghanaian obtained a university post, his whole family descended on him to share his good fortune, not just his wife and children, but all his 'sisters, his cousins, and his aunts'.

I was, however, in the first few weeks taken 'up-country' by Richard Yorke. He introduced me to the dubious pleasures of driving hundreds of dusty miles in extreme heat in a Land Rover over roads which were hardly more than cattle tracks, destroyed by the rains each year. He did, however, show me something of the countryside and the people. In some villages the younger children had never seen a white man, and ran away screaming when they saw us. There were very interesting antiquities and digs to be seen, and I quickly absorbed something of the nature of life in Ghana, and of its archaeology, knowledge of which was still very limited.

I was impressed by the general air of happiness and gaiety. There was a high level of euphoria about, since it was only a year since the fall of the now-hated dictator Kwami Nkrumah, with many fearsome rumours of his evil doings.

I was also taken to Kumasi, the capital of the Ashanti, one of five 'nations' which had been welded together to make Ghana, with English a *lingua franca*: a useful hang-over from the colonial days of the Gold Coast. I found here a splendid city, with spacious parks and gardens. It was difficult to believe that the British had been besieged here in my father's lifetime.

Nkrumah was somewhat afraid of the power of the Ashanti, and had lavished much money on Kumasi. Among other benefits he had made an Olympic-sized swimming pool, in vain expectation that Ghana would host the Games one day. This was now an élitist feature for staff at the University of Kumasi, and very welcome to me! He was also very keen to westernise the country, even to the unfortunate extent of forcing Ghanaian women to wear clothes at the market.

In the countryside there was plenty of ethnography for my camera to record: houses, pottery-making and even fetish-houses, the latter rather dangerous to be seen photographing. There were strange open places, where it was said that ritual dancing took place, and where the surrounding caves exhibited patterns of owari-boards: sequences of cup-hollows cut in the rock.

In Kumasi, the Museum had many exhibits dating back to the seventeenth century, to the days of Osei Tutu, the first ruler of the Ashanti. Here too is the royal mausoleum, a concrete building guarded by concrete red lions and *armed soldiers*. It was said that 'no white man has ever been inside'. It seems that there are here the skeletons of all the rulers since Osei Tutu, held together by gold wire; and that when a new Asantahene is proclaimed, he has to shake hands with all their bony fingers. I could only stand outside and wish!

On our brief travels we stayed at uncomfortable 'guest houses', shacks for travellers; the mosquito nets had many holes, to allow the insects full access to one's body. Well north of Kumasi was a small town called Kintampo where we saw a cave with extensive signs of burning on its roof, floor and walls. This was rather surprising as Africans fear caves, as places where dangerous wild bees and other beasts are likely to lurk (not to mention spirits!).

It was suggested by the University authorities a week or two later that £500 had been allocated for Begho, and should be spent; and would I like to do some excavation? All I could think of was the Kintampo cave, which looked promising as a possible settlement site; and I knew it was in a pleasant area. I was allocated a Land Rover, a driver (Ibrahim), a surveyor/photographer (Torgbor), and a foreman. The latter was the redoubtable Quansah, who had taken part in many previous archaeological expeditions, and knew the ropes. We were due to make the 400-mile trip to the north on a Monday. On the Saturday before, I hired a small car from the University and went down to Accra to see some traditional dancing; on the way back to Legon, I crashed it into a lamp standard on an unlit roundabout. As the car hit and went over I wondered if I'd come all this way just to die. I was thrown about amid big CRUMPS, and when the car finally stopped I came to and found blood pouring down my face. I was not dead, but thought I'd be disfigured for life. I'd stocked up on food to take north, in the (correct) expectation that I'd have difficulties with the food my colleagues ate. This food was spread out all over the roundabout. I was pulled out of the wreck by the military police, who appeared in the dark as if by magic, and gathered the food up safely. I was whisked away to the military hospital and given the once over: all I had was a broken nose.

The next morning, the police called and charged me with dangerous driving. They took me to the crash site — the car looked as if it had been sat on by an elephant. It was clear that the lamp standard had *bent* under the impact (being Ghanaian), thus saving my life.

On the Monday, duly bandaged up, we set off, myself a little shaky. Quansah was extremely efficient. He got us a house to live in with a paraffin-driven refrigerator; this would have been very useful if it had worked. My staff soon acquired local (temporary) wives to see to their culinary and other needs; it was some weeks before they persuaded me to do likewise ('Meesa Raas, this ees Mrs Raas') (**39**). I found myself looking out over a sea of trees right to the horizon; and the only white man in a town of 7000 people. Religion they had, but wore it lightly — pagan, Christian or Muslim — with no conflict.

To expedite the dig, we first had to visit the local chief. We all sat round in his courtyard: my staff, the chief, his brothers and hangers-on. Quansah produced a bottle of gin — I'd wondered what this was for; now I knew (or thought I knew) I was wrong. The bottle was passed around; each man poured a little into a glass, and then, to my surprise, threw it on the earth floor. It was a communal offering to the spirits of the earth, air and water; and secured the full collaboration of both the gods and the chief. He provided us with 20 really good men, very strong and with good eyesight, which proved useful in the event (**40**).

39 Mamunaatu Mahamadu (Mamima)

We set off each day to the dig at 5.00am, met our men by the Baobab tree, and work began about 5.30. By noon, it was too hot, so we stopped for the day. After lunch I went for a swim in a small reservoir, kindly built by the British Army in earlier years (there were four British graves in Kintampo cemetery); a pleasure shared only with water-turtles; except for one memorable afternoon, when I persuaded my driver Ibrahim to have a dip; and ended up teaching him how to pronounce English as she is spoken, using Agatha Christie's novel, *Cards on the Table*. In the dusk, I read, or washed and marked finds, and wrote up my excavation records.

The cave was high up in the side of an inselberg, a mass of limestone rock. Its roof looked rather thin and dangerous, so I first got all my men to stand on it, hanging on to trees and jumping — the rock survived. The visible burning was reflected in the upper layers of deposits in the cave floor; there was a lot of burnt wood, burnt stone, stone dust and chips. As we proceeded down, we realised there was interleaved strata of burning and rubble; with half-finished stone objects and quartzite hammer-stones. I didn't know what it all meant, but the staff knew; we had stumbled on a place where food-grinding stones were being made (saddle-querns); used for the trituration or mashing of food; the men knew because they were still using them; they had them in the house.

40 The excavation at Kintampo, Ghana, 1966; my team (Quansah 3rd from right, top row)

Rather abashed, I realised what had happened there, having gone down some four metres through these layers. The cave had started off lower down, nearer the ground level. It was filled with brushwood and set afire. Water was then thrown on the hot walls and roof; this brought down large slabs of rock which could then be worked into grindstones using the harder quartzite hammer-stones. The process was then repeated until the roof, now higher up (as the floor also rose), became too thin.

What about the date of this manufactory? I knew it was pre-colonial, as there were no clay pipes, ubiquitous in Africa on sites of the seventeenth century and later. There was pottery, about which I knew nothing. I didn't even know which millennium I was in; this was working from first principles with a vengeance. It was not until several months later that radiocarbon dating of the charcoal (among the first half dozen such dates then available for Ghana) at the University of Birmingham gave a reading about the beginning of our era, in the first century AD.

But more was to come; below the grindstone-making debris were cave earths, with quite different pottery, fine flint flakes and small greenstone axe-heads. This is where the men's eyesight came in useful. They could see the tiniest flints. Again, I had no idea of the date, which radiocarbon later put at about 1500 BC — contemporary with our British Bronze Age (**41**).

The grindstone factory was at that time only the second to be found in Africa. The stone and pottery assemblage from the lower levels made Kintampo a type-site, in later years giving its name to the 'Kintampo culture'.

Socially and anthropologically it was also a great experience. Work songs kept the dig moving fast; boulders were shifted by the gang pulling on a rope, with Quansah as the cheerleader. The men were paid 7s 6d a day (*c*.35p). The social system in Ghana was such that no money was needed for daily subsistence or housing. The money earned on the dig was for two deeply-felt needs: transistor radios and football boots. I watched a few of the matches, but never saw one end, except in a fight.

I lost weight, due to the food problem; but was able to replenish my stocks when I spent a weekend in Kumasi, 150 miles distant. I also, through the kind offices of someone I met on the boat, who was a lecturer there, delivered the first lecture on archaeology ever given (and possibly the last) at the University of Kumasi. It was principally a scientific university, so my lecture was appropriately on 'Science and Archaeology'.

41 The excavation in the cave

By Christmas, the dig was over, and we returned to Legon; my staff to their wives, who were very anxious to know how their husbands had been looked after by their temporary wives; and me to England and problems; not now on a ship, but one of the two large aeroplanes run by the State of Ghana. Taking off at 10am from Accra, one cleared the coastal area, the canopy forest and the savannah in an hour, and then there were seven hours across the Sahara: blue sky, snow mountain, black rock and yellow sand: the first intimation I had of the vast extent of the desert. And then suddenly the reappearance of houses and roads, the Mediterranean and a quick descent to Zurich airport, with ice and snow all around the runway, and a temperature of 50 degrees celsius below that of Accra.

I was gratified to have made, after such an inauspicious start, such a positive contribution to African archaeology, so far removed in every way from my British pre-occupation.

A nice tailpiece to this is that in 1994 my son Sebastian visited Legon, and met Quansah in the Department of Archaeology; he was very pleased to meet the son of his former colleague of earlier Kintampo days.

6 The later years at Birmingham; the big digs of the 1970s (1969-78)

I take up the story of my closing years at Birmingham (from where I digressed) in 1969. I had by this time become fairly well known, especially in the West Midlands (one has to live in London to be at the heart of British archaeology, and be on the powerful Committees, Councils, etc). My very small part in the administration in the School of History left me with the opportunity to do plenty of fieldwork. The excavations we organised gave ample scope for those History students who showed an interest in excavating, and attracted a wide range of other helpers.

The excavations at Upton came to an untimely end in 1968, when one of our helpers left the farm gate open; the cows took advantage of this to trample all over the farmer's garden; we were given notice to quit.

It so happened that there was a new opportunity in the offing. This was at Bordesley Abbey, a Cistercian foundation of 1138, in fields which were gradually being absorbed into the new town of Redditch, in Worcestershire, some 10 miles south of Birmingham. Nothing remained above ground of the abbey buildings, but there were conspicuous earthworks over some 36ha of the valley of the River Arrow.

Excavations in the nineteenth century had shown that the largest earthwork was the church of St Mary, with substantial foundations and floors beneath turf. Although the excavator, Frederick Woodward had published a fine monograph in 1866, this had been largely forgotten a century later. The New Town planners were reluctant to believe that there was really anything worth saving beneath the 'bumps and hollows'; they would have liked to flatten everything and create new playing fields. Strenuous efforts were made by Philip Barker, single-handed, in a passionate speech to the planners, to persuade them to change their minds, and fund excavation. He was successful, and digging ensured under the direction of Kate Pretty (then a teenager, now Principal of Homerton College, Oxford) and Trevor Rowley (now Deputy Director of Extra-Mural Studies at Oxford) to demonstrate the quality of what was buried, by excavation. They were successful — even a Development Corporation knew what a church was. They were now persuaded that to have a major 'Ancient Monument' in their New Town would be prestigious, useful for public and school education, and would be an attractive focus for recreation and dogs.

They offered to provide £400 for a further season of excavation in 1969; Rowley was no longer available; Philip Barker asked us if we'd be interested. Since we had been thrown out of Upton, we needed a new training dig for the students, and here was welcome finance: so I accepted. Rodney Hilton was rather horrified; as a Marxist, he was strongly anti-clerical; in his famous book on the medieval West Midlands, there was no chapter on the Church as a major landowner or participant in trade, or industry of the region. I remember students I told about this didn't believe me! He was eventually reconciled to the value of Bordesley as a training excavation, incorporating architectural as well as archaeological studies; he came out to help in later years.

It was decided to continue work on the church, as likely to provide the most impressive remains. Had there not been this political imperative, we would probably have tackled other features of the monastic complex more related to social and economic medieval history. A great deal is known about Cistercian churches and the claustral complex, but little on the other buildings; landscape features, such as boundaries or fish-ponds were evident among the earthworks.

Mick Aston, then a graduate student at Birmingham, now of *Time Team*, did a survey of the whole 36ha and showed that the Abbey complex was complete and largely undisturbed; he also made very useful hypotheses as to its development over the four centuries of Cistercian use, which were to be confirmed in later years.

Excavation of the church showed that there was a great deal surviving below the ground. Although the Abbey had been robbed of its stone for Redditch buildings after the Dissolution in 1538, this robbing was only down to the latest floor level. Because of the wet conditions in the valley, the ground had been successively made up in the thirteenth and later centuries, floor after floor, burying the lower metre or more of the masonry and columns. This led to the preservation not only of successive architectural alterations, but also to the preservation of the layout of floors, with their evidence of changing liturgical needs and the pattern of movement within the church. Thus stratification was thus linked to structural sequences — excellent experience for ourselves and for the students.

I was fortunate enough to have very good lieutenants at this time: Grenville Astill (now professor at the University of Reading), Susan Wright and Susan Hirst (**42**). The latter had been initiated into archaeology at Hereford (39A), and was now living with me in Birmingham. We also had Daryl Fowler and Ian McCaig as surveyors, measuring the intricate remains; and David Walsh (from the University of Rochester, USA). He dealt with the masses of loose stone, and the architectural aspects of the building (see chapter 10).

Over the next 10 years we excavated about a third of the church, which was then consolidated by the Redditch authorities. Sue Hirst and I published a full report on the first five years (74) and a popular version for the increasingly interested public (75). Mary Berry and her 'medieval' choir from Cambridge gave (over 24 hours) the first performance of the whole Cistercian Office (the sung parts of the daily services) since 1538, in the now opened Abbey ruins; all dressed in white Cistercian habits.

At Bordesley, too, the graves were very informative, although destructive of stratification. Inside the church, they included those of secular patrons; local aristocracy who had made financial contributions in exchange for having masses said for their souls, with their families. Outside the church, to the east, were graves of the first generation of monks who had built the first wooden church in the 1140s before the main stone building programme began later in the century. Planks from their wooden church were laid over their bodies, and were preserved in the wet soil providing us both with information on the wooden structure and (by tree-ring dating) precise dates for the tree felling.

42 Digging at
   Bordesley Abbey,
   Worcestershire,
   1981. Sue Hirst
   on the left and
   Sue Wright in
   foreground
   (copyright
   Birmingham
   Post and Mail
   81/7548/B/5)

I gave up substantial involvement in Bordesley in 1978, when I moved to York; but it continued under the direction of Astill, Hirst and Wright. They have dug more of the church; but Astill has also undertaken (with his Reading students) a major excavation of the watermill and industrial complex in the lower part of the valley, together with an examination of the whole water management. Here again, major wooden structures survived, and many pieces of the mill machinery, precisely dated by tree-ring sampling.

Bordesley, from somewhat unpropitious beginnings, has become a model for the examination of medieval monasteries, principally because of its combining archaeological (stratigraphic) studies with those of the 'above-ground' (in this case buried!) remains, and its well-preserved evidence of medieval monastic technology.

As an 'extra' to the larger excavations, in 1971 we took a select team of students to St Mary, Deerhurst, a famous Anglo-Saxon church near Tewkesbury in Gloucestershire; here we spent a week excavating a small ruined area at the east end. I knew little about Anglo-Saxon churches at this time, but I had begun to include them in my Birmingham courses. My eye was caught by a footnote in a paper by the doyen of these studies, Harold Taylor (see chapter 10). In a discussion about Deerhurst, he asked a simple question: 'Did Deerhurst ever have a corridor crypt?' (this is an ambulatory set at a low level around the east end of some churches, such as Brixworth, Northants; from it, circulating pilgrims could view relics under the inside altar, through a small tunnel). I realised that this was indeed a straight question, which excavation could easily answer; within a few days, we had decisively shown that the answer was in the negative; Deerhurst never had a corridor crypt. Being on the site every day for a week gave us an opportunity to get to know the church well, and to look at it in detail. Every member of the team noticed something new, something that had never been reported on by the numerous scholars who had written substantial books and papers on the church. This was immensely stimulating to students, to realise that archaeology of a standing building was not a closed shop: anyone could contribute to research; they all went on to success in later years; the best teaching/learning experience I've ever had (**43**).

The small area we excavated was an apse, part of the east end of the church which had become ruinous in the Middle Ages; it had been later used as a pig-sty and as a cider-mill; it is now part of Deerhurst Farm. It had been examined before, in the 1920s, by the well-known ecclesiologist, W.H. Knowles, in a search for further elements of earlier churches inside the ruined apse; the area was 'thoroughly trenched, but nothing was found' (sic). Luckily he had not dug it all: from what survived we were able to deduce a good deal, later published, not in a one-line comment, but in a 59pp monograph (73).

43 Group at the first excavation of the church of St Mary at Deerhurst, Gloucestershire, 1971; top row: Sue Hirst, Grenville Astill, Sue Wright, the late Alan Hannan, Steve Hughes; front row: David Bowcock, PAR, Gill Gordon, Jeremy Jones

We duly communicated our views to Harold Taylor; we met and decided to plan further work together; later joined by my old friend Lawrence Butler. Thus began a collaboration which went on for 14 years, leading to a major monograph in 1997 (172); a large piece of the lives of my wife and myself.

The later years at Deerhurst involved again a major survey by Mick Aston (in 172) not only of the environs of the church and village, but the surrounding parish, and the estates of the Priory on both sides of the River Severn. With students and other volunteers, we excavated much of the ground outside the west door of the church (it is the only door, so worshippers had to 'walk the plank'), and along the north exterior; we also sectioned the monastic boundary on the west side, and dug test holes further away from the church to determine the extent of Roman occupation, and the general landscape.

Inside the church, we attempted some very small problem-orientated excavation, but soon encountered problems of stability in the dry and powdery soils caused by graves. We also stripped extensive areas of Victorian plaster, which was concealing important Anglo-Saxon features. This also caused dust problems — the organ was never quite the same again. Most time-consuming, however, was the stone-by-stone drawing of all visible Anglo-Saxon masonry, aided for higher areas by photogrammetry (photographs taken by two camera positions and computer-corrected for perspective).

It was by no means a total study (we never succeeded in getting any analysis of the geology or mortars); but we did set an agenda for later generations (72, 191).

The church is a complex structure, with no less than 34 Anglo-Saxon openings, much sculpture, and major architectural detail. A Roman origin is witnessed by nineteenth century records of burial urns and a coin under the nave floor; and by brick-tempered mortar incorporated in a newly-discovered foundation outside the west end; we believe that there must be a Roman villa very close, with perhaps the church site as a mausoleum (pagan and/or Christian?).

In our final synthesis, we were able to define six periods of construction, between probably the eighth century and the Norman period (**44**). To show anyone round Deerhurst St Mary (including all floors in the tower, and going onto the roof), or to go round with our book as a guide, is, we reckon, a two-day experience; few will attempt it.

Our work there really indoctrinated us into Anglo-Saxon church archaeology (see also chapter 10) and gave us valuable experience when in 1994 we embarked on another famous Anglo-Saxon church — that of Kirkdale (see chapter 14).

The other great enterprise of these years was Cadbury Congresbury, in which Peter Fowler, Keith Gardner and myself developed an excavation of this Dark Age settlement site, an Iron Age hillfort which came back into use, with refurbished defences. Of all the digs with which I have been involved, this was probably the best, the most challenging and historically important, and successfully carried through to very detailed publication (152). I outline the background to this excavation in chapter 9, both in relation to the general state of research and its objectives at that time, and the particular circumstances which led to the initiation of this excavation in 1968. Our interest in the site was principally aroused by the finding of Dark Age imported Mediterranean pottery by Gardner; and we hoped to find evidence of the settlement which was using this. There was the added attraction that

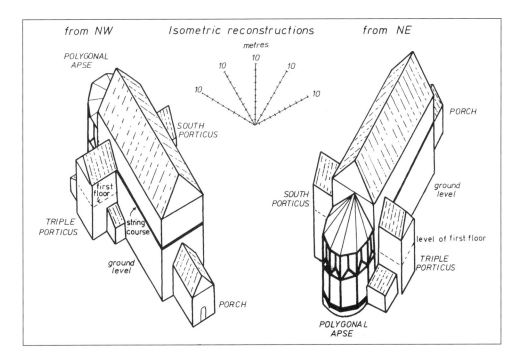

44 *Deerhurst St Mary: isometric reconstruction of the church as it may have been in the ninth century*

a cemetery had been found on a very closely-neighbouring hill (Henley Wood — see chapter 9) which was also of Dark Age date — possibly the very people who had lived on our hillfort.

Our first season was in a wet fortnight of September 1968 with volunteer help (**45**). The bedrock here is a fissured carboniferous limestone, with a very thin soil cover; it was difficult to find features in this. Only on the north side, where there was a degraded defensive rampart, was there any depth of material. In an area 20 x 12m, however, we were able to define a large circular building with a very wide entrance, its wall-line represented by a shallow trench cut in the rock, with impressions of post-sockets. We eventually interpreted this as a shrine. There was also a rectangular building marked by post-holes cut in the rock. We recovered many finds of prehistoric, Roman and Dark Age date; the densest concentration of Dark Age finds (principally pottery and glass) in Britain (except for Tintagel and Whithorn — see chapter 9). This was a very promising start. We published a first report very promptly (46), and further seasons took place in 1970-3, covering over 1200m² — a large area, but still only 5% of the total area enclosed by the ramparts of the hillfort. We located several more circular and rectangular buildings, and a very large number of finds of many materials.

In all this work I played an unusual role, being in charge of finds recording, classification, and drawing; every find, except animal bone, was recorded three-dimensionally. Peter Fowler directed the excavation very skilfully (**46**), while Keith

45 Cadbury Congresbury team, 1970; Peter Fowler on left, PAR on right, Peter Leach by PAR, Sue Hirst below PAR, Ian Burrow in front row left, Ann Woodward next to Sue Hirst

Gardner looked after the administration — a good triumvirate! Peter and I did, however, discuss the strategy of excavation frequently; and there were daily site tea-time expositions of our decisions, whether they turned out to be the right ones, and 'what it all meant'. Nearly everybody camped on site, with food prepared by the Fowler family.

Basically, this was an Iron Age hillfort, and there was ample evidence for this, and of earlier prehistoric use of the hill in layers below those of Dark Age date. We did not explore these fully, a decision for which we have since been castigated. The substantial defences were of this date, but there was a final, rather slight Dark Age enclosure of timber and stone construction, but not necessarily defensive.

At one point the Iron Age and Dark Age use of the site interacted in a dramatic way. In an area on the edge of the defences there was a deep level of rubble; here were human skull fragments dated by radiocarbon as not later than 390 BC. But in this same layer was a sherd of North African Red Slip Ware of the sixth century AD. There were no other parts of human skeletons in this area. It appeared that there had been some structure incorporating human skulls, which was tumbled down a millennium later. The rubble layer had been roughly levelled off. In the surface of this was what appeared to be a pit, full of soft dark soil. We saw this as an 'emplacement', a setting for a large timber post or more probably a tub-like container. In the dark soil was an astonishing number and variety

46 Peter Fowler demonstrating delicate excavation techniques at Cadbury Congresbury, Somerset, 1970; his father, Bill Fowler, is at the back

47 The finds department at Cadbury Congresbury, 1974 — Gillian Swanton (left) and Jane Everton

111

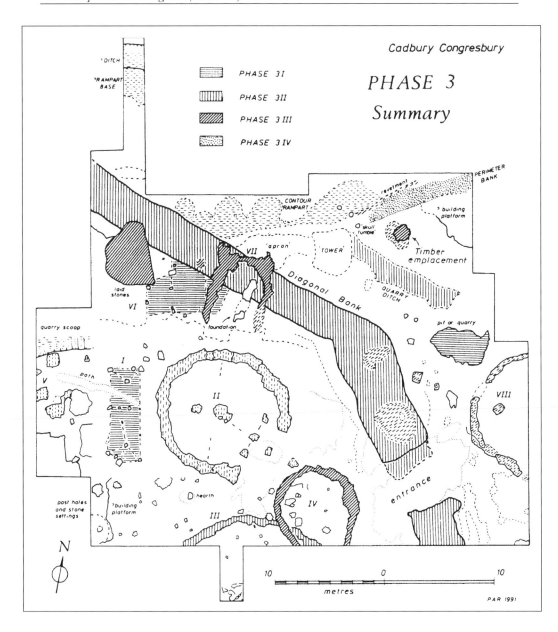

48 Plan of Dark Age structures at Cadbury Congresbury

of Dark Age finds of almost every class found on the site; almost as if someone had gone round the settlement picking up a sample of every aspect of the material culture of the site. We saw all this as 'part and parcel of the same event horizon, the desecration of one ritual focus and its replacement by another, perhaps a Christian one' (a baptistery?).

We were hard put to it (as always in Dark Age archaeology) to put a neat 'label' on the Dark Age aspects of Cadbury Congresbury (**48**), whether it was a defensive stronghold used by a Dark Age chieftain of high status in contemporary society; or a religious or ritual complex, with a transition from pagan to Christian observances; or a monastery (the site is traditionally associated with St Congar, a local saint — hence the name); or a complex that included all these characteristics. Even massive further excavation might not clarify the situation; though I personally think it would. The combination of numerous buildings, masses of exotic finds, and a nearby temple and cemetery, make this a site of the highest historical and archaeological potential. I look back on our seasons there as one of the richest episodes in my archaeological career.

In Birmingham too in the late 1960s and early 1970s I developed an interest in the Saxon towns of the West Midlands, then part of the Kingdom of Mercia (80). The first dig in these towns was Hereford in 1968, where I defined for the first time in a lucky rescue dig the sequence of defensive earthwork, ditch and wall (39A); and then at Tamworth in 1971. Here, mechanical excavation for a car park had located preserved timbers at some depth. In the hope that they might be part of Tamworth's ninth-century defences, we organised a dig, and duly uncovered a splendidly-preserved wooden structure, which was indeed of Anglo-Saxon date. It did not however look anything like a defensive structure. The clue as to its identity came (as at Butcombe, p53) with the finding of a number of fragments of millstones, some of local stone, and some of lava imported from Germany: the structure was a watermill.

Now I knew nothing about watermills. I'd seen a number of recent ones, in which a huge wheel, turning slowly with gears, was driven by water filling buckets, directed usually from above (overshot) or at the base (undershot). The Tamworth mill clearly didn't work in this way. It was Ken Sheridan who wrote to me after the dig, and pointed out that this was a mill whose wheel did not lie vertically, geared down to turn the mill-stones, but horizontally, with one turn of the wheel making one revolution of the mill-stones. Light dawned! I looked at my drawings and photographs (which I had not been able to make any sense of) and all fitted beautifully into this new hypothesis.

This opened up a whole new field of interest — the horizontal-wheeled mill (or Norse, or Greek mill; 49) with the Tamworth example now precisely fixed by tree-ring dating to the middle of the ninth century. This new understanding led to a number of publications: the Tamworth mill itself (153), a paper on medieval milling in general (96) and one on the names used in different languages for the parts of such a mill (81). Not only this, but this new interest led us to look at working examples elsewhere in Europe in the 1970s: in Turkey, Greece, France and Spain. The type had long been extinct in England, and in Ireland, but survived into recent centuries in Scotland, Orkney, Faroe and Scandinavia: but examples could still be found working in Crete and Galicia (north-west Spain). In Crete, we recorded several dozen ruined sites (96), but were very pleased to find one still in full operation at Zaros (near Festos) (see chapter 11).

Alas, Tamworth also literally brought me to my knees. Lifting too many buckets of heavy wet mud slipped a disc (**50**). Through the summer of 1971 I could only crawl around on my hands and knees (I participated in Cadbury Congresbury that summer on a stretcher). I was put on the road to recovery by two weeks being stretched out in hospital

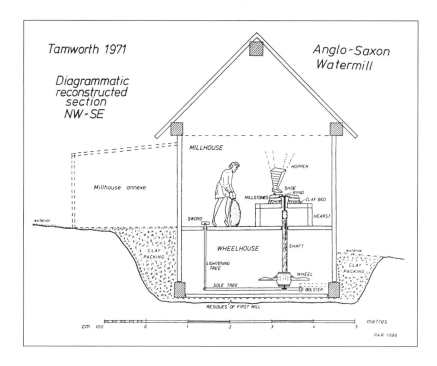

49 *Tamworth: diagram to show working of a horizontal-wheeled water-mill*

50 *A slipped disc: sorting out Tamworth millstone fragments, while lying on an air mattress, 1971 (photograph by Mick Aston)*

(traction), which left me straighter but weak. In September of that year I struggled with Susan Hirst (**51**) to Brâc, in Yugoslavia, where a combination of bottles of Slievovic (plum brandy) and throwing myself into a cold sea, did the trick; but I remained in some pain well into 1972, wearing a steel corset, an undignified and unromantic garment. But I had learnt a lot about watermills.

The origin of this type of watermill is still unknown. It certainly wasn't a Roman invention — all Roman mills have vertical wheels. The earliest known mills of horizontal type are those that have been excavated in Ireland, of the seventh century AD. So Tamworth wasn't by any means the earliest mill of this type to be found in Britain. Did the Irish invent them, or did they get the idea from somewhere else? The problem remains open.

51 Susan Hirst, 1971, in the early days of her career

With increased experience I was able in the 1970s (**52 & 53**) to embark on some synthesis of particular topics — notably Dark Age Somerset (51, 62, 88, 99) (see chapter 9), Anglo-Saxon buildings and rural settlements (68, 69) and churches (see chapter 10), Mercian towns in general (80) and cemeteries and graveyards (71, 82, 84).

The work on Anglo-Saxon buildings included the monastery at Whitby (70), and palaces. This used data from Cheddar and Yeavering, but also from yet another 'palace', this time one in the home territory of the West Midlands, at Hatton Rock, near Stratford-upon-Avon (48, 52). The enquiry here began with an air-photograph, and culminated in a rescue observation of a pipeline, in the snow.

Oddly enough, it was not these worthy enterprises that attracted wider attention, but my first attempt at humorous writing. 'How likely is likely' (65) — see Appendix C — started as a fringe paper to a West Midlands conference, written in half-an-hour, and enlarged and polished up for *Antiquity*. It suggested a 'probability scale' for archaeologists' range in print (rather like weathermen's definitions of wind-speed from a gentle zephyr to a full gale). Archaeologists delight in the whole gamut in their writings, from 'just possible' to 'certain' and I proposed that these should be put on a numerical scale, so that the reader might know just what these literary efforts meant. I realised, however, that it wasn't so simple to 'translate'; archaeologists said 'possible' when they were quite sure in their minds that their conclusions were correct; and 'certain' meant there was no evidence whatever — the scale was inverse! Other sayings in print too had to be 'translated': eg.

52 The family in 1975, Bristol; now three generations; Wendy Rahtz (my first wife) second from left in standing row

'there was no evidence of post-Roman levels' meant 'we bulldozed off the top ten feet' (in towns); 'the sections showed' (on one side of the baulk anyway) etc. etc. — the trump-card in persuasion being 'no reasonable person can doubt . . .'.

Like all successful humorous writing, it prospered because it contained a high element of truth; and made me famous (at last!) in Australia. I also wrote a piece satirising Philip Barker's attention to detail: on 'how to get an excavation finished' (86) by not digging carefully (Appendix C)!

Turning back to my academic career, I had (by being active in the field and prolific in publication) achieved promotion: not without repeated opposition by establishment characters who regarded me as a maverick. So I was well placed to try for a chair; and in 1977 happened to hear (literally) of one coming up at York. The story of that must however be preceded by a relevant event of 1977, which increased my chances.

I was in the habit at the end of each digging season of blowing my own trumpet, and informing the world in general what archaeology in the School of History had amounted to in that year, by compiling a multiple-copy report summarising the work. It happened, in that year, to include an account of an excavation at Kenchester, a Roman town which preceded Anglo-Saxon Hereford.

This report, as usual, I circulated to colleagues in the School and to other archaeologists in the West Midlands and beyond. To my amazement, my paper was attacked by Rodney Hilton (see p90) with whom I had not been on the best of terms since the cessation of our joint enterprise at Upton. He also circulated a memorandum. 'What', he said, 'was the Lecturer in Medieval Archaeology doing, excavating in a Roman town, as recounted in his self-congratulatory memorandum etc. etc. How was this contributing to

53 PAR in 1976

the core research of the Medieval History Department of the School, which was medieval social and economic history?' (nobody had ever told me this, let alone suggested I should join in, and subscribe to this field of enquiry).

I had a defence of course. Archaeology was indivisible . . . it was about the history of humans the world over . . . from hominid origins to modern times and (to be particularist), how could one understand early medieval Hereford without knowing about its Roman predecessor? I went to see my boss, Professor Ralph Davis, and asked his advice. He took Rodney's censure quite seriously and thought it might 'come up before the Dean' (of the Faculty of Arts) so I wrote up my defence in full; it never got mentioned again. But, being forced to think it all out, I was clear in my mind what archaeology was about, and medieval archaeology in particular. Armed with this, I sent in my application for the chair at York; and the story of that follows in chapter 7.

The later 1970s were also a time of sadness. My first wife, Wendy, died in 1977, aged 61, of a heart attack. She had been suffering from arthritis for many years; she had been seriously weakened by the powerful drugs used to combat this.

7 Becoming a professor: the Department of Archaeology at York (1978-86)

I had never had any ambitions to be a Professor; I was rather surprised to have been elevated to a Readership. I had however, become respectable, with FSA (Fellow of the Society of Antiquaries) after my name, and an MA acquired by thesis from Bristol, using the Cheddar Palace material. When I applied for the chair at York, I did so rather to test the water, hardly expecting to be interviewed. I was, however, put on the short list (I subsequently gathered that I was a late addition).

The University of York was one of the new academic institutions created in the 1960s, and soon won a reputation for style, thanks to its Registrar, John West-Taylor, who carefully designed such crucial matters as the notepaper and colour of the vans. The founding personnel were drawn largely from Oxford, and York became known as 'the little Oxford of the North'. The original Vice-Chancellor, Lord James, deliberately excluded Archaeology from the subjects to be developed, but there developed an interest in the 1970s arising from both History and Biology. After much lobbying, it was decided that Archaeology should be sponsored; and wisely this was to be a separate department, not brought under the wing of History; no period label such as medieval archaeology was to be attached, though close links with the historic centuries were expected; and there was to be a separate chair.

The interview (in April 1978) went reasonably well; I expatiated on my belief that Archaeology was a subject concerning the whole world, in all periods (p135), which didn't go down too well; and that a strong practical element was needed, so that students should understand the nature and limitations of archaeological evidence.

Each of the candidates being interviewed was assigned to a member of staff to be shown round the University campus, library, etc. I was passed to an eminent historian, very much an Oxford man, and I got the distinct impression that he took one look at me and decided that I was most unlikely to get the job, and need not be taken very seriously. Indeed I came away with the feeling that I was not quite what they were looking for. I did not even bother to collect my post the next day; but when I eventually did so, there was a *fat* envelope from York, not a thin one, offering me the chair and position of head of department. My scalp crawled. My first reaction was that this joke had gone far enough, and I was quite unsuited to such a responsible position. I was, however, persuaded by my colleagues to accept (perhaps they wished to be rid of me!). One mitigating circumstance was that I wouldn't have any students until the autumn of 1979; and I thought perhaps that (since I was the oldest candidate at the age of 57) I was chosen so that if the subject didn't take off, I could be quietly retired. It turned out that I had impressed the

*54 PAR and Lorna
   Watts after getting
   married; Hereford,
   April 22, 1978*

interviewing committee, not the least because, alone among those interviewed, I had well-thought out ideas on the teaching of undergraduates, as well as research.

The summer of 1978 was spent digging as usual, thinking about the new degree, and especially about theory. I realised that one couldn't start a new degree course without being right up to date on the present state of archaeology in Britain; and especially the profound changes in theory that had been fermenting since the advent of the so-called 'new archaeology', in which I had been hardly involved (see chapter 8).

The move to York was a change of life in more ways than one. I married again in 1978, to Lorna Watts (**54**). We had a great party (**55 & 56**) to celebrate my promotion and a new mode of life (**57**). We set up house in a rented seventeenth-century apartment in the King's Manor in York, which is part of the University.

The move was accomplished with some relief at a new start, a higher income and more independence of action. As I have said, I had a whole year to design the new degree, and to learn about administration, and how a University works, affairs of which I knew next to nothing. We were given temporary quarters in Chemistry, but the smells were too obnoxious, and we settled not on the campus, but in town, in a fine Georgian house in

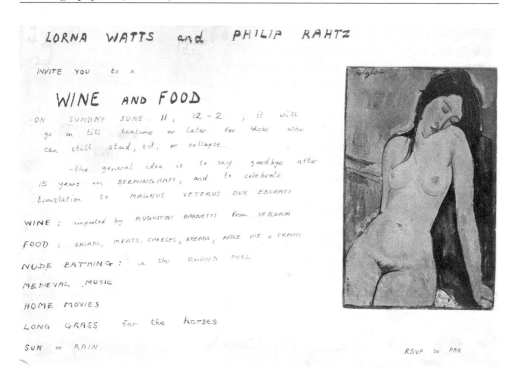

LORNA WATTS and PHILIP RAHTZ

INVITE YOU to a

WINE AND FOOD

ON SUNDAY JUNE 11, 12-2; it will go on till teatime or later for those who can still stand, sit, or collapse.

— the general idea is to say goodbye after 15 years in BERMINGHAM, and to celebrate translation to MAGNUS VETERUS DUX EBORACI

WINE: imported by AUGUSTINI BARNETTI from VERONA

FOOD: SALADS, MEATS, CHEESES, BREADS, APPLE PIE & CREAM

NUDE BATHING: in the ROUND POOL

MEDIEVAL MUSIC

HOME MOVIES

LONG GRASS for the horses

SUN or RAIN

RSVP to PAR

55 The great party, June 11, 1978, Birmingham; the invitation

Micklegate. There were problems for staff and students in being in town; but that was after all where the archaeology was, thanks to Peter Addyman and the York Archaeological Trust, and we felt very much at the heart of things.

I was initially given a secretary, and was promised a lecturer for the start of the academic year in late 1979.

I had ideas about the new degree course (85). I still believed that archaeology was concerned with all places and all periods. This was impossible in a three-year course. The compromise was to have *themes* such as death and mortuary behaviour, urbanism, or rural settlement; and while using Britain as a case-study (the students being more familiar with its geography and cultural background) examples could also be drawn from other parts of the world and from all periods from the Palaeolithic to modern times.

The second idea was to cut down formal lectures to a minimum, and to initiate seminar-type teaching, with each student being given a case-study to study and expound. The latter also helped in teaching students how to talk. Part of the final examination was to be a slide-assisted lecture and the chairing of a seminar.

I was happiest if prospective students wanted to be archaeologists, so practical classes in drawing were instituted, and compulsory participation in fieldwork and excavation. Not all of them, of course, did become archaeologists — there were not enough openings; but the education and mind-training were wide-ranging and made our students better-fitted to choose any career than those reading more narrowly-based disciplines, such as history.

56 At the party: Lin and Mick Aston

When I went to York, one of the proposals from the University was not only a single honours degree but also a combined archaeology/history degree. Here I saw an opportunity to develop a degree in which medieval topics could be studied from the dual point of view of written sources and archaeological evidence, with tutors of each department jointly present in all sessions. Alas, this was not to be; it was not at all what History had in mind; their resources did not allow such profligate use of staff time! So the combined students had to choose discrete courses from each discipline, destroying the whole point of the exercise.

Since it was a new degree, and unknown, we enrolled only nine students in the first teaching session of 1979-80, six of single honours and three combined. All went well, and one of our first students, Ken Dark, is now an established academic at Reading. By 1980, the second intake, we had our full complement of students. Another student of these early years, Roberta Gilchrist is now a professor, also at Reading.

We needed to incorporate archaeological theory in the course (chapter 8). We used the classic Clarke study of the Glastonbury Lake Village as part of this. Each student had to write a seminar paper on some aspect of the site.

I was joined in 1979 by Tania Dickinson and we made a very good teaching duo. She, with her Oxford background, brought some tone to the department and smoothed our

57 Ian Burrow's farewell cartoon, 1978

relationship with other departments. Later we were joined by Harold Mytum and Steve Roskams, and were a well-balanced team (**58**).

In designing the fieldwork element, we still had Bordesley Abbey in the early years, excellent experience; and on a lesser scale, the Anglo-Saxon church at Deerhurst (73, 172). To these we added Wharram Percy. In 1978 this excavation was already in its 28th season, progressing from a research project primarily concerned with the deserted medieval village aspect, but developing into both a landscape study of that part of the Yorkshire Wolds, and a multi-period study when prehistoric, Roman and Anglo-Saxon phases of the site were found in extensive excavations (see chapter 8 in 114).

The work there was directed by Maurice Beresford (*see* **72**) and John Hurst (*see* **71**). The former I knew only slightly, as a great landscape historian. I'd known John Hurst since the early rescue days in the 1950s. Maurice and I did not get on very well, but we developed a mutual respect. John and I had always got on, and he was very pleased at our involvement in the project.

We began with a study of the memorial stones in the churchyard (103) and (with our first students) did a rescue excavation of the Wharram-Le Street Roman Villa (115). Our main effort was, however, an area excavation of the North Manor complex, which went on for several years. Here were sealed Iron Age, Roman and Anglo-Saxon features of great interest. A mass of data was recovered, which is still (2000) being processed for publication (185).

Wharram offered a useful opportunity for a part of our excavation training; another advantage was that it had a well-established logistic basis of accommodation, food and social cohesion. The latter was not easy at first: our students (**59**) were regarded by some of the 'old hands' as interlopers, muscling in on their long-established province. A brilliant pageant, in which we were the 'Vikings' and the rest the 'Anglo-Saxons' (under King Egghurst) did much to ease these potential tensions (**60**).

To return to the Department, we flourished as well as might be expected in a competitive world, under the extremely valuable guidance of our secretary, Priscilla Roxburgh (still there in 2000) who saved my sanity during those stressful years (**61**).

At York, all new Professors were expected to give an inaugural lecture. Mine was delivered in 1980 (94). Tania Dickinson, Lorna Watts and I also sought to publicise our Department by organising a very successful conference at Oxford in 1979 on 'Anglo-Saxon Cemeteries' (90). This again included aspects of theoretical approaches, and also papers on Sutton Hoo.

Here I must digress and explain how this last topic came to be included. Sutton Hoo had remained one of the most prestigious early medieval cemetery sites since 1939, as a result of the immense range of treasure found in the Anglo-Saxon ship burial. During the intervening years, Rupert Bruce-Mitford had compiled three great volumes on 1939 and later work, under the auspices of the British Museum. By 1978 these were nearly complete, and he (and other scholars) were anxious to see a resumption of work there.

58 Student field trip to Cheviot, 1981; Harold Mytum in foreground, Steve Roskams top right

59 *A wet day at Wharram Percy, 1981; Trevor Ashwin top right, PAR lower right, John Bateman on left*

60 *Wharram Percy group 1981; Maurice Beresford with dog; John Hurst and PAR upper left*

61 Priscilla Roxburgh, my secretary at York

In 1978 he asked me to have lunch with him at the Athenaeum; this was not my scene at all, and I wondered what on earth this could be about. It turned out that he wanted our new department to be involved with him in new excavations at Sutton Hoo. It was an attractive proposition, which could bring fame (and students!) to us.

I recently found a copy of a letter I wrote to Tania Dickinson (21.12.1978) in which I outlined (among other things) my ideas on how we might be involved in Sutton Hoo. I repeat these verbatim, as they are of some historical interest in the light of the great campaign that ensued in the 1980s and '90s:

> 'The Society of Antiquaries [who had been approached by Rupert and myself] believe, as we all do, that the British Museum must be involved, as long as they can be prevented from dominating . . . my intention is not to have any "posh" objects for at least three years. My strategy is to clear up the area partly examined by the British Museum in the 1960s, and re-excavate the mounds trenched by Basil Brown. R.B-M may wish to dig a ship, but if I and the proposed committee don't agree, he can't. It seems unlikely that excavation will begin in 1979, but survey might be done, and headquarters established. I envisage now the development of a small part-time professional team, contracted for say 3 months p.a. for 5 years — I have in mind Angela Evans and

Catherine East [from the BM] Susan Hirst, Susan Wright, Lorna Watts, Ann Woodward, Peter Leach, and ourselves.'

How naive this reads now!

I soon, however, saw the red light. Neither of us were young, nor were we exactly up-to-date in method and theory. Rupert thought that with his experience he was as good at excavating ship-burials as anyone else. I could see that I would be doing all the logistics and he would be down the hole! I accordingly persuaded him that the new director should be a younger person; that we should set up a committee, who would raise funds and secure technical back-up; and we should eventually advertise for a full-time Director. The steering committee consisted of Rosemary Cramp, Barry Cunliffe and the two of us. The idea was that the new enterprise, on a large scale, should be jointly sponsored by the Society of Antiquaries of London and the British Museum.

There was a problem, however. The BM would not have anything to do with a project in which Bruce-Mitford had any part. The then Director had been daggers drawn with Rupert for many years, one of the most virulent feuds in British archaeology; the reasons for this enmity were difficult for outsiders to fully understand; though neither Rupert or the BM Director were the easiest people with whom to collaborate.

We needed the resources of the BM, notably those of conservation, but they were adamant. Our master stroke was to ask the Ashmolean Museum in Oxford if they would like to join with us and the Antiquaries, and provide the technical backing; and they agreed. In the face of this, the BM backed down, and a formula was found where Rupert would be the 'honorary advisory consultant'. The BM and the Antiquaries agreed to fund a number of years of work very handsomely, with other donors. The Committee was enlarged, ultimately to include the powerful personality of Sir David Attenborough, who did his best to pour oil on troubled waters.

The announcement that we were going to excavate further at Sutton Hoo led to a furore among other archaeologists. This was, they declared, merely a treasure hunt to further enrich the BM. The site was, they said, safe and protected, and there was no need to touch it (92). It was included in our 1979 Oxford Symposium (90) to try to explain why, on balance, it would be a good thing to proceed; not least because it was thought that Britain needed a 'flagship' project to excite public and academic enthusiasm.

I have described elsewhere in this book (p202) how Martin Carver was appointed Director and carried the whole thing through in a very modern way to a fine conclusion. Rupert Bruce-Mitford visited regularly; when he died in the final years, many of his ideas were shown to have been highly perceptive; and Carver had found his advice very useful.

In 1981 I was invited to give the O'Donnell lectures in Wales. This involved giving the same lecture on five successive weekday evenings at the five Welsh University Colleges. At each venue we were royally received, for evening hospitality and lecture, and spent the days looking at Welsh archaeology.

The subject had to be something to do with the Celts; I interpreted this liberally as Dark Age Somerset (what else?) with the title of 'Celtic Society in Somerset AD 400-700' (98); though whether there were any Celts there remains dubious.

All went well on this trip; the only hiccup was at Aberystwyth where, after a dinner-party (put on by the Vice-Chancellor), the late Professor Emrys Bowen went off home with my glasses — a thing, it seemed, he was prone to do; a mad rush the next morning got them back.

There was also time to travel, to France, Holland, Majorca, Morocco, Spain, Greece, the Canaries, Orkney, Turkey and Tunisia. While these were partly holidays, but they were also valuable in looking at watermills (p113) and generally in collecting ethnographic data — slides, pottery and other objects (chapter 11).

One especially rewarding long trip was in a Land Rover, camping, from Lourdes, over the Pyrenees, down the long pilgrimage route to the great medieval shrine of St James at Santiago de Compostela. This resulted in a substantial picture-essay (113) as an offering to a *Festschrift* for Harold Taylor (p107).

What with running the degree course at York, excavating, lecturing, and travelling, the period of 1978-86 was a busy eight years. I enjoyed them, but by 1986 I was decidedly tired, and ready to retire; I was then 65; I could have gone on two more years, but decided not to. It was a wise decision, as around this time University administration became more financially orientated and there was an unpleasant trend towards such horrors as student assessment of their lecturers, and a general 'ranking' of staff, departments and universities,

62 After the presenting of Peter Addyman (centre) for the degree of Doctor of the University; the only photograph of me in academic dress, 1984

63 *My successor at York: Martin Carver, a father again*

to the detriment both of teaching and research. I got out at the right time. My successor was Martin Carver, and although he has made a great success of a much-enlarged department, it has been a difficult time for him, especially since he continued to direct Sutton Hoo as well; and undertook major tasks such as the editing of the large volume of the York Minster excavations (170).

I conclude this account of my tenure at York by reference to the 'other' archaeology at York, the very successful York Archaeological Trust. This was founded in 1971 by Peter Addyman, formerly a lecturer at the Universities of Belfast and Southampton. He gave up an academic career to tackle the major problem of the increasing threat to the archaeology of York by modern development; and (ably assisted by Richard Hall) has carried through a major programme of excavation, research and publication. One of the Trust's major achievements was the world-famous Coppergate Viking period dig, which was used subsequently as the foundation for one of the best 'Heritage' experiences in Britain, the Jorvik Viking Centre. This has been immensely successful, giving a vision of archaeology to millions of people, and enabling the Trust to survive in difficult times.

Peter Addyman would have liked to have been the first Professor of Archaeology at York; he was one of those interviewed for the post. He wanted, however, to incorporate the Trust with the new department, which was not at the time what the University had in mind (though it might take a different view in 2000). Fortunately for our subsequent relationship, he had been my assistant on digs and summer schools in earlier years, and had some respect for me as someone senior to himself, at least in years.

The new department was, nevertheless, seen as something of a rival in the archaeology of the city, though we were careful not to encroach on their preserves. In the early years they did some teaching for us, and I sat on various bodies of the Trust. In 1985 I had the pleasure of presenting Peter for an honorary doctorate of the University (**62**). In my speech I recounted the story of the squeaky postcard sent to me from Sewerby (p80) to the assembled audience of several hundred parents, and guests, and squeaked the postcard: surely a first in the presentation of honorary degrees! He has recently been awarded the CBE.

As noted at the start of this chapter, my wife and I lived at the Kings Manor (the latter now the home of Martin Carver's department). I knew I would have to give this up when I retired, so in 1983 we began looking for a new home. We favoured some spacious redundant medieval church to convert, but no such thing was to be had; instead we acquired in1984 a redundant school at Harome, a village in Ryedale, some 28 miles north of York, where we still live. For two years we commuted from here to York, pending a decision on where we should retire to in 1986.

When I left, my colleagues and students gave me a splendid send-off, and I was happy to leave what I had created in the more-than-capable hands of Martin Carver (**63**) and retire (chapter 14).

PART TWO

Aspects of a life in archaeology

8 Theory and method

Theory

As in many subjects, there has been a continuous debate in archaeology on the relationship between theory and practice. This dialectic has been valuable in shaping the discipline, and giving it a sound academic basis.

In earlier days, the basis of archaeological research was straightforward. Study of field monuments or objects, by survey, excavation or other means, was carried out for several reasons (cf 150); principally:

1　To find out about our ancestors; laudable enough, and satisfying our natural curiosity about the past.

2　To enrich private or museum collections; or to enrich individuals or institutions.

3　For anthropological or historical research; this has gradually gained ground in the last century, at least among academics and professionals.

After the days of treasure-seeking etc., General Pitt-Rivers was one of the first to pursue a theoretical procedure, using anthropological and ethnographic parallels, and building up an avowedly educational collection.

In the first half of this century there was much bad and some good archaeology; the good archaeology led to major syntheses of European prehistory and history (by such major figures as Flinders Petrie, Gordon Childe, Christopher Hawkes, Graham Clark, etc.), theory as we understand it today.

There were formerly certain assumptions in British archaeology which were taken for granted, but which have since been discarded, not only as ill-suited to the evidence, but also on theoretical grounds. Among these we may note, as examples, the belief that observed changes in the archaeological record in Britain were the result of 'waves of invaders'; that all things Roman disappeared almost instantaneously in AD 410 (cf 82, 88); and that the Germanic peoples who laid the basis for England dispossessed or killed all the former inhabitants.

When I began archaeology, I was hardly aware that it had any theoretical basis; I have always found that it is very stimulating to find something that has been hidden a long time, and was last seen by people of many generations ago. Unlike Wheeler, who believed that archaeology was wholly about people, I actually like finds for their own sake, and more particularly for the processes that enable one (with experience) to identify them, to determine their function and their meaning, even if this is only explicable in human terms (**64**).

64 Problem of perception: Anglo-Saxon ornament? Or ring-pull?

I'm also increasingly interested in origins — in cosmology, astronomy, space-time, etc. and in the Darwin/Dawkins schemes of evolution; and in the early hominids and the debate concerning regional evolution from *Homo Erectus*, or a new move out of Africa of *Homo Sapiens c.*200,000 years ago. All are of the greatest interest in looking at the origins of technology, language, society, co-operation, virtue and vice, nomadic and sedentary societies; and in recent times the development of the anthropogenic (humanly altered) landscape (though I still get a thrill out of seeing unaltered landscapes, that look nearly the same to us as to Palaeolithic people).

I have slowly graduated over the years to a wider and interdisciplinary perspective (**65**), if not of formal theory. I have been personally interested in finding out what had happened in the past on a particular site, and (subsequently) comparing it with others; and assessing its contribution to the understanding of certain aspects of the discipline, or certain periods; notably in my case, the Dark Ages in Western Britain (see chapter 9). These seemed quite enough in earlier days. One accumulated data, looked at them and made particular and general conclusions. The more that was dug, the more we knew about the past. There were major gaps in our knowledge, it seemed, but they could and would gradually be filled by acquiring more data (**66**).

This was mostly a straightforward procedure. Most sites in the pre-Second World War decades were chosen for research, either to explicate the monument (by State archaeology), on abbeys and castles, etc; or for academic research, such as the work of Wheeler at Maiden Castle, or Hull and Hawkes at Colchester.

When the percentage of sites being destroyed by non-archaeological factors was small, the loss was not regarded as serious, an acceptable concomitant of natural causes (such as the sea), of land exploitation (such as ploughing), or development (roads, quarries, etc).

By the 1950s, however, when I began work, the losses were becoming so great as to raise grave concern (55-57, 61). It seemed that what appeared to be an infinite reservoir of buried archaeology could all be drained within a short time. Thus *rescue* archaeology was seen as an attempt to save data for posterity (as was the case with many of my own excavations). There was no question such as 'to which research topic is this work going to

ARCHAEOLOGY
and OTHER SUBJECTS

Resources : WATER
SOIL *(pedology)*
ROCKS *(geology)*
POWER ~ gravity,wind,water,solar, fire *(technology)*
WOOD and other plants *(botany)*
ANIMALS - land and sea *(zoology etc.)*

Techniques : DEVELOPMENT OF THEORY *(philosophy)*
PROSPECTING, DISCOVERY *(geophysics, chemistry)*
IDENTIFICATION and ANALYSIS *(geology,*
chemistry, botany, zoology etc., metallurgy)
DATING *(physics, chemistry, geology, botany)*
STATISTICS, PATTERNING, ORIENTATION etc.
(mathematics, computing, astronomy)

Artefacts and other residues *(below and above ground)*
FOOD, MEDICINE *(zoology, botany)*
TOOLS, CONTAINERS, WEAPONS, BUILDINGS,
VEHICLES, FURNITURE, CLOTHING, JEWELLERY,etc.
(geology, metallurgy, botany, zoology, technology)
COINS *(numismatics)*
RITUAL OBJECTS *(anthropology, theology)*
MUSICAL INSTRUMENTS *(musicology)*
ART *(art-history)*
MAPS *(cartography)*
INSCRIPTIONS *(epigraphy)*
DOCUMENTS *(history)*
HUMAN and ANIMAL REMAINS
(human biology, zoology, etc.)

INTERDISCIPLINARY COLLABORATION

65 The relationship of archaeology to other subjects

contribute?'. It was just a matter of piling up data on any topic or period; it was assumed that posterity would use this stockpile for their future research, perhaps when there was nothing left to dig.

There were problems, however. The volume of data was too much to cope with, synthesise, publish or read; museums were alarmed at the mass of finds they were being asked to conserve and store. Such was the situation by the 1970s, when RESCUE was founded (61). The ethos of rescuing the past was, however, beginning to be questioned. The concept of steady progress in understanding was felt to have been abandoned. New questions were being asked about the past, which were not always answerable by the data being collected, either by research or rescue. There was an intellectual revolution in the subject, influenced largely from America, where archaeology is not primarily historically-

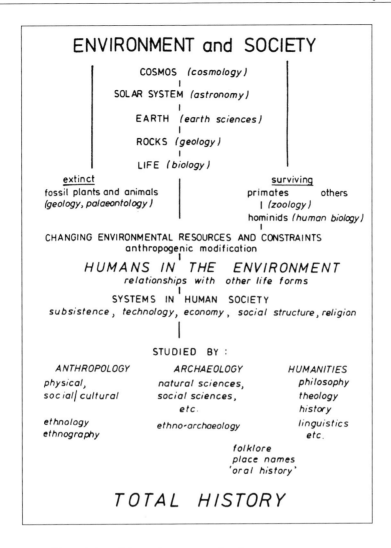

ENVIRONMENT and SOCIETY

COSMOS *(cosmology)*

SOLAR SYSTEM *(astronomy)*

EARTH *(earth sciences)*

ROCKS *(geology)*

LIFE *(biology)*

extinct   surviving
fossil plants and animals   primates   others
(geology, palaeontology) | *(zoology)*
                hominids *(human biology)*

CHANGING ENVIRONMENTAL RESOURCES AND CONSTRAINTS
anthropogenic modification

HUMANS IN THE ENVIRONMENT
relationships with other life forms

SYSTEMS IN HUMAN SOCIETY
subsistence, technology, economy, social structure, religion

STUDIED BY :

ANTHROPOLOGY   *ARCHAEOLOGY*   *HUMANITIES*
physical,   *natural sciences,*   *philosophy*
social/cultural   *social sciences,*   *theology*
                etc.   *history*

ethnology   *ethno-archaeology*   *linguistics*
ethnography   *etc.*

                    folklore
                    place names
                    'oral history'

TOTAL HISTORY

66 The structure of knowledge, of the environment and society

based, as it is here, but is closely allied to anthropology — in fact as palaeo-anthropology. In Britain, the principal exponent of this movement was David Clarke, who wrote highly influential books such as *Models in Archaeology*.

All this ferment became known as 'The New Archaeology'. It had as its basis not only a more holistic view of the past, involving eg. the study of *process*, and a strongly environmental and ideological mode of enquiry. Fundamental at that time was the concept that it was no use digging up lots of 'answers', when the questions (especially the 'right' questions) were not being asked. The idea was to set up hypotheses to 'explain' the past, and then seek the 'right' data to test them. Inevitably, this led not only to new approaches (backed up by rapid progress in the archaeological sciences, radiocarbon dating, etc), but to selectivity — which ran counter to the 'rescue' ethic of saving everything.

67 Ann Woodward c.1975 (then Ann Ellison); my principal mentor

This selectivity began to be applied not only to site data (influencing methodology) but also to site selection. 'League' tables were drawn up by committees, deciding what 'we need to know' and what should have low priority (on a regional or national) — a process which continues today in state-funded projects.

As a data-accumulator, I was quite satisfied with the results of my research, whether in the field or (after 1968) in synthesis (eg. 37, 39, 51, 53, etc). I was not very interested in process, or in hypothesis construction or testing. It was apparent to me (and still is) that grandiose hypotheses and research designs are largely based on data that are already available! I was still primarily concerned with answering the simple question of looking at a site and asking 'what is there and when was it put there?', and then finding out, and asking the further questions of 'why?' (very pregnant!) and how it related to our understanding.

In my heart, I still feel the same basic motivation. I did increasingly get to appreciate the value of certain facets of the new theoretical approaches, and they doubtless influenced my work in the 1970s.

All this changed, however, when I was appointed to the Chair in York in 1978 (see chapter 7). At Birmingham, there was no need to do more than teach fairly conventional archaeology, and do it; but now I faced a major dilemma. How could I possibly design and mastermind a new degree course without knowing enough of theory to be able to

68 Cadbury
Congresbury
data: the agenda
for interpretation

CADBURY CONGRESBURY DATA

Subsistence   *Fauna*
              Artefacts directly related to subsistence
              Features and structures .. ditto ..
              Artefacts features structures related to secondary production
              Site catchment, resource, space, and energy analysis
              Contemporary landscape features
              Demography

Exchange   *Central place theory ~ social hierarchy*
              Artefact distributions ⟶ exchange networks
              *   (household local, regional, national, international)*
              Fall-off patterns

Social   *C P T etc as above*
              Spatial patterning of artefacts within and between structures
              Structure type and detail
              Analysis of Henley Wood burials

Technology   *Typology etc. ~ pot, metal, stone, glass etc.*
              *   (definition of production :~ household, part~, and full-time)*

Political   *Size of settlement unit*
Legal   *Ranking of structures and sites*

Religious   *Ritual and votive artefacts*
              Graves at Henley Wood
              Ritual structures and features

Psychological *Vernacular Irish texts*
              Spatial analysis, dimensions ~ areas, structures

incorporate a course on it? Increasingly, the younger generation of archaeologists were becoming theoretically minded, reacting against the ideas of the establishment figures. Many books and articles were based on theoretical approaches, using an incomprehensible vocabulary (now thankfully less evident).

The students who were to begin at York in 1979 not only had to be able to read the new literature, to follow papers at conferences (such as TAG, the Theoretical Archaeology Group) but to be up-to-date in preparation for future career prospects. I would have been guilty of a gross dereliction of duty if I had buried my head in the sand, and pretended that the New Archaeology didn't exist.

So I had to read it up; it was clear that many of its approaches were of great interest; and especially to what was intended as the major theme of the new degree — Medieval Archaeology. Most of the progress of theoretically-based archaeology had up to this time been developed in America in the study of non-literate pre-Columban societies; and in Britain in the study of prehistory.

At that time, the new approaches had not been applied to Roman studies, or to medieval archaeology. Here then was my opening. I explored all that had been written on theory in post-Roman archaeology, and delivered my inaugural lecture in 1980, 'The New Medieval Archaeology, or King Arthur and his Random Number Table' (94). In the next year, Richard Hodges and I gave papers to the conference on 'Twenty-five Years of Medieval Archaeology' (i.e. since the Society for Medieval Archaeology was founded) (102). We had a hostile reception from an audience who were largely traditionalists, who

SITES	ATTRIBUTES						PERIOD	NEO-BA	IRON AGE	ROMAN	POST-ROMAN	ANGLO-SAXON
	HILLTOP SETTLEMENT	SHRINE	TEMPLE	CHURCH	MORTUARY EVIDENCE	FINDS						
CADBURY CONGRESBURY	□ ?△ ●	●			□+	○ □ △ ●	HILLTOP SETTLEMENT	●	●	○	●	○
SOUTH CADBURY	○ □ ● ✼	□	?△	✼	□	○ □△●✼	SHRINE		○	○	●	
HENLEY WOOD		?□	△		●	□△	TEMPLE				●	
CANNINGTON CEMETERY		△●		?	○ ?□△ ?△ ✼	○ □ △ ●✼	CHURCH			○	○	●
CANNINGTON HILLFORT	□△ ?●					□△	MORTUARY EVIDENCE	○	○	●	●	○
GLASTONBURY TOR	?△ ● ✼	?△		✼	●	○ △ ● ✼						
MAIDEN CASTLE	○ □ △ ?●	□●	△		□●✼	○□△✼		○ MINOR			● MAJOR	
BREAN DOWN	□		△		●	○□△●						
PAGANS HILL	○□△	●?	△?●	?●		○□△●✼						
NETTLETON		●	△		?△ ●	△		**PREHISTORIC TO HISTORIC IN THE WEST COUNTRY**				
ULEY		○●	△	?●	△	○□△						

○ NEO/BA   □ IRON AGE   △ ROMAN   ● POST ROMAN   ✼ ANGLO-SAXON

69 Inter-site comparison: the attributes and chronology

saw no need for theory in their subject. I also came under fire from a few younger theoretically-orientated academics, who dismissed my efforts as naive and badly informed (they probably were, given my background!).

It should be pointed out (*contra* my critics) that my intention was never primarily to espouse the cause of theory, but merely to plead for some open-mindedness, suggesting at least the application of theory that *had* been tried by others to the world of medieval studies; and asking medievalists to consider seriously whether any aspects of the new approaches could enrich their own research.

Cadbury Congresbury (152) was a good breeding ground for discussion on theory in the field and elsewhere, its relevance to our work on the Dark Ages on that site, and more generally in the south-west. Peter Fowler, my co-director there, was very good at making everybody think about what they were doing, and what it all meant. One of our excellent team there was Ann Woodward (**67**). She considered the data accumulating from the site (**68**) into a wider theoretical framework, both in theme and time. The point here was to suggest that the wider perspectives would help us to fill in the missing column, on the Dark Ages (**69**). Ian Burrow provided a pictorial version (**70**).

A further facet of this was to ask whether the historical and archaeological background of the British Dark Ages had any analogues with cultures in another place and in an earlier time. Colin Renfrew (1979) had constructed a scenario on the decline of Mycenean civilisation, which we were able to compare with Dark Age Britain. The general idea

70 *Beyond theory: Ian Burrow's cartoon of Cadbury Congresbury, which is probably nearer the truth than conclusions arrived at from formal analysis and theory*

expressed here was that societies in any part of the world, at any time, develop in similar ways: given certain pre-conditions and other factors. That is, if no 'disasters' intervene, such as climatic downturn, volcanic eruptions, flooding, or asteroid impact! (cf end of chapter 9).

Another way of developing theories about the fate of societies is the writing of science fiction, in which I have had a minor role (110, 132, 155 and p232). I used this mode in considering the 'meaning' of memorial stones in churchyards. My wife Lorna and I had made a study of those in the Wharram Percy churchyard as part of the overall Wharram Research Project (103). Under the pseudonym of Rilip Phahtz, I postulated a visit in the distant future by Martian archaeologists (among them Boris Meresford and Hon Jurst) who studied the gravestones without prior knowledge of their Christian cultural background. What could the Martians make of them from first principles? I gave this as a paper in Oxford at a conference on Medieval Villages; it brought the house down. It also brought down on me the wrath of one leading medievalist, who walked out, believing I was making fun of Wharram Percy and belittling its achievements and those of Hurst (**71**) and Beresford (**72**). It was, however, included in the resulting volume (110).

In the new department we incorporated a course on theory. Among other items, we ran for several years a very successful seminar, designed to illustrate many facets of the new archaeology, using David Clarke's brilliant chapter in his *Models* book, on the Glastonbury Lake Village, in which he used all data accumulated over 50 years by the Somerset archaeologists, Arthur Bulleid and H. St George Gray (the latter had worked for

71 John Hurst, 1987

General Pitt-Rivers in his youth). If they had known what Clarke was to make of their work, they would have been extremely horrified.

The relationship of history to archaeology was another topic I explored in another paper: the 'Nuer Medieval Archaeology' (106) in which I poked some innocent fun at Ian Hodder, the most prominent modern theorist in England, who had done anthropological fieldwork among the Nuer people in Africa.

I also drew on my lifelong addiction to determinism to comment on a paper I heard at TAG, on the choices available to a potter, suggesting that his/her decisions were based wholly on available resources at each stage of the process, a process of trial and error, rather than a 'freewill approach' (128).

In the event, many facets of the New Archaeology were 'old hat' by 1978, and there has, in more recent years, been a sharp reaction. This is usually represented as due to the massive influence of structuralism and post-structuralist approaches. I believe that at least part of this reaction was the emphasis given in the 'Old New Archaeology' to the holistic view, in which environmental determinism was apparent (see pp37-8); and it was, in addition, too difficult! The general feeling among the young Turks (but not, alas, in

72 *Maurice Beresford at*
   Wharram Percy,
   c.1989

Turkey) was that the human *mind* had not had enough emphasis in the 1960s schemes; again a reaction to determinist approaches, which seemed to denigrate humans to merely another animal and that what they do might be predicted; people don't like to think they're animals!

Theory has thus moved far from what was considered revolutionary in the 1960s, the emphasis being very much on ideology and the mind, and on a unity of the mental and physical experience in our ancestors, in an attempt to gauge how the world seemed to them; and the extent to which this can be worked out from the material culture represented by the remains of their monuments and their rubbish; these new approaches are known as post-processualism.

Dr Woodward has, since Cadbury Congresbury, collaborated with me in several publications, and we exchange a regular correspondence. She is in the forefront of archaeological research and its theory, especially in the Iron Age. She has kept me up-to-date on theory and how it changes rapidly (TAG is the shop-window for this). She has recently initiated another new way of looking at site data: the sensory approach, where one suggests how all archaeological evidence can be interpreted in terms of sight, hearing,

141

smell, sound and touch; this is, after all, how our forebears experienced life. Can we read this in their rubbish?

I followed up our theoretical approaches to Cadbury Congresbury with an attempt to introduce theory into Wharram Percy (see pp122-3). I suggested ways in which the mass of data from some 40 years of work could be ordered and analysed in a more holistic way. I wrote and published from the new department two editions of 'Wharram Data Sheets' (91 and 97) which set out what I meant. In the very traditional society of the Wharram team, all this fell like a lead balloon. Maurice Beresford was not responsive to new approaches to Wharram; John Hurst's reaction was (and still is) 'all this nonsense — why doesn't everyone just get on with it' i.e. continue as we always had. Jean Le Patourel, another historian, said 'But, Philip, what does all this tell us about Wharram that we didn't know already?' The answer was obvious: nothing, but we can look at it in different ways which may lead us to increased understanding. Wharram Percy has escaped theory; but it will come into its own when all the data are synthesised in coming years.

I thus remain interested in and sympathetic to theoretical development even though my own work has been more traditional. In spite of my earlier efforts to introduce some open-mindedness into medieval archaeology, there is little support; the Romanists (the older ones anyway), lag even further behind. I don't think, however, that anyone takes me seriously as a theorist!

Method

Theoretical approaches have changed over the decades. So too have methods: partly in an effort to extract more from data observed in or recovered from the ground; and partly to provide the kinds of data relevant to the new questions about the past that were being asked.

The differences in method during the twentieth century are obvious to anyone who compares the work of most nineteenth-century archaeologists with those of the present day. The major changes relate to an increase in preparatory work on a site; survey and mapping, especially geophysical; an exponential increase in the recording of excavation data; the electronic revolution; and the methods of excavation.

When I began digging I hardly knew what 'recording' meant; I made plans, drew sections, took photographs; even plotted the position of such finds as seemed to be 'important'. Such observations were written (no, not on backs of envelopes! — well not often) in a site notebook or diary. This was all very well when one was the sole recorder, as in many of my early digs. But a more systematic approach had to be adopted with increasing delegation, and especially in training. Hence the development on my digs (as elsewhere) of standardised recording forms, of which we designed quite a few, with spaces to put in all detail. They were best if they were designed for a particular site (such as Cadbury Congresbury) or type of site (such as the Cannington Cemetery or Bordesley Abbey).

I have tried all kinds of excavation techniques: test-holes, trenches, quadrants, grids and area excavation. The temple at Pagans Hill was excavated in quadrants (when it was thought to be a barrow, for which this was considered appropriate). In the event this proved very suitable, giving radial sections while observing large areas. There were trenches there in other areas; and the well demanded special techniques of pumping, baling and pot-holing. Chew Valley (79) was a combination of very large mechanical excavation (using massive machines lent by the reservoir constructors), trenches, and grid excavations (the latter the result of influence from Mortimer Wheeler).

Here, however, I was encouraged to try open area excavation on the Moreton medieval village, by John Hurst. In his famous work on deserted medieval villages, he had been impressed by the good results of this method in Denmark, and adopted it at Wharram Percy. As a result, I adopted it for several excavations (such as Holworth, 9) and actually became associated with this stripping technique; I was referred to as 'Gypsy Rose Rahtz' (older readers will remember Gipsy Rose as a famous stripper!). I was a very minor figure in developing this method, however; primary credit must go to John Hurst and later to Philip Barker, who employed it with such devastating success at Hen Domen and Wroxeter (for the latter see chapter 9 and Barker *et al*, 1997); his approaches have been very influential in recent archaeology.

In the recording and analysis of field data, the computer, both in the field and study, has been of immense value, but not to me. I'm innumerate in this respect, though others have used computers in the analysis of Cannington (181). I am thinking however, of trying to learn more in my final years (chapter 15).

All in all, in both theory and method, I am on the fringes, still basically working with the same paradigms as I had in the 1940s.

9 How the Dark Ages in the West were won

Introduction

The late- and post-Roman centuries in the West of Britain have been an abiding interest for me, stimulated both by the inherently romantic and intractable nature of the topic, and by my own rather fortuitous involvement (**73**).

My middle name is Arthur, and so is that of my old friend Philip Barker; he also has devoted a large part of his life to the urban aspects of this study. Perhaps it was this that provided for us both a signpost to the future. As I have recounted earlier, my first girlfriend Bobbie told me (when I met her 50 years later) that I was always interested in King Arthur as a teenager; and Tintagel was a favourite place for the family to visit.

For those readers who were not familiar with the background to this rather esoteric topic, it may be as well to set out the relevant agenda which a number of archaeologists have addressed, something of the history of their endeavours, and the present state of research.

The time period concerned is of several centuries, from Late Roman times (the fourth century) to the time of the political consolidation of the English settlement (seventh to eighth centuries); from the general currency of Latin (however barbarous) and spoken Celtic in its various forms to the establishment of Old English as the principal language, at least in the southern and eastern regions.

These centuries have long been considered as 'Dark', principally because there are very few written sources available, and these of a difficult and ambiguous nature; not until the eighth century and the writings of Bede do we move again into a documented society. This, however, is an historical darkness. Archaeology should have an unlimited role in increasing our understanding; but, as we shall see, this too is difficult to interpret. Although no new historical documents relating to this period are likely to turn up (except inscriptions on stone or metal, from excavation), the younger generation of historians have been very successful in re-interpreting known texts, such as those of Gildas and Bede.

There has been a welcome tendency among historians to accord archaeology a bigger role in enlightening the Dark Ages; and not merely to regard archaeology as useful only if it is directly relevant to basic historical concepts. Indeed the modern advice from historians to archaeologists is 'try not to interpret your data in a historical framework, but *keep it separate*, as a different medium with which to increase understanding of this period'.

Both historians and archaeologists (as well as other romantically-orientated people) have used a series of names to describe this period. *Sub-Roman* is an adjective useful for

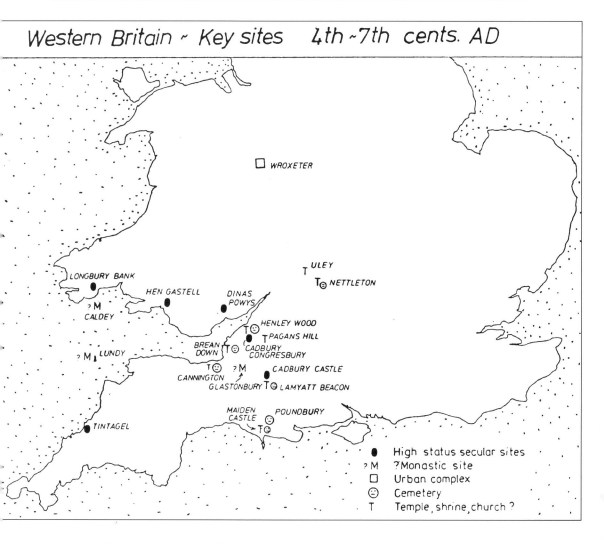

Western Britain ~ Key sites   4th~7th cents. AD

WROXETER

ULEY
NETTLETON

LONGBURY BANK
HEN GASTELL
DINAS POWYS
? M CALDEY
HENLEY WOOD
PAGANS HILL
BREAN DOWN
CADBURY CONGRESBURY
? M LUNDY
CADBURY CASTLE
CANNINGTON
? M
GLASTONBURY LAMYATT BEACON
MAIDEN CASTLE POUNDBURY
TINTAGEL

● High status secular sites
? M ?Monastic site
☐ Urban complex
☺ Cemetery
T Temple, shrine, church ?

73 Map of key Dark Age sites in the west of Britain

some aspects (such as indigenous pottery or art) which owe more to Late Roman predecessors than to any new society. *British* is a convenient word to describe the west of Britain, and is better than *Celtic*. The latter strictly only refers to language (such as Gaelic, Cornish or Welsh) but is often used, notably in relation to art, Christianity and the Church, and people. *Arthurian* will often be found in popular writing, but is best reserved for those aspects of literature and popular archaeology which are especially concerned with the development of myth, rather than history. Finally, *English* or *Anglo-Saxon* are used to discuss the language, institutions and people associated with infiltration of settlers from Germanic areas east of the North Sea.

The geographical extent of the areas concerned in this chapter includes principally Shropshire, Wales and (especially in my own involvement) the West Country, from the

West Midlands to Cornwall. An outlier which must now be included is the important complex of Whithorn near the coast of western Scotland.

The unifying factor is that these western areas were remote from the gradual movement of English settlers, ultimately from the Low Countries and Scandinavia. In some areas as much as three centuries passed between the decline of Roman influence, and military and political domination by the English. This allowed ample time for a new society to develop and flourish; it is sometimes thought of as a 'heroic age', which belies the concept of it being dark.

There is of course a much bigger agenda for this period in the far west and north of Britain. Although Scotland was largely un-Romanised, there are major changes in its archaeology and history during these centuries, which have been the especial concern of one of my great heroes and mentors, Professor Leslie Alcock. The same applies to Ireland, a vast field of study, the understanding of which is beyond the reach of most English archaeologists and historians; but which is vital to a wider understanding of the period.

The Roman and earlier background

The archaeology of post-Roman western Britain is sometimes seen as more akin to the long sequence of indigenous settlement of Britain, extending back to at least the sixth millennium BC and culminating in the tribal kingdoms of the Iron Age glimpsed in Roman literature.

In this view, the four centuries of Roman Britain are seen as an exotic interruption, restricted largely to lowland England, but with military arms extending through southern Scotland and Wales.

The fourth century AD must nevertheless be our starting point. Towns, developed in earlier centuries, were largely in decline, but the countryside flourished, with agricultural and industrial production mostly centred on villas, of a scale ranging from small farms to palaces in classical style and amenity.

The archaeology of Roman Britain is often taken to end in the early fifth century, with the 'withdrawal of the legions', and the virtual cessation of a money economy and all that it supported. Coinage did, however, continue to be minted in other parts of the Roman Empire. One of the most curious features of Romano-British archaeology has been the almost total failure to realise that even if coins later than 400 were rare in Britain, much of the Roman way of life, as it was experienced by 'ordinary' people, did go on. In report after report, we find the assertion that since coinage ceased, so did Roman Britain. Doubtless to those that knew about other parts of the Empire, this seemed true; and also to archaeologists in this country who had chosen to study Roman Britain. Even where there was clear evidence of stratigraphical sequences and structural changes after the 380s, it was only suggested that 'occupation may have continued into the early fifth century'. Such use of a site as could be archaeologically demonstrated was dismissed as the squalid activity of 'squatters'.

One major change was the loss of technical skills in building in stone, and a widespread use of timber or other organic material. To recover the plans of such structures demanded excavation and recording skills that were beyond those of the average Roman archaeologist, used to the relatively easy archaeology of mortared walls, heating systems, mosaics, etc. We shall see, later in this chapter, the serious results of these shortcomings at Wroxeter.

In more recent decades, it has come to be recognised that a Late-Roman way of life, albeit more localised, and based more on subsistence/exchange than a trading economy, continued to (say) *c*.AD 500. What is clear is that a great legacy of Roman material culture remained, notably the ruins of substantial buildings, streets, boundaries, and personal possessions, notably (for archaeology) millions of iron and copper alloy objects, and pottery vessels.

The last-named especially seem to have continued in use, being found as vessels or sherds, in contexts as late as the sixth century AD, and even in later graves. Only in the east of England do we encounter major changes in the material culture, introduced by new settlers from overseas in the fifth and sixth centuries, and widely adopted by the indigenous Britons in those areas, who had recently been semi-Romanised.

Pagans and Christians

An important legacy of the Roman world which continued to be a potent factor in the post-Roman centuries is a firmly-established religion; firstly pagan beliefs, based on the Greco-Roman pantheon of Mediterranean origin; and secondly that of Christianity (**74**). The latter seems to have taken strong root in fourth-century Britain; some elements of this may have survived into the fifth and sixth centuries, ultimately to be absorbed into new movements of Christian evangelisation from Ireland; and from Rome in the later sixth century. In the western areas with which we are here concerned, there may have been more Christians than the archaeology might suggest; the rather 'difficult' sixth-century writer Gildas seems to assume that at least the local rulers were Christian by his time; though he bemoans their lapse from the faith.

Society and Politics

It is generally believed that post-Roman society in both west and east was increasingly the product of opportunist power-struggles between powerful groups or individuals, culminating in larger groupings such as those described by Gildas and Bede; they name some of the emergent rulers, both British and English. The new kingdoms in the west may have been akin both to those visible in the pre-Roman Iron Age (sometimes with similar names, e.g. Dumnonia) and the numerous small kingdoms of Ireland, ultimately grouped in the five major agglomerations of Ulster, Munster, Meath, Leinster and Connaught.

With that very broad introduction, we may now proceed to the archaeological work that has been done in the last seven decades.

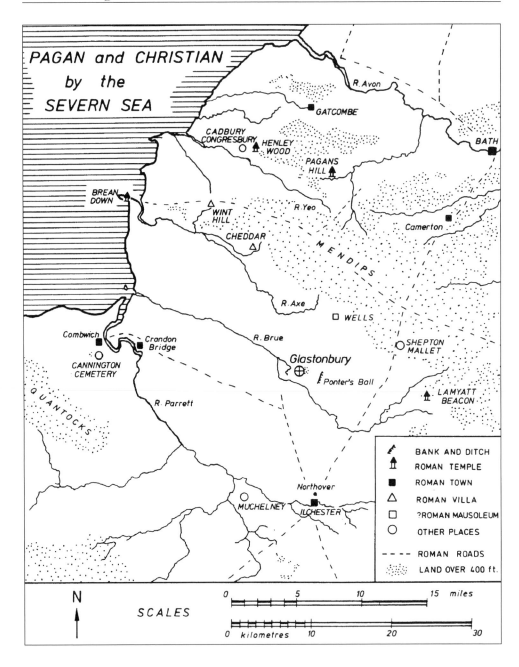

74 *Pagan and Christian by the Severn Sea: sites of religious significance*

The archaeological evidence

Tintagel

Until recent decades, the principal evidence for Dark Age rulers and priests came from the inscriptions on stone monuments in Ogam (a form of stroke-coded writing), and Latin. There have, however, now been excavations at a number of sites which have revolutionised our understanding of the Dark Ages in many ways.

It all began with the late C.A. Ralegh Radford's work at Tintagel, in north Cornwall, in the 1930s. Traditionally, Tintagel was renowned for its myths about King Arthur (it was said to be his birthplace) and his magician, Merlin. Radford's excavations led him to believe that the spectacular headland was not the stronghold of these times but a 'Celtic monastery'; he found buildings that he thought were monastic cells, and a scriptorium (a 'building' where monks created manuscripts); and he believed that the standing chapel ruins on the headland were built on those of the monastery. This was a major change of interpretation, but the local people didn't notice: the village still lives on its bogus Arthurian past — Camelot, King Arthur's castle, and a 'hall of chivalry' where one can get 'knighted' for a small fee. Car parks, fish and chip restaurants and bars all have Arthurian names and live on the Arthur legend.

Radford dated his 'monastery' principally to the sixth century; not by any coins, jewellery, or locally-made pottery, but by the very remarkable finding of thousands of sherds of amphorae (wine or olive oil containers) and fine red tableware from the Mediterranean, datable by Byzantine coins in their centuries of origin. These he recognised because of his wide experience abroad; dramatic witness of a long-distance trade in wine, olive oil and fine pottery, from Asia Minor, Greece and North Africa; and possibly other more perishable items such as silks and spices. Much has been written on these distant connections; it would seem that a profit was to be made by bringing these exotic items by sea, through the western Mediterranean and the Bay of Biscay and up to the seaways approaching western Britain; it is supposed that what these courageous captains wanted in return was tin, silver, gold, slaves and other valuable items which Britain could supply and for which there was a demand in the eastern Mediterranean (**75**).

When I began to take an interest in the Dark Ages in the 1950s and '60s, I was rather sceptical of Radford's 'monastery' — the evidence was decidedly thin. At a conference in Edinburgh in the early 1970s, on monasteries and settlements, I egged on my graduate student, Ian Burrow, to ask a few questions of Radford, who was present. 'Where exactly had the famous pottery been found, in relation to the buildings classed as those of a monastery?' Radford replied at once: 'There is no doubt about the association of the buildings with the pottery: it was *on* the floors, *in* the floors, *under* the floors, *by* the walls, and *in* the walls'. There was a dead silence. Everyone present (except Radford) realised at once that the pottery had nothing to do with the buildings; it was lying densely all over the area, and had been incorporated in all subsequent (medieval) building layers. And so it was later shown; recent excavations by Professor Morris of Glasgow have totally destroyed the 'monastic' hypothesis and — ironically — restored the popular idea that it was an important secular site, the resort of 'kings' and other important people — perhaps

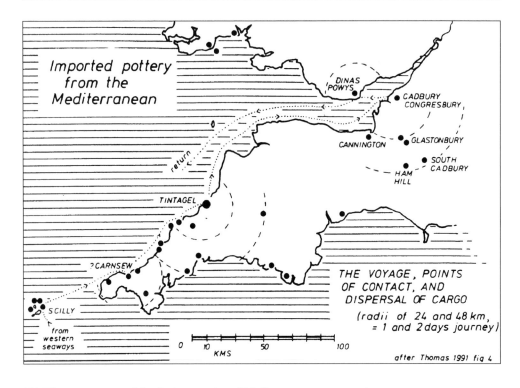

Imported pottery
from the
Mediterranean

DINAS
POWYS

CADBURY
CONGRESBURY

CANNINGTON

GLASTONBURY

SOUTH
CADBURY

HAM
HILL

TINTAGEL

?CARNSEW

SCILLY

from
western
seaways

THE VOYAGE, POINTS
OF CONTACT, AND
DISPERSAL OF CARGO

(radii of 24 and 48 km,
= 1 and 2 days journey)

0   10   50   100
          KMS

after Thomas 1991 fig 4

75 *The routes suggested for the importation of Mediterranean pottery to the west country*

a seasonal meeting-place; people who controlled the Cornish resources of tin, etc, and who valued the luxury and Roman-ness of wine, olive oil, glass, and fine red plates. Not King Arthur, but someone of equal status! All this is excellently discussed by the great Cornish archaeologist and scholar, Professor Charles Thomas in a very readable book (Thomas 1993) (159, 163).

Although Radford had misinterpreted the site, his work at Tintagel set the scene for the remarkable excavations that were to follow in the later part of the century. The Mediterranean pottery was to be the key material for subsequent recognition of settlements of the post-Roman centuries.

Pagans Hill

Although I knew Tintagel well from pre-war years, I don't think that when I began in archaeology I was aware of what Radford had found there, nor its wider implications. My own interest in the Dark Ages, though long-established in a non-scholarly way, was dramatically stimulated by the discovery of the seventh-century glass and bucket in the Roman well at Pagans Hill, as I have described in chapter 2. I was very impressed by the implications of this discovery. There was clearly some relationship between a Roman temple that had flourished in the fourth century and the use of the well and the deposition of a highly exotic glass vessel some three centuries or more later. What had happened in the meantime? The numerous coin series ended as usual with issues minted in the latest fourth century. All we could say (with the Romanists) was that 'occupation may have continued into the fifth century', but if it did, there were no finds that could be dated to the fifth or sixth centuries specifically; nor any trace of subsequent timber structures or 'squatters'. The temple and its surroundings remained 'clean'.

But, and this is the major point here, the building itself survived; archaeological evidence showed that it was still standing, with its roof at least partly intact not 200 years later, but at least 800: medieval pottery was found *on* the temple floor *under* fallen Roman roof slates. It would have been as an impressive icon in the countryside, some 20m high and wide, that it had a continued significance, such as to attract a major re-use in the seventh century; but what for? As a religious building? Was it a Christian use? Pagans Hill showed (especially to me) that all did not end in 410; and that the archaeological evidence for such continuing use or significance could be found on a temple site.

Although I did not find the crucial Mediterranean material, I was now firmly hooked on to Dark Age archaeology; I began a crusade against the blinkered Romanist attitudes, which continue to this day; in this I have been joined by many others. By the time I became a professional in 1955, I knew about the pottery at Tintagel and its importance; and now came exciting news from the other side of the Bristol Channel.

Dinas Powys

In 1953, the small hillfort of Dinas Powys, in South Wales, was chosen for long-term study, and as a training ground for students taking the new archaeology course at University College, Cardiff. The work was initiated by Leslie Alcock. Initially the site was believed to be Iron Age; and while there were phases of this period, and possibly of Roman times, Dark Age material was also found: more Mediterranean pottery, Dark Age glass, and later sixth- or seventh-century pottery of a different type originating probably in south-western France.

These finds aroused great interest in the 1950s, and was the cause of a major change in Leslie Alcock's life. While not totally abandoning the archaeology of earlier (and later) periods, he became the best-known exponent of Dark Age archaeology; and of its history from written sources. After publishing Dinas Powys (Alcock 1963), he wrote the best seller that British archaeology has ever known: *Arthur's Britain* (Alcock 1971). The magic name ensured its success (over 100,000 copies sold) but it has remained the best and most readable introduction to Dark Age history and archaeology, it also paid for all Leslie Alcock's subsequent holidays! In later years he became the principal authority on Dark Age Scotland, from his new base at Glasgow.

Nettleton

Following hard on the discoveries at Dinas Powys was the excavation of another temple, at Nettleton in Wiltshire. Part of the complex had been dug in 1938-40 by W.C. Priestley (it will be remembered that he visited Pagans Hill, see p54); but he discovered only those buildings of the temple complex on one side of a stream, where it was crossed by the Fosse Way.

In 1955, the then curator of archaeology at Bristol Museum, the late Leslie Grinsell, was invited by the landowner to look at some ruins he had found in a wood, on the other side of the stream from where Priestley had dug. I was in Bristol at the time, 'resting' after a hard summer of my first professional work outside Somerset. Grinsell asked me to go along with him, to back him up. To our astonishment, we were shown a ruin nearly two metres high, with purple plaster on the walls, and obviously of Roman date; such survival is very rare in Britain. We offered such advice as we were able, but neither of us was in a position to follow up this discovery, even if we had been asked!

Another archaeologist, Bill Wedlake, did however seize the opportunity. He had had wide experience as Sir Mortimer Wheeler's foreman in the 1930s and had been running a successful local society at Camerton. They had excavated a large part of the Roman settlement there; and he now embarked on Nettleton, working there until 1971.

The building we had seen proved to be part of an octagonal temple, with many other buildings around it, of a large religious complex. Several inscriptions and sculptures showed that the temple was dedicated to Apollo (as may have been the octagonal temple at Pagans Hill) (143).

Apart from the temple, there were no less than 32 other buildings and many other features, including cemeteries and tombs. There were very complex stratigraphic and structural sequences. The temple itself had gone through a number of changes. Bill Wedlake interpreted these as firstly an adaptation to Christian use, then a 'relapse' into paganism, and finally a re-use as a homestead ('squatters'). During the 1960s, news of these very important discoveries and their interpretation spread, and everyone awaited the detailed publication with eager anticipation (Wedlake 1982).

Not surprisingly, in the light of what I have said in my introduction to this chapter, Wedlake, being a 'Roman' archaeologist, believed that all this remarkable sequence had ended about 400, allowing for something still going on into the fifth century. In the light of the archaeology of other later excavations, notably the temple at nearby Uley (see below), we would now lengthen this dating by perhaps 300 years. There were no finds or other dating to confirm this; no Mediterranean pottery has been found beyond the reaches of the estuary of the Bristol Channel, in Gloucestershire or Wiltshire; but there were at Nettleton a number of sherds of hand-made local coarse wares and copies of late Roman forms. The report needs a major re-working, going back to the site archives and finds, and especially to reconsider the series of religious structures and cemeteries.

Bath and Ilchester

It has been generally believed that urban life was a casualty of 'the end of Roman Britain'. In Somerset there are only two Roman towns, Bath and Ilchester. At the great Roman temple and baths complex at Bath, there are phases which suggest some post-Roman ritual use of some kind, extending into the sixth century, but lack of Roman style maintenance had caused flooding; and severe later destruction has largely removed the evidence (see 184, p4).

At Ilchester, however, the late J. Stevens Cox reported in the 1950s not only a few Mediterranean sherds but also (extremely rare in Britain) two sixth-century Byzantine coins; none, alas, in stratified levels; but Ilchester is a likely candidate for Dark Age survival, in view of all the other evidence from the area.

Brean Down and Lamyatt Beacon

The final excavation of the 1950s was yet another temple, on the magnificent headland of Brean Down projecting into the Bristol Channel. This was excavated by Arthur ApSimon, primarily a prehistorian; he had been one of our colleagues in the Chew Valley work and its subsequent publication.

He uncovered the (square) temple totally in 1956-8 (ApSimon 1964-5). It was built in the middle of the fourth century, and in ruins by *c*.400. The temple itself was orientated north-east/south-west, but a secondary smaller building was aligned east/west. This might suggest a change from pagan to a Christian use of the site; if so (i.e. if this building was a small chapel or hermitage) it would be by far the earliest Christian evidence from Somerset. The use of this little building is unusually well-dated. A number of coins on its floor were of the latest fourth- or early fifth-century date, and worn, indicating a fifth-century date for some use of this building.

Potentially of equal significance, but not directly associated with the temple, was a cemetery of east/west graves in the great sand-cliff which is banked against Brean Down on its south-east corner, a few hundred metres east-south-east of the temple. These have been further excavated in recent years, and are dated to the Dark Ages by radiocarbon determination (Bell 1990).

A similar situation was encountered at Lamyatt Beacon in the southern part of Somerset. Although badly destroyed by looters, a square temple there was also followed by a small east/west building with graves directly associated (Leech 1986), of sixth- to seventh-century date.

Henley Wood

It was in the 1960s, however, that the Dark Age West really took off. Brean Down and Lamyatt Beacon had shown that it was not only finds such as Mediterranean pottery, or the glass jar from Pagans Hill, which could indicate post-Roman occupation; but also skeletons, which could be independently dated scientifically. For every dead person, there had been a live one — here we glimpse the *people* in an area, irrespective of their having dropped pottery or other rubbish. This was even further demonstrated at Henley Wood but in a wider context.

By 1961 I was engaged in extra-mural teaching; one of my classes was at Clevedon on the Somerset coast. One of its members, Jim Pullan, brought some human bones to show me; he'd found them on a hilltop nearby, which was being destroyed by quarrying. He took me to see the site, at Henley Wood; burials were visible, cut through rubble of a building; this was evidently of Roman date, as there were also coins and pottery in the rubble. I alerted the then MOPBW; they arranged for the quarrying to be temporarily diverted, so that a proper excavation could take place in 1964-9; it was directed by my old friend Ernest Greenfield (see chapters 2-3). He did not live to write it up, but all his records were passed to my wife, Lorna Watts, who (with Peter Leach) produced the final report (Watts and Leach 1996).

Henley Wood proved to be yet another temple (they seem to grow in Somerset!), again of double square plan, with a long history of earlier shrines (**76**). The temple was orientated north-west/south-east; it was flourishing in the latest fourth/early fifth

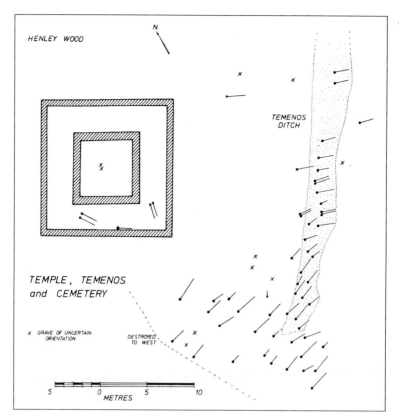

HENLEY WOOD

N

TEMENOS
DITCH

TEMPLE, TEMENOS
and CEMETERY

x GRAVE OF UNCERTAIN
ORIENTATION

DESTROYED
TO WEST

5   0   5   10
        METRES

*76 Henley Wood,
the Roman
temple and
Dark Age
cemetery*

centuries; subsequently a cemetery of about 50 west/east graves developed, with graves cut in the ruins of the temple, in the open area to its east, and in the eastern enclosure ditch. The skeletons were again dated by radiocarbon to the fifth and sixth (and possibly seventh) centuries; yet more evidence of continuing use of the temple complex by people living nearby (**77**).

It is of particular interest that in this case we can at least suggest *where* at least some of the dead people lived: for Henley Wood is only *c*.200m from an adjacent hillfort, of Cadbury-Congresbury, also used in the Dark Ages, to which we shall return.

Cannington

I have described the excavation of this site earlier in the book (chapter 3). The *c*.500 graves we excavated in 1963 onwards became the type-site for these Dark Age cemeteries. To recapitulate, there was a shrine on the hilltop (hardly to be dignified by the name of temple) which was apparently associated with the beginning of burials. Again there is a hillfort close by, where we postulate that the dead people lived, but this has yet to be proved (**42**). Dating for the graves was provided by an extensive series of radiocarbon dates, by a few sherds of Mediterranean pottery, and sherds of a 'native' Dark Age pot made in Cornwall; we have here a local sequence extending from late Roman times onwards.

The range of radiocarbon determinations made it clear that the burials at Cannington, unlike the other cemeteries of this class began, not in the Dark Ages, but in the second half of the fourth century; yet, by and large, the cemetery is homogeneous. The final graves were of latest seventh- or eighth-century date; and here we have the evidence not only of radiocarbon but also of finds — two small groups of grave-goods buried with infants, and taking us into the datable world of Anglo-Saxon and later Western British metalwork; but these still included a Roman coin, albeit pierced for suspension.

The radiocarbon ranges cover three and a half centuries reasonably evenly; there is little doubt that the population was represented throughout the Dark Ages; if the settlement site (or more than one) were to be confirmed, it would be most informative to see what there was apart from residual Roman material.

It took forty years to achieve publication of Cannington, but this finally happened in 2000 (181).

Public and academic interest centred, however, not so much on the cemeteries, though they alone covered the whole period, but on the 're-occupation of hillforts', a theme of wider import, suggesting the possibility of a 'regression' or reversion to a society not unlike that of the pre-Roman Iron Age. This general interest led to two great campaigns on hillforts: the two Cadburys.

77 Bronze statuette from Henley Wood (first century AD but very worn)

Glastonbury Tor

Before we consider these, however, we turn to a very dramatic place, Glastonbury Tor, another hilltop, but not fortified. I have described in chapter 4 how I came to be involved at Glastonbury, in a somewhat problematical ethical role (comparable to the rather different problems faced by Leslie Alcock at Cadbury Castle — see below).

In the light of the sites I have discussed elsewhere in this chapter, to find Dark Age material and structures on the Tor in 1964 was an enormous stroke of luck — it made me prone to belief in destiny. True, there were only a dozen Mediterranean sherds, but they were crucial in dating this phase of the Tor's history and its contacts with the western seaways; and starkly in contrast to the absence of such material in the extensive excavations undertaken at the Abbey — the supposed cradle of early Christianity in the West. The possibility that the Tor is one of the earliest monasteries or hermitages in the West (after the debunking of Tintagel!) is still a very open question. Here was this exotic and alien

78 Leslie Alcock at Dunadd, ?1975; Sebastian Rahtz in foreground, looking rather bored!

material in a very different context from that found in 're-occupied hillforts' or cemeteries (unless perhaps some local chief was holding court in that inhospitable and wind-swept place!) (158).

We now return to the major hillfort campaigns in the later 1960s.

Cadbury Castle

During the 1950s another site yielded Mediterranean pottery and post-Roman glass. This was a famous place indeed, the most massively-defended Iron Age hillfort in Somerset. It has a system of great banks and ditches around a large open hilltop. It is known by various names; firstly as no less than Camelot itself, the mythical court of King Arthur. This identification was averred by local people as early as the beginning of the sixteenth century: a tradition recorded by the great antiquarian traveller John Leland ('The people can telle nothing ther but that they have hard say that Arture much resortid to Camalot'). The identification as Camelot survived into modern times; on the Ordnance Survey map the hillfort is named 'Cadbury Castle or Camelot'.

Field-walking by Ralegh Radford and the late J Stevens Cox recovered sherds of pottery and glass, 'an interesting confirmation of the traditional identification of the site as the Camelot of Arthurian legend' — a bold statement linking archaeology to myth. Interest in Dark Age archaeology in Somerset was becoming stronger, especially its Arthurian association. Accordingly, plans were laid for a research excavation. The Camelot Research Committee was set up in 1965, with Radford as Chairman, Sir Mortimer Wheeler as President and Geoffrey Ashe as Secretary. By this time, I had become archaeologically and academically respectable (see chapter 4). I was known to have developed an interest in this period, so I was invited to be a member of this Committee, though I rather deplored its name.

It was, however, financially necessary to keep Arthurian names firmly in the forefront, to raise money for the excavation. There were also, on the Committee, representatives of various 'Arthurian' societies who sat rather uneasily with the academics.

We invited Leslie Alcock (**78**) to cross over the Bristol Channel to direct the work; with Dinas Powys now published, he was in an excellent position to expand his Dark Age experience. As always, he was cautious and scholarly in his approach; while sympathetic, as a historian, to some reality behind the legends.

The excavation was brilliantly carried through from 1966-70. Inevitably, such an impressive site was primarily prehistoric. Neolithic, Bronze Age, Iron Age, Roman, and medieval layers and structures took up the great majority of resources, and provided a vast number of finds; somewhat to the disappointment of the Arthurians, who were, however, elated by the discovery of a bronze letter A.

There was, nevertheless, a major Dark Age phase, represented by an encircling defensive timbered bank over a kilometre in length, a timber gateway, and a possible hall and other structures. Nearly a hundred finds of fifth- to seventh-century date were recovered; a significant assemblage, but few compared with the thousands found at Tintagel; Cadbury Castle is after all some way from the coast and any port of entry for the Byzantine ships.

A popular book (Alcock 1972) swiftly followed the conclusion of the excavation. Alcock justifiably entitled it 'By South Cadbury' (the village close by), 'is that Camelot', a direct quotation from Leland; the publishers, however, dishonestly put in bold letters on the spine, 'Cadbury-Camelot', to ensure its sale. The final definitive report on the Dark Age aspects of the site was published by Alcock in 1995; by this time he had retired from his chair at Glasgow, and was able to update the whole by reference to the other Dark Age sites discussed in this chapter, and his now wider experience.

Cadbury Congresbury

In 1959, a local archaeologist, Keith Gardner, dug some test-holes on the hillfort above Congresbury before Henley Wood had been discovered; he was fortunate enough, in very small-scale work, to find sherds of Mediterranean pottery, which suggested yet another re-occupation of an Iron Age hillfort.

In the later 1960s I also met, at Bristol, Peter Fowler (then in extra-mural studies) who shared my enthusiasm for Dark Age studies; he was a very stimulating person with whom to work; we rather egged each other on. In 1968, we joined with Keith Gardner in an excavation of a small area of this Cadbury: we had had a covetous eye on the site ever since his 1959 discoveries.

The results were very encouraging: a density of Dark Age pottery and finds second only to Tintagel; we felt we had a worthy rival to 'the other Cadbury' where Leslie Alcock had begun work two years earlier. There was personal rivalry too. We exchanged visits between the two sites, not without some acerbity. We took the rather arrogant view that we were digging objectively, without any preconceived pseudo-historical notions; in this, of course, we were quite mistaken; we were as much indoctrinated with the cultural baggage of the Dark Age syndrome as anyone else. We poked mild fun at the other Cadbury, suggesting that Leslie Alcock had an Arthurian tin can tied to his tail, which he would have a job to shake off: and so it proved, except that he is a great enough archaeologist to give an effective shake. We even had an extended satirical chronological chart pinned up in our shed. Leslie did not take too kindly to this when he visited our Cadbury; his only reaction was a wan smile, and some retort about the uselessness of Dark Age archaeology if not linked to history.

We published a first report in 1970 (46) at 50p; very few copies of this were bought by our digging team, even at this price; they really came for the digging, it seemed, and didn't want to know too much about 'what it all meant' or our brilliant thoughts about it.

We excavated large areas in 1970-3, with very positive results thanks to Peter Fowler's skilful direction (**79 & 80**). I count Cadcong (as we slangily called it) as technically one of the best excavations in which I have been involved. The data were, however, massive as well as of great importance (*see* **48**); it took many years to produce the definitive monograph, but this was finally achieved in 1992 (152). We cited the authorship as CADREX, to emphasise the team nature of the enterprise: Peter Fowler, Keith Gardner and myself (collectively known as P.K.P. FOWLGARAHTZ), Ann Woodward (then Ellison), the late Anne Everton, Lorna Watts, Susan Hirst, Ian Burrow and Peter Leach. The name was also meant to be a play on the Cad-element and 'King' (even King Cong — the local ruler!). But alas this attempt failed. The publishers (British Archaeological Reports) put all our names and CADREX in the fly-leaves; but on the spine it was 'Rahtz et al'!

All of these excavations had aroused considerable interest in the Dark Age West, in which not surprisingly I shared; and I was beginning to realise, as an academic, that some preliminary synthesis might be attempted. I began in 1968 with a brief discussion of the cemeteries and then, at the same time as our collaboration over Cadbury Congresbury (in 1968) a seminal paper with Peter Fowler on 'Somerset Dark Age Problems' (39). This was followed by a fuller exposition on 'Somerset 400-700' in Leslie Grinsell's *Festschrift* of 1972

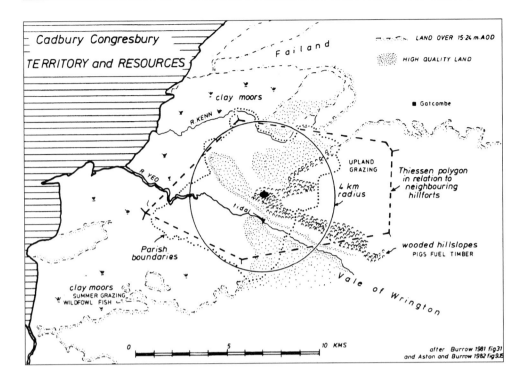

79 *Cadbury Congresbury, territory and resources: the nearer horizons for the inhabitants of the hillfort*

(51). Although this is 27 years old, we still see this as setting an agenda for future research, even though it needs updating.

I also wrote a rather malicious little piece, lampooning another pseudo-historical project, that of Ralegh Radford at Castle Dore in Cornwall (50). Luckily, however, I'd written it so 'straight' that only a perceptive few appreciated the irony; I also attempted to outline what little we know about pottery in Somerset between the Roman and Norman periods (62); and, looking further afield, whether any of our Dark Age people might be Irish immigrants (76).

All the cemetery excavations I've described above brought up the rather fundamental question of why most of the graves were west/east; and more generally why were graves deliberately orientated at all; this led me into a much wider discussion on orientation in 1978 (84), venturing into both anthropology and the quicksands of religious belief. I also looked more widely then Somerset in extending the whole subject of Late Roman and later cemeteries, which put the west into a wider context (82); and (with my wife Lorna Watts) a more general synthesis of Roman temples in the west and what happened to them (88). In this we added an appendix on a modern shrine in Co Donegal — again venturing into anthropology and ethnography.

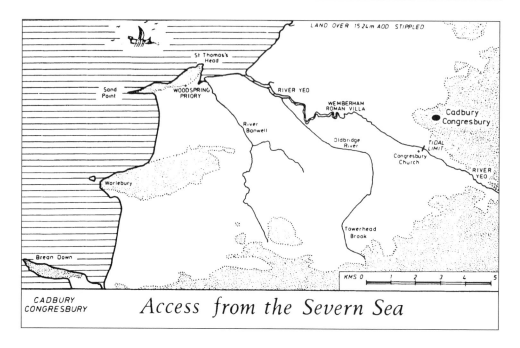

80 Cadbury Congresbury: the way from the sea, in times of a lower sea level in relation to the land

I have in this chapter dwelt more on Somerset rather than the west in general; and have included little that had origins later than the cessation of work at the Cadburys in the 1970s. The 1960s and '70s were the golden age of the big Somerset digs. I have said nothing about Devon; a few coastal sites there have yielded Mediterranean sherds. The focus of attention in the last ten years, has, however, been in Wales, where various sites have been found with Dark Age imports, amplifying the evidence from Dinas Powys.

I will conclude this chapter by moving outside the south-western counties into areas further north. We have already considered the excavations of 1935-71 at Nettleton and their problems; another temple in the Cotswolds has recently been excavated to very high standards. This is Uley; the directors were Ann Woodward and Peter Leach. Like Nettleton there was a series of some 20 structures in this ritual complex covering the prehistoric and whole Roman periods. The principal building was another square temple; finds were very rich and numerous (8,000 objects, 67,000 sherds of pottery, a quarter of a million animal bones) all recorded meticulously. There was also sculpture associated with the principal deity, Mercury. Parts of the cult statue were found carefully buried; these included a second-century head of Mercury (**81**), one of the finest pieces of sculpture ever found in Roman Britain. This is in a very accomplished style reflecting the prototype of the Greek sculptor Praxiteles: his statue of the Greek equivalent of Mercury (Hermes). When Ann Woodward told me about this, I travelled up to Uley to see it. I was taken to the landowner's house where it was temporarily in safe keeping in a cardboard box. When it was lifted out, I experienced that very rare feeling in archaeology, a prickling of the scalp. It

81 The head of Mercury: Roman sculpture from Uley

wasn't just that it was a work of art of the highest quality, but that it emanated an 'aura'; Ann had had it in her excavation caravan, and had the same feeling as she slept with it so close. It is now one of the prime exhibits in the new Roman gallery at the British Museum.

Relevant to this chapter, Uley exhibited important phases after the fourth century: the temple was partly destroyed or fell about 400, and was converted into a new form in the earlier fifth century. This was succeeded by a timber basilica, interpreted as a Christian church; there were also baptisteries, and subsequently a small stone church and other structures. Associated with their demolition were fragments of red-streaked window glass of seventh- or eighth-century date.

The cult-sculpture was carefully buried in these later phases. The head was found 'crisp and quite unweathered'; although over two centuries old 'it does not seem to have been exposed at all to the elements, and may have been protected by a cloth, a bag, or a box. The implication is that the statue head had been curated, preserved, and possibly venerated, during the lifetime of the timber basilica . . . the head may have been placed in a recess within the basilica, hidden in a chest, or even placed or sealed inside the altar itself . . . the head of Mercury himself may have seemed a too dangerous and profane item in the eyes of these early Christians . . . Alternatively, the head may have been rescued by individuals of pagan leaning and buried secretly next to the new Christian shrine.' There was suggested at the time a further possibility: that the head may have been perceived or presented as representing the head of Christ himself, or of a local saint or martyr.

Uley thus encapsulated, in far greater detail, the sparse evidence for Dark Age religion that the earlier temple evidence (especially Nettleton) had suggested. If my readers of this chapter are inspired to read more, the Uley monograph (Woodward and Leach 1993) is an essential beginning, demonstrating the power of modern scientific archaeology to reconstruct Dark Age sequences; even with no coins later than 400!

On the other side of the Bristol Channel, opposite the Cotswolds, another great temple complex had been dug at Lydney in the 1930s by Sir Mortimer Wheeler himself; but he dismissed the post-400 phases (which included a new enclosing earthwork) as in 'some period of recrudescent barbarism', a conclusion which we castigated in an appendix to our paper on the end of temples (88); and which Uley confirmed acutely. In this same paper, we also re-interpreted another 1930s Wheeler temple excavation, at Maiden Castle in Dorset.

Further north, in the West Midlands, the problem of the continuing use of towns was tackled by Philip Barker (**82**) at Wroxeter (Roman VIROCONIUM CORNOVIORUM) in Shropshire. This great city had been extensively excavated in the past, from 1859 onwards. In the Baths area there is a surviving wall standing many metres high: 'The Old Work'. The site of the Baths Basilica by this was examined by Dame Kathleen Kenyon in 1937, and again by Dr Graham Webster in 1955-66; he is one of England's leading 'Roman' archaeologists. The general method of all these excavations were by trenching, and removing all 'loose rubble' etc. until a substantial wall or floor was revealed. Not surprisingly, the work uncovered in part much of the plans of Roman period buildings (or the stone-based ones). In 1966 my contemporary Philip Barker, who is one of Britain's most famous archaeologists (his textbook on techniques of excavation is now a classic), joined Webster as his assistant. He was given the job of excavating a small area alongside the earlier excavations where a new bungalow was to be built for the site custodian. Using more cautious and meticulous techniques he had developed at Hen Domen (a timber castle site in Shropshire), he defined *fourteen* phases above the highest remains recognised by previous excavators. The archaeological world was shocked; the implications for the upper levels of Wroxeter were profound; and for all other Roman towns; and more importantly for the whole debate on the continuity of urban life in the fifth century and beyond.

Barker went on to re-examine the whole of the Baths Basilica area, a very large excavation, until 1990. Much had been irrevocably destroyed by the earlier trenches, but he was still able to define 70 buildings and structures. Radiocarbon dating and a very high standard of recording pushed this sequence into the seventh century (virtually all finds were fourth-century or earlier). The structures were of timber, and represented an entirely new campaign of town planning under the control of some powerful individual. The structures were built on platforms mostly made out of rubble and were defined by meticulous observation and photography of the differing colour textures and degrees of wear. They were not humble buildings, however. Some were very large hall-like

82   Philip Barker and Maurice Barley, ?1994

buildings; a whole length of a Roman street had, moreover, been bodily removed and replaced by sifted gravel and sand.

The inhabitants of the city, right down to the final occupation (at least in the city centre), clearly thought of themselves as 'Roman' or at least 'Romano-British'. A large central building, constructed between *c*.530 and 580 has the plan of a symmetrical villa; there is no resemblance to anything in the British West, or to those of Germanic areas further east. Even more significant is that analysis of the ground plan measurements of the timber buildings of the later phases showed that they were in multiples of Roman linear units — the *pedes monetalis*; whoever designed them was still thinking in Roman terms.

Most professional archaeologists visited the site at one time or another during Barker's fifteen seasons. Only the Romanist die-hards were sceptical. Many, including myself, were initially dubious, but came away convinced: firstly by Barker's careful and logical site exposition (he is a great teacher), and secondly by being persuaded to mount onto a high photographic platform, from where the outlines of the buildings could be discerned by variations in colour and the nature of the stony platforms; these were made from the debris of Roman buildings.

A great deal of Wroxeter Roman city remains unexcavated; but no one will dare to trench it any more, nor we hope any other Roman towns! The work of analysis went on for some years, but resulted in a massive volume with a box of A3 fold-out plans in which every stone was drawn; its publication has been one of the major events of recent years (Barker *et al* 1997); reviews are awaited with interest!

It had rather been assumed that the geographical extent of the Mediterranean imports (both of primary 'landing places' and of dispersion into inland areas such as Cadbury Castle) was restricted to south-west England, Wales and Ireland; as we have seen, it did not penetrate beyond the Bristol area into Gloucestershire or Wiltshire; the only exception was that of a very few sherds from the famous early Christian monastery at Iona. This supposition has, however, been recently given the lie by the finding in 1984-91 of large amounts of imported pottery and glass again in western Scotland, at another famous monastic site, that of Whithorn, near the coast of Dumfries/Galloway. Although historically associated with the early saint Ninian, the area from which this material comes is described as a 'monastic town', a place which saw extensive trade and outside contacts (Hill 1997, see 180). The full implications of this have yet to be considered.

It will be clear from this brief historical sketch of Dark Age archaeology in the west that an enormous task of synthesis lies ahead for some brilliant scholar in the next millennium. I would like to have attempted it but I am not brilliant, nor sufficiently in touch with modern archaeology to attempt it, and I doubt if my energy would now stretch to that daunting task.

The last such attempt at such a synthesis was the piece that Peter Fowler and I wrote in 1972 (51); but that was only in Somerset, and now well out-dated, as is my 1982 paper on 'Celtic Society' (98). The religious aspects have been discussed at length by Ann Woodward (Woodward and Leach 1993) and there are long general discussion sections in Cadbury Congresbury (152), in Thomas 1993 (Tintagel), in Alcock 1995 (Cadbury Castle), in Watts and Leach 1996 (Henley Wood), in Barker et al 1997 (Wroxeter) and in our Cannington monograph (181). We all seem to have been chewing over the same problems and material, but there is no shortage of data, or of reading matter, for those who wish to enter the scrum!

Apart from these serious discussions, there have been more slender reviews such as my chapter in the Somerset popular book (99), the final words on Pagans Hill (143) and in what I consider to be my most evocative title, 'Pagan and Christian by the Severn Sea' (151).

No attempt has been made in this chapter to consider all the data thematically; the agenda for the Great Syntheses can conveniently be thought of under four main headings: the environment, politics and power, settlement and economy, and religion.

For the first of these, there is increasing evidence for changes in the landscape, vegetation, sea-levels, etc.; and there is now a joker in the pack. This is the evidence from dendrochronology, radiocarbon and ice-cores that there was a major climatic disaster in the years around 540, brought about either by major volcanic activity, perhaps in Iceland, or possibly by an extra-terrestrial impact. This disruption has been discussed by Professor Mike Baillie of Belfast (1999), and he believes, on the basis of analogous disasters, that there was air pollution, crop poisoning, wintry summers, food shortage/famine, disease, depopulation (in this order), and a loss of confidence in the ruling class, leading to anarchy and the fall of dynasties. Although this scenario has not yet been widely accepted, there is clearly a need to consider all the archaeology and history of the western Dark Age (and other contemporary events further east) in the light of this suggested massive crisis.

I am unlikely now to take any further active role in these studies, except as an onlooker. Some of us would like to extend the database by opening further areas at Cadbury Congresbury, but this is at present little more than a pipe dream. But if it does happen, I hope to live long enough to see it!

10 Church archaeology and graveyards

I have been involved in the archaeology of fifteen churches and chapels. This has not been an intentional emphasis. I am not a Christian, unlike a number of other British archaeologists, whose Christian belief has drawn them to the study of churches. It is difficult, for someone who has been concerned with rules of evidence, to abandon these in favour of faith. Short of personal visionary experience, belief in external controlling forces or life beyond death does not come easily. I have always been puzzled by the large numbers of highly intelligent scientists who are also Christian; and I have never heard a convincing explanation of how they reconcile science with religion; one gathers that to some extent it results in some compartmentalisation in their minds.

On a more prosaic level, I would find it difficult to adhere to a belief system that was not cosmic and universal. To belong to any particular religion would appear to involve rejecting others, involving at worst aggression and active intolerance, at best, a toleration which can appear patronising. If in the future there is scientific evidence of 'supernatural' forces and existences (i.e. not compatible with the present laws of physics, etc.), and this seems unlikely to occur in my lifetime, it would be in the realm of what is currently called science fiction, in which higher forces were seen to emanate from another planet vastly in advance of ours; maybe even being responsible for the development of hominids on Earth. Science fiction will become scientific fact, and believable, however humbling and demoralising to those who take pride in hominid 'achievement'.

Nevertheless I was born and brought up in a western European society, in a country where Christianity was nominally the official faith, and in a home where church-going was customary, and moral principles were based on biblical precepts rather than the (to me preferable) laws of humanism (see Appendix A, 'Letter to David').

I had been, moreover, exposed to churches and cathedrals as places to visit, admire and study, with all their bits and pieces. In the course of archaeology, this interest in the buildings has increased, and I have been especially intrigued by those of pre-Norman date. I also find churches and monasteries of major interest as the expression of spiritual beliefs and ideology in Western European society. For the same reason I have also been concerned with pagan temples and shrines of an earlier period. Both may be said to appeal to me as an essentially romantic archaeologist, though it has not deterred me from being heavily involved also in what might be regarded as the more mundane topics of a secular nature, settlements, buildings and the associated environment.

As an academic, I found that in the late 1960s churches were (and are) part of the 'heritage' that was threatened in the RESCUE scenario. Churches were in danger. They had been through many crises as a result of political and religous upheaval. Many were in ruins (notably in Norfolk). But a great crisis was now becoming apparent, which is still with us; the rapid decline of the Christian faith in Britain, in the limited funds available at national level, and especially in the unwillingness of local communities to pay for the upkeep of churches they rarely or never visit.

Many churches became redundant. The best were taken into care by the Redundant Churches Fund as heritage monuments. Many others were converted to houses, factories, workshops, cinemas, or destroyed to make space for secular development (often with disastrous consequences for the graves under and around them).

In some cases, archaeologists could at least record what was being destroyed, but this could be only partial. I was at that time principally concerned with the political and rescue aspects of churches and even wrote a paper for the Institute for the Study of Worship and Religious Architecture at Birmingham University on the crisis (55).

My academic interest in church archaeology was, however, neither of worship or religious architecture; nor did I have the appropriate expertise. As an excavating archaeologist, I nevertheless had to be involved in the above-ground aspects of churches, in the general predominant ethic that there should be no division of interest between below-ground and above-ground archaeology. Perhaps fortunately, of the churches in which I have been involved only five were standing in part or in whole. When it comes to understanding the finer details of the architecture of stone buildings (or even the upper parts of timber ones; see 100), I am a veritable tyro. It is as much as I can do to follow Pevsner in his peregrinations around the buildings of England, or hide behind my camera abroad as a substitute for *looking* at buildings (cf 113).

Being essentially a below-ground archaeologist, I have been primarily concerned with stratigraphy, rather than architectural history. Even though much if not all of the evidence recovered below-ground is of direct relevance to the understanding of what the church was like above-ground, I had been content to let others draw such conclusions. All I could do was to present the evidence from the excavation in as clear a form as possible for those who would wish to use it.

There is a school of thought (if not indeed a majority opinion), that one only finds what one is looking for; i.e. that certain evidence will only be noted and recorded if the excavator is not only knowledgable about building construction, but is thinking about it all the time during the digging. I may thus have missed a good deal, especially of the more ephemeral traces of timber structures.

In more recent years, however, I have been willy-nilly forced to integrate the two, and to educate myself in architectural matters, at least as far as individual buildings were concerned. We shall see below how this came about.

How then did I get involved in churches? The first was an accidental discovery of the foundations of the Chapel of St James at Moreton, in the Chew Valley (79), in rescue excavation of the shrunken medieval village. There was no previous published reference to this; and oddly enough I only accidentally found a reference to the chapel when I was tracing the manorial descent in the library: it was not even in the index to the volume I was consulting. Also at Chew was the Nunnery of St Cross, a moated site with a chapel; though the identification of the particular building was somewhat tenuous, more by exclusion in relation to other buildings than by any positive evidence. Curiously enough, neither of these first excursions into the field of churches had any burials. These, although a fundamental attribute of churches, are a bane to the archaeologist. The digging of graves has destroyed 95% or more of the stratification both outside and inside the church. The excavation of burials poses its own problems, both archaeological and ethical (136, 144).

Broadfield (64) was another by-product of the examination of a medieval village. The castle chapel (83) at Pleshey was an accidental discovery; that there was a great chapel in this important castle was well-known from written sources, but not where it was within the bailey. Our big trench was meant to be an examination of the defensive earthwork around the bailey, but it encountered the chapel on the inside.

The Chapel of St Columbanus at Cheddar was a ruin; its excavation was part of the palace work; the earliest great hall lay beneath it (87, 119).

On a very different scale was the excavation of St Mary-le-Port (112), one of the big churches in the centre of the old city of Bristol. Worship ceased here a few hours before it was gutted by Nazi bombs in the great fire-bombing of 1941. As part of the conservation of the area, Bristol City Museum commissioned an excavation of the ruins. The foundations of several successive churches survived the most determined efforts of grave and vault diggers within the church, so we were able to reconstruct the ground plans in outline of the various stages of the church. We were, however, taken to task in a review by one of the greatest of church archaeologists (Warwick Rodwell) of having taken no account of the ruins above the ground! But someone else can do that (if they remove the Victorian cladding) — the ruin is still there!

The burials here were rather gruesome. Before we began work, Bristol Corporation had employed workmen to 'clear the graves' — not in those days seen as an integral part of the archaeology. The workmen's principal interest was not in the bones or coffins, but in scrabbling for wedding rings, etc. The bones were bundled out into wooden crates and cremated elsewhere. Lead coffins were also sold for scrap, but not before one had been vandalised by a visitor, with highly unpleasant results.

The examination of the ground-plan residues of the church of St Michael in Glastonbury Tor (49) was again not considered with the standing tower, which was given only cursory attention in our report, but again is still there. 'Fortunately', the other Glastonbury chapel at Beckery (60) had been reduced by robbing to the foundations, so there was no problem, and we did manage to suggest possible 'artist's reconstructions' (158).

With these reservations on my limitations as an architectural historian, should I work on churches (or even buildings) at all? I felt happier in dealing with timber buildings, where reconstruction was highly speculative; or with buildings of which only foundations survived, where I could at least provide data for those who were concerned mainly with the above-ground elements. So how could I continue with a clear conscience?

The answer was of course teamwork — archaeologists working with architectural historians. This at last happened in 1969, with the initiation of excavations at the Cistercian Abbey of Bordesley, Redditch (74) (see chapter 6). Apart from the revealed architectural features, there were tonnes of mouldings: decorated and carved pieces which were useless for stone robbers to build with, but invaluable as evidence of the church in its various architectural changes. As ignorant archaeologists we could not evaluate the significance of these mouldings, so we put them on one side, covered them with soil against the time when we could enlist the help of an architectural historian. Fortunately one was forthcoming. One of my fellow-diggers at Split (p206) was David Walsh, of the University of Rochester, New York, an art and architectural historian whose very specialism this was, with particular interest in the Cistercians. So he took over this whole study, and from our tonnes of carved stone, coupled with what survived *in situ*, he was able to make splendid drawings and paintings of what the church had looked like in the Middle Ages.

The next crucial influence in marrying archaeological evidence with that of church architecture came when we met the late Harold Taylor, who with his wife Joan in the 1960s, produced the two definitive volumes on the Anglo-Saxon churches of England. They had visited and measured every one of the 400-odd pre-Norman churches in England; or what they could see of them above the ground.

Harold was primarily, in his academic career, a mathematician, with a keen interest in mountaineering (which came in very useful when he had to scale high ladders to look at detail in the upper parts of churches — alarming to onlookers). He came to England from New Zealand, and had a distinguished career in academia, including being Vice-Chancellor of Keele. He was also, however, a devout Christian. He realised that the study of Anglo-Saxon churches would be a worthy project. He dedicated his third synthesis volume to God, 'in whose honour these humble buildings were erected by our ancestors' — a very positive motivation for his great study.

At the time when I first met him in the late 1960s, he was becoming increasingly aware of the crucial evidence for the architecture and structural sequence preserved below the ground, often in better condition after a millennium than the parts above, which had been subjected to rebuilding, mutilation and re-pointing.

We agreed to collaborate on a major research project, supported by the British Academy and the Society of Antiquaries of London, on one of the most remarkable Anglo-Saxon churches in the country, that of Deerhurst in Gloucestershire (73, 172, 191). Over many years, we excavated around the church, stripped plaster and drew all the important early wall-faces stone-by-stone. While I was able to deal with the archaeology, I always had it in mind that Harold would do the great architectural synthesis, sorting out all the evidence and organising it into different periods. Lawrence Butler (now at York) was the third member of our triumvirate, dealing with the history and the post-Norman phases of the church (see also chapter 6).

Alas, when the time came to draw it all together and publish a definitive monograph, Harold (who was some years older than us) was stricken with Alzheimers disease, and could no longer hope to participate actively in the post-excavation analysis; all this had to be done by Lorna Watts and myself, including the architecture. Only too conscious of our lack of expertise, we took deep breaths and got on with it. Harold spent two days with us in the closing stages; and although in poor mental health, he was able to go through the whole text and drawings, and express his satisfaction that all was well; and that our collaboration over many years had been successful (172).

More recently, feeling more confident of our ability to handle both architectural and archaeological data (at least of the Anglo-Saxon period!) we began a similar, though

83 *Will Scarlett, the man behind the graveyard; he buried five queens and lived to be 98. The tools of his trade (pick, shovel, keys to vaults, dog-whip) are accompanied by a skull. (Photo from a painting in Peterborough Cathedral)*

84 The lighter side of graveyard life (from a painting by Thomas Rowlandson); the gravestones depicted are caricatures of typical stones of the eighteenth century, with skull/crossbones and cherubs

smaller-scale study of Kirkdale, in North Yorkshire; but this story belongs to chapter 14, that of my retirement.

Involvement with churches led not surprisingly to an interest in grave memorials, a rich source of evidence for many aspects of life and death in recent centuries (95) (**83 & 84**). Whereas there are ethical problems in disturbing the dead, even in the name of science, no such caveats apply to gravestones, or the spatial arrangements of the graveyard in relation to the church; or to the study of internal memorials.

Recording and analysing data above-ground from graveyards (71) is also non-destructive and repeatable, so it is a very respectable mode of research. The range of enquiry is wide: geology and the use of stone by the monumental masons; who and where they were working; the design and decoration of the stones, changing with time (eg. the transition from deaths' heads to cherubs in the sevententh to eighteenth century) (**85**); the changing attitudes to death and the after-life, in the epitaphs; and the names, sex, date and age of those buried beneath them.

We became interested in this as a result of continuously seeing the splendid examples in the churchyard at Deerhurst (see above). One of the Birmingham students (Jeremy

*85 Grave memorial stone of Lussod Watkins. The Welsh shawls have been transmuted into angels'
wings*

Jones) working with us there became especially interested; he recorded them and used the
data for his B.A. dissertation. We realised that a wider facet of this study was the use of the
data in teaching classification and statistics. It quickly became obvious that standardisation
of data was needed, and in a form which was suitable for computerisation. So Jeremy and
I designed a recording card to indicate the data that needed to be noted.

Recording of gravestones has long been a favourite pursuit of people living near a
churchyard; but usually it amounted to no more than a list of people commemorated
(with, in the best cases, some plans and photographs). The recording of gravestones was
now, however, becoming a matter of local and national concern. There were reckoned to
be 20 million or more stones in Britain. Natural erosion by wind, rain and sea-spray was
being accelerated by air pollution. Graveyards were being levelled and the stones used for
paths and walls, and replaced by rose bushes; ironically to enable a village to compete in
the 'best-kept churchyard' contests. Vandalism was rife: this was a dwindling resource.

Accordingly, Jeremy wrote, in collaboration with us, a little book to go with the
recording card, *How to Record Graveyards*. It was published by the CBA and has been into
many reprints. It has done a good deal to rescue gravestone data in hundreds of graveyards
in Britain.

In later years, when my wife and I joined in the Wharram Percy epic (p122), our first
contribution was to make an exhaustive and loving study of the churchyard memorials.

Luckily, there were only 35 of them (in a poor rural area) and they were not a very exciting group; their study was only viable in the 'holistic' content of the Wharram campaign. To basic card recording and photography we added what was known of these people from church registers (of birth, baptism, marriage and death) and, rather to our surprise, found that the whole amounted to a monograph (103), seen by some as overkill!

One rather surprising offshoot of our work on these stones (which included some restoration and tidying up of this disused and overgrown churchyard) was to put all the archaeology of Wharram into good favour with local families, whose forebears were among those commemorated; so that it now became a common thing for the children to be brought to see 'great-grandad's gravestone'; a social act enhanced by the restoration of a yearly service in the ruined church.

11 Ethnography: living archaeology in other countries

Ethnography proper is a part of anthropology, the 'social' side (as opposed to 'physical', the study of the people themselves as living flesh and blood, and dead skeletons). Social anthropologists were (and are) primarily interested in the whole systems by which people live: rites of passage (birth, marriage, death), property and inheritance, power and ranking, religious belief and art. With notable exceptions, they did not until recently study material culture: the technology, possessions, rubbish (**86**). The latter is the stuff of archaeology, and much has been lost by the failure of anthropologists to record these data before they were destroyed.

Social anthropology has moved a long way from its rather superior attitudes towards inferior 'primitive' peoples; anthropologists are sometimes seen, along with missionaries, traders and soldiers, as agents of oppression and exploitation; or conversely, and equally mistakenly, the people being studied are viewed, patronisingly, as 'noble savages'

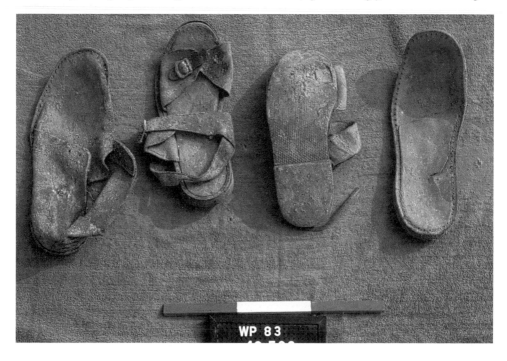

86 John Hurst's sandals; found at Wharram Percy in a 1950s rubbish pit, re-excavated in 1983, so soon does rubbish acquire a historical significance

174

87 St Agnes, Scilly;
Atlantean
sculpture, 1976

untouched by the horrors of civilisation. Things have changed: with the decline in a general belief in the ethics of colonialism, and increasing scepticism about our own society, there has developed a much greater respect for the diverse lifestyles of the Bushmen, Inuit, Amerindians and Aborigines. The latter are especially regarded nowadays as one of the most successful human settlers, in having achieved a balance with nature for 40,000 years or more. This has in turn resulted in a greater interest in their material culture.

Not surprisingly, this has led scholars to wonder if the diverse technologies or beliefs encountered in living people could offer any guidance in the archaeological study of past peoples. If one finds, in a settlement of earlier millennia, a particular tool whose function is quite obscure, and then compares it with one still in use in the Arctic, whose function is known, it is very tempting to interpret the ancient tool as having been used for the same purpose. This is ethnoarchaeology. I wrote a chapter on this in my *Invitation* book (114, chapter 6); the subtitle of this was 'how to avoid boring holidays'; the idea was that now we all travel widely in Europe and beyond, a great deal can be learnt by merely looking and photographing, about how people and how things work — an antidote to basking on

88 Sitia, Crete, 1976; morality picture (see text)

the beach in the sun, which can be done in a million identical places wherever there is a coast and a warm climate.

My own travels have been very educational to me as an archaeologist. Only in one case was this undertaken deliberately as archaeological research — ten weeks spent in Crete and the Cyclades looking at mill sites, in a term of study leave in 1976. Other trips have been more in the way of holidays, but we have never failed to find not only 'ruins', but ways of living and doing that have long been extinct in north-west Europe; one problem has been that this generated not only thousands of photographs and slides, but mountains of paper, and pottery and other objects which decorate every shelf and fill every space in the house.

Apart from Spain, where for a few years we owned a house, we have rarely gone to the same place twice. We are not great travellers, such as the ever-increasing hordes who get to all parts of the world; but we have been to all the southern Scandinavian countries, Holland, France, Italy, Russia, Bulgaria, Israel, Egypt, Turkey, Greece (especially her very diverse islands), Yugoslavia, Tunisia, Morocco, Portugal, Malta, the Canaries and Madeira. Some of these places were visited on cruises; not, I hasten to say, as a paying passenger, but as a lecturer-in-residence on the P&O Princess (see chapter 14).

This was itself an ethnographic experience, studying the behaviour of rich Americans abroad. One does not need money, language or expertise to do ethno-archaeology: just eyes, ears and a camera. Some of the photographs are included below.

89 Spain, the ideal family (see text)

One also sees strange things nearer home, in semi-distant places like Orkney, Ireland and the Scillies. The latter is a candidate for the lost civilisation of Atlantis, and one can still see examples of the great sculpture of the giants who lived there (**87**).

One final example of ethnoarchaeology, as it is related to modern society, is the role of pictures in attempts at moralisation, by state or society. My first example (**88**) is a picture hung on the walls of a rather run-down taverna in Crete seen in 1976, one of several similar around the walls, and doubtless commoner everywhere in the earlier decades of the century; presumably they were supplied by the state to try to improve public attitudes. The picture shows two men; the one on the left is living in a derelict house, with a paraffin lamp, plaster is falling off the walls, and unpaid bills are on the floor, and he is down-at-heel, with no tie, thin, and highly distraught. The message here is clearly 'this man is unsuccessful, and it's his own fault'. On the right, however, is a very different character: a well-fed, well-dressed man (with tie) in a well-maintained house, lit by electricity, with books, telephone and 'vases'. This was clearly the ideal to be aimed at. But oddly, half-a-century or more later, he would be the villain, the Maxwell, the mobster, the worst product of a capitalist economy, while his poor companion would be the goal of social reform.

My second example (**89**), from recent times, is a type of postcard that can be bought which exemplifies the ideal family to which all should aspire — the prosperous man, the heavily-made-up wife with a henna-blond wig, and two arch children. Who buys such postcards and who do they send them to?

I will end this chapter with an account of our most extended tour, to Crete and the Cyclades. It illustrates how one *does* ethnography as part of one's travel.

Lorna Watts and I spent ten weeks in April-June 1976 on this trip. I had been given study leave from Birmingham for the whole term. We had been told by Anthony Bryer, the Byzantinist at Birmingham, that there were horizontal-wheeled mills in Crete; we had become interested in this technology in attempting to interpret the ninth-century mill we had excavated at Tamworth in 1971 (see chapter 6) (153).

We did not have enough money to travel in style; everything had to be done as cheaply as possible; the entire cost for the ten weeks was under £500 for both of us. The first economy was to go on what was then called the Magic Bus, a cowboy outfit operating between London Victoria and Athens; I believe it was £24 return. It left Victoria at 9am on a Saturday and arrived at Athens at 4pm on Monday. At Victoria there was chaos, with Greeks returning home for Easter, laden with enormous packages; the driver refused to take these, which led to fierce altercation and delay. The trip, right across Europe, was non-stop except for short breaks to grab food and go to the lavatory; or tumbling out of the bus in some remote spot where there was a water-tap and bushes. There were two drivers; one was supposed to rest while the other drove, but this was not taken very seriously.

It was uncomfortable, but the long transect across western Europe, the Alpine passes, Yugoslavia and northern Greece were memorable. On arrival at Athens, we had a taxi from the bus terminal to Piraeus and caught the night boat to Crete, arriving there at breakfast time. For most of our travel, we camped in a small lightweight tent; or had a village room, still very cheap at that time.

Our point of entry was Heraklion, where having 'done' the museum, we embarked on another bus to the south coast, where it was warmer in April. Crete is a big island, 114 miles long, and we had no expectation of being able to see it all. We fell in with what would nowadays be called 'travellers' who guided us to a superb beach named Como not far from the famous hippy cave-dwellers of Matala.

Here was a remarkable sociological phenomenon, a naturist beach community of a dozen or two people of various nationalities presided over by a 'patron', a bearded German and his partner. They lived in a cave which had been utilised as a German gun-emplacement during the occupation of Crete in the latter part of the 1939-45 war. They lived by selling pictures in Germany, to which they returned for a month each winter. Everyone else camped; the nearest shop and taverna was at Pitsidia, about 2 miles away; the beach itself was hardly visited by tourists, and gave superb bathing on sand, and a free pitch for our tent.

Some of the community earned a little money by offering casual labour to local farmers. One of the latter visited the beach frequently; not however with his wife, but to see all the naked girls. He also played the traditional Greek role of conspicuous hospitality, bringing a barrel of retsina, bread, and half a lamb for a beach barbecue, in which everybody joined.

We stayed at Como for three weeks, using it as a base for travelling round that part of Crete. We moved by local bus, walked, or hitchhiked. We hit on an ingenious way of getting to remote areas: having successfully got a hitch from some American couple

90 Storage jars at Knossos

wealthy enough to hire a car, we successfully persuaded them that where we wanted to go was far more interesting than where they had intended to go when they set out. On arrival at our chosen spot, we gave them a 'horses-mouth' exposition of why we wanted to go there; they were duly impressed, and sometimes asked if they could pick us up the next day.

In this way we visited the standard 'ancient monuments' of both Minoan and classical date, admiring the large storage jars at Knossos (**90**); or the singularly beautiful mountainous sites of Greco-Roman towns, such as Lato; and we managed to do the great walk down the gorge at Samaria (**91**); at one point one has (at this spring time of year) to wade the river as it passes between 400m cliffs in a 4m channel.

A German visiting Como invited us to join a party venturing into the high mountains above Festos, still snow-capped in April; he had a large passenger-carrying truck. The first night, on the way up, we had a feast of rabbit, Greek salad and retsina at a remote village, and spent the warm night in a field in the open, under a tree, in which a nightingale sang till dawn.

We visited the great cave of Ida which has yielded a hugh haul of Greek and earlier votive offerings; it was believed to be the entry to the underworld, the Kingdom of Hades.

We spent a night on an upland plain (**92**) just below the snow line. Here was a remarkable economy, with ethnographic overtones. Around the rim of the plain were little stone-built farms, consisting of no more than a single living chamber and a corral for a few dozen sheep and goats. Each day the shepherd and his 'lad' led them on well-marked

91 The narrowest part of Samaria Gorge in Spring

routes around the plain, milking them twice a day. The milk was processed into cakes of the famous soft cheese known as 'mesithera', by heating the milk in pans. Every Saturday morning the shepherd took his cheese down the steep descent to the market town of Mires (a feast of marketing ethnography), where he bought sardines, bread, wine and cigarettes to supplement the mountain diet of lamb or goat.

The heat was provided by bottled gas, brought up to the plain each week by lorry. Originally the shepherds would have used wood for burning, but the area had long been stripped of trees; apart from the gas, the scene had probably looked similar for hundreds if not thousands of years.

As the season advanced into May and June, the snow receded, uncovering higher and higher small farms, and new pasture for the animals. One drawback of such ethnographic experiences is the need to partake of local customs. On our arrival on the plain we were greeted warmly by a hoary old Cretan shepherd; he demonstrated his hospitality by offering us a drink of warm sheep's milk, and a slice of a smoking sheep's heart. He was very taken with the blonde Lorna, and tried to lure her away from the party; doubtless she would have provided a welcome change from sheep.

All this was, of course, only a summer activity. In the winter the shepherds and their lads returned to their wives and families, to while away the cold months at their local taverna.

Mires was also memorable in that we were witness to a total eclipse of the sun in May 1976. Not a lot of interest was taken by the locals, but everything went strangely dark and

92 Upland plain with shepherds' hut, Crete

dead; even the birds stopped singing; and everyday bustle virtually stopped in a great atmosphere of depression until the sun returned.

The kinds of ethnography I have described in earlier pages were very frequent: there were numerous examples of threshing floors (**93**) and of the no-longer-used *tribulum* or threshing sledge studded with flints, in remote farms; but also, cleaned up, for sale in tourist traps. The pastoral shepherd sleeping in the midday heat was still a common sight, again of great antiquity. Hand-mills were still in use in 1976 in villages, even though the onlooking lads ate commercial ice cream.

93 Threshing floor, Crete, 1976

In the churches were many votive offerings, mostly with small plaques of metal with an embossed depiction of the whole person, or an organ, such as a heart. They were offered either in hope of a cure, or as thanks for one. They can still be bought in drapers' shops; and (sadly enough) also in tourist centres as souvenirs.

Crete has a very thorny scrub, hence the traditional garb of the older men, the stout boots, leggings and clothing of the traditional Cretan 'warrior', who played a prominent part in the Battle of Crete in 1944. A further reminder of that disastrous episode (for the British) was a visit to the port of Chora Sfakion, from where much of the British army were evacuated by destroyers in the nick of time, before the Germans could cross the mountains from the north coast. In a village near the town of Castelli in the north-west of the island, there was (and probably still is) a clock in the square, with four clock-faces. Three indicated the correct time, the fourth was set permanently at 4.50pm. We were told that this was the time when the entire male population was mowed down as a German reprisal for the murder of one of their soldiers; the clock-face was stopped permanently. In that area there were still at that time tavernas that would not serve Germans, so bitter were the memories of thirty years before.

We left Como under rather unhappy circumstances. The German couple in the cave were expecting a baby, which they intended to have baptised by the local priest; they were very integrated into local society. One day, however, on returning we saw them being helped up the cliff-top; she had (or threatened to have) a miscarriage, and was being taken to Heraklion hospital; it was time to leave.

One postscript to Como; it was not only a beach, but (unknown to us at the time) on the verge of a well-known Minoan site. In recent years, Professor Peter Warren of the University of Bristol carried out a major excavation there; but refused to start until the Greek police expelled all the naturists; a sad end to an idyll.

We now embarked more seriously on our 'research' on mills. Local enquiry directed us (usually by a very old American-speaking returned emigrant) to a ruin, and we soon recognised the characteristic shape of the horizontal-wheeled mills: a stream or mill-pond fed water into a narrow channel on top of a tower (**94**) (sometimes two, operating in parallel); a little barrier of sticks prevented branches and other debris from fouling the wheel. The water descended into a circular 'sink' at the end of the channel, and dropped several metres down a chimney, into a wheel-house far below; here, with considerable force from the drop, the water passed through an angled pipe, and was directed onto the paddles of a wheel, one after another, causing it to rotate, gradually accelerating to *c*.60-120 revolutions a minute. A shaft in the centre of the wheel extended upwards through a (waterproof) floor, through the centre of the lower (stationary) of a pair of mill-stones in the mill-house above, turning the upper stone one revolution for each revolution of the wheel below, there being no gearing. Above the millstone assembly and its housing was a 'hopper' filled with grain; from this, grain was fed through a wooden 'shoe' into the central aperture of the upper stone (helped by an ingenious device, the miller's 'damsel', vibrating by bouncing on the upper stone). The grain then found its way between the two stones to emerge as flour through a spout into a collecting box.

The majority of the fifty or so mills we recorded (see 96) and photographed in various parts of the island (probably about a quarter of the total) had been ruinous for several decades. Part of American post-war help to Crete took the form of modern diesel-powered mills, which now produce most of the flour needed.

The ruined mills, of sixteenth- to

94 Water-mill: the top of the tower. The water runs along the channel, and disappears down the 'chimney' at the far end, descending at increasing velocity to strike the paddles of the mill-wheel far below; a small gate traps floating debris

95 Horizontal mill-wheel in wheel-house below abandoned mill, Crete

nineteenth-century date, were useful in providing us with much basic data on the type, to help us understand the Tamworth mill of a thousand years before (153). Crawling into the overgrown wheelhouse, sometimes through water overhung with orange trees, located the decayed wheel (**95**); and in the mill-house were remains of some of the hoppers and mill-stone housings; and sometimes the lifting gear, a giant pair of callipers, to enable the stones to be lifted out and 'dressed' to keep them 'sharp'.

We were, however, extremely lucky to find two mills which were still working; where the water supply was so abundant that it would have been folly to substitute a fossil-fuel power source. One was in the east in the village of Zakros above the famous Minoan site. Here the mill-structure was modern, being made of concrete; and although clearly a working establishment, we could find no one to show us round. The second was, however, all we hoped for. This was at Zaros, near Festos. We had been tipped off that there was an active mill there, driven by a powerful stream coming down from the mountain. As we drove up the road (another hitch-hijack) there was the mill, with water gushing out of its outlet, and a price-list pinned on the wall; this showed the price per kilo in *leptera* for milling different kinds of grain (varying from animal feed to fine flour).

Here was the whole shebang. Inside the mill was one room in which was the whole milling assembly, hopper, millstones and flour-bin. Close by were all the maintenance tools neatly arranged. There was also a raised store at one end (with a prominent cat to keep the rodents at bay); and at the other end the living area of the miller and his family — a chair hung on the wall, bed, fireplace and cooking area.

184

We were able to talk to the miller with the aid of a friendly interpreter. He explained that he was a full-time miller in the sense that he served Zaros and other local villages, who brought their grain to him by donkey; but he also had a dozen hens, a vegetable garden, and a small vineyard. He explained that the principal expense was that of the millstones. They cost (in 1973) *c.*£140 per pair, and lasted only 4-5 years. He stopped the mill by operating a lever which controlled a baffle which was drawn across the water-jet in the wheelhouse below. He started the mill by withdrawing this, and there ensured a very satisfying roaring, whirring noise, and a slight smell of friction 'burning'. In the floor was a spherical metal ball sealing a hole, through which the miller could look down into the wheelhouse. I innocently asked if I could look; a slight smile crossed his face as I lifted the ball and got a very wet face — there was quite a maelstrom below.

While we were there, a lad from a nearby village came with a donkey to collect his flour, the miller loading the sack for him.

We now had a thorough understanding of this type of mill, at least in Crete, and this was reinforced by later travels (see earlier pages).

After eight weeks in Crete we moved on, fairly tired after our journeying in what is a 'strong' country, as regards the heat, wind, colour and people. We took a boat to Mykonos — an island not of water but of windmills. Here we relaxed for a few days; we were intrigued to be told that beyond the popular Paradise Beach there were three more, reached by walking or small boat hops. The first was, we were told, a mixed naturist beach, the second for gay men, and the third for gay ladies. We thought this must be folklore, but when we reached them, it was even more explicit than we had been led to understand in terms of beach behaviour. We spent a fine couple of days camping behind the first beach.

We also took a boat from there to the incredible island of Delos, then (and hopefully still) very carefully preserved from tourist development, with its wealth of monuments of Greco-Roman times — one of the greatest ancient sanctuaries in Europe. Since this autobiography is not a guidebook, I restrict myself here to a picture of me with one of the ancient ladies (or part of one) (**96**).

Our final move was to Santorini or Thera, the site of a gigantic volcanic explosion in prehistoric times. The village is set on the rim of a huge sea-filled crater. There has been an enormous amount written on the archaeological implications of this great explosion, in particular the extent to which it was related to the destruction of the Minoan civilisation and the rise of the Mycenean; there have been fierce arguments about the date of the Thera disaster and the precise chronology of the associated east Mediterranean chronologies (and the Egyptian dating to which they are linked).

A spanner has recently been cast into these works by Professor Mike Baillie of Belfast, one of Britain's leading tree-ring-dating experts (see also chapter 9). He believes that his studies, coupled with data from polar ice-cores point to 1628 BC as the date of the explosion, a date not currently acceptable to the traditional authorities on Mediterranean archaeology. He goes further in postulating that the height to which the debris ascended made it visible from the Nile delta in Egypt; and, startlingly, it could be linked to the Biblical myth of the Exodus, the erupting volcano being 'the pillar of cloud by day, and the pillar of fire by night' — the guide to the Israelites (Baillie 1999). Baillie thus ventured into

96 PAR with female statue, Delos, 1976

three hornets' nests at one stroke: those of Mediterranean, Egyptian and Biblical chronologies; he is currently being badly stung.

We visited the more direct result of this or associated eruptions, the amazingly-preserved Minoan town of Akrotiri, where houses were found with two or three stories intact, under metres of volcanic debris. The Greek excavator, Professor Marinatos, was killed when he stumbled over one of the walls he had uncovered, and now he is buried in a grave dug in one of the rooms (**97**).

*97 The grave of Professor Marinatos, in a room of the house he excavated in the Minoan ruins of
Akrotiri, Santorini (or Thera), Greece; tended with red roses*

We finally returned to Athens for our return trip to England. A last night here was
enlivened by a display of street rioting and military reprisal, our first (and hopefully our
last) experience of the stench of burning rubbish and tear gas; we were glad to escape the
next morning, when our Magic Bus left without further incident. Well nearly — our two
drivers could not find their way out of Athens, and were clearly the worse for alcohol. On
the way north through Yugoslavia, they took the rest/drive rule even less seriously than on
the way out; one driving while the other sat by his side, swigging Greek brandy. I found
myself in the uncharacteristic role of getting up and haranguing the other passengers
about the danger the drivers were putting us in, on this extremely dangerous 'motorway';
until we all protested so violently that the drivers were abashed. We got back to London,
and Birmingham, safely, very fit and stimulated by a great journey.

12 Getting into print:
writing, drawing and publication

When I began archaeology, it seemed obvious that there was no point in just digging things up if one didn't make a record of all that had been done and found and make it available by publication in some form. I had as a model the great volumes of General Pitt-Rivers in the later nineteenth century, in which he published literally everything — every sherd, bone and nail — setting an important maxim that the more ordinary and common a find was, the more likely was it to illuminate the history of the site. Few followed him in this, however; the importance of some publication was accepted in the 1950s, and emphasised in the 'bibles' I had relied on, Richard Atkinson's *Field Archaeology* and in Mortimer Wheeler's *Archaeology from the Earth*.

But no one any longer believed in the publication of such detail as that in Pitt-Rivers. I remember being told in the 1950s by the fine archaeologist Philip Corder: 'one important thing to remember on Roman sites: don't treat the pottery as finds' — by which he meant there was too much of it, and only those pieces should be published which were crucial to the stratigraphic and structural interpretation.

As I have already stressed, I had to learn how to write up digs to survive as a professional archaeologist, and it was my abilities in this field among others which led to an academic career. By the time I was appointed to a post in Birmingham, I had written over 20 reports.

I had also realised that there was a widespread lack of knowledge of just how to set about the writing. This was not true of the leading figures in the subject — their shortcomings were more culpable — but among the hundreds of amateurs, some of whom were students in extra-mural evening classes.

In Bristol, Alan Warhurst, Leslie Grinsell and myself began to give classes to help amateurs to write up their digs, following in Graham Webster's footsteps. In 1962 we made our lectures available in a book, which went through four revised editions (19, 28, 32, 59). The final version fortunately included a chapter I wrote, on the future of archaeological publication, which presaged the major changes that are now taking place (see below).

The book was influential and useful to those who were ready to follow its advice. The only rather quizzical review was by one of Britain's greatest but least-known archaeologists, Brian Hope-Taylor. To him the compilation of an archaeological report was a work of art; and to him we had reduced this to the level of 'How to write a business letter'.

In the second half of this century, the amount of archaeology being done vastly increased, principally because of the accelerating pace of destruction in the 1960s onwards; with a corresponding volume of data. It began to be questioned whether all these data were really of any use (*contra* Pitt-Rivers), or whether we should begin to be selective (a potentially dangerous approach!).

Moreover, however assiduous archaeologists were in ordering data, there were increasing problems in persuading editors of journals to publish them. This was made especially acute by the fact that, in Britain especially, many of the media were local or county journals. Their readers were increasingly irritated by the boring detail being put in; so editors were under pressure to reject it.

As a tyro in archaeology, I tended to publish as near to a total record as was possible, since I was in no position in earlier years to decide what was 'important' and what was not. What seemed irrelevant in the 1960s and 1970s to the then generation of scholars may well be crucial to later workers with different theoretical approaches. Some of my publications (such as the first monograph on Deerhurst) (73) were criticised for their excessive detail.

Even with a site as important as Cheddar, where I believed (and still do) that every detail and find were crucial in assessing interpretation, I had difficulty in getting it published. It was turned down by the then Department of the Environment (formerly MOPBW who had paid for the excavation!), by Phillimores, by Leicester University Press, and by Bristol Museum. No one ever insinuated that there was anything wrong with it; it was just too big (411pp). Eventually it was accepted by *British Archaeological Reports* (BAR); for this, Sue Hirst and I were able to design it to some extent: BAR merely mass-produced it in facsimile and marketed it (87).

Another problem that has been getting worse in recent years has been the increasing pressure on university archaeologists not only to do more intensive teaching, but to do research, and publish it. They have inadequate time to read in detail even monographs and articles that are germane to their own special fields of study. Few people actually read or study the vastly increasing number of volumes that have resulted from the major expansion in British archaeology, let alone relevant material from all parts of the world.

Not many copies of the more technical kinds of reports are produced, usually no more than 300-500 in Britain, and even these are difficult to sell, and are hardly read, except superficially — unless the reader has some special interest in the subject. It was therefore a matter of some gratification to me to find that one person at least had not only read *Cheddar*, but studied it in detail, and even gone back to the finds in Taunton Museum. This was John Blair, a medieval historian in Oxford who is equally at home in archaeology. He did so in pursuance of a hypothesis concerning the relationship at Cheddar between the palace and the Minster surviving as St Andrews Church, where we had also done some digging (36, 54). Part of his argument (Blair 1996) was that my published chronology was wrong — he wanted it all to go forward by some 50 years. He wrote to me about this; not surprisingly I did not agree with him, but I was very pleased that *someone* had read *Cheddar*, and opened up a debate. Dialectics of this kind are very desirable in archaeology. Radical differences of opinion were expressed in the York Minster volume (cf 170) and in our paper on the Kirkdale inscription (174).

Reactions to the problems of the dissemination of data have been varied. The first, in the 1970s, was to formalise different levels or qualities of data; the highest to be printed, the lower ones to be in microfiche or in an archive. The latter would be deposited in two or three major institutions such as the National Monuments Record (NMR) and copies could be made available. Microfiche, however, needed a special reader, and few people had or used them; librarians hated microfiches, because they were loose in a pocket at the back of the volume.

Increasingly, therefore, there has developed a tendency to publish only the synthesis and interpretation, backed up by only those data which are directly relevant — again a procedure inimical to scholarship. In the case of Deerhurst (172) we again published much detail, but there was no microfiche. An indexed archive (of which two copies are available) is several times larger than the published book.

But now there is a curious reversal of this. Electronic publication, on CD-ROM, DVD-ROM or the Internet, has again allowed full 'publication' of all data, but in successive levels, but now under the control of the user. He/she can now call up data at any level at the touch of a button. Landscape to site, site to building plan, plan to posthole, posthole to finds in three dimensions: in colour if one has the gigabytes! Clearly by 2010, electronic archaeology will be easily available. As in all fields the book will become rarer (especially when one can browse on a laptop in the train!). It may be that the printed volume will become only a menu — an index to the electronic data, and a guide to its efficient study.

This mode does not appeal to me at present — I'm not of a generation to gaze at screens, and like the feel of a book and the smell of printed paper. But I am excited by the realisation that I can (theoretically) *talk* to a computer, see my words on the screen, and print them out. This should speed up my output, at present done in longhand.

The other aspect of publication is *illustration*. My photographic experience has been useful in producing half-tone and colour pictures of the actual dig and finds, but graphics require different skills. As I indicated earlier in this book, my early efforts at drawing sections and plans were somewhat abysmal. In earlier decades, many archaeologists did their own drawings, which expressed their own personal viewpoint and emphasis. This was true of Wheeler, who had had training in graphics, and also of Brian Hope-Taylor, who was a commercial artist before becoming an archaeologist. The tradition was carried on by Barry Cunliffe and Mick Aston; and I have also followed Wheeler in preferring to do my own drawings. One also develops a style which is instantly recognisable, even where I have not put PAR 19— in the lower right-hand corner.

In recent decades, however, few archaeologists have done this; partly from a trend to de-personalisation — a more 'objective, scientific' approach (reducing the personal equation); and partly from pressure of work and the scale of the enterprise. Draft sketches are passed on to a 'draughtsperson', who then (in consultant with the archaeologist) produces neat drawings for publication. The result is a dull uniformity applied to any excavation, anywhere, of any period. The dreary appearance of many modern drawings is further exacerbated by the use of applied transfer 'tones' (shading, stipple, symbols, etc.) rather than doing them all lovingly by hand. If I had a pound (or Euro) for every dot I have done in stippling, I'd be a rich man.

Lettering, design and dynamic are things that I had to learn by long experience. Nasty hand-lettering gave way to tedious tracing of alphabets. Then transfer-lettering, which you will see on earlier drawings: this was elegant but expensive, and transfer lettering sheets have a habit of using up particular letters, making the remaining 90% useless. So I ended up with a range of stencils, not so attractive, but clear and efficient and coming in a variety of sizes, and in upright and italic (I like the latter best).

The basic drawings for the site record are plans and sections. The former are either plans of stages of the excavation, or of phases of activity worked out after later analysis; or both.

There are basically two approaches to section drawing (of an exposed face of stratification). One is to make a drawing that clarifies what is visible, either in terms of the recording of the contexts that comprise the units of stratification, or of the interpretation of the sequence in terms of phasing or historical events (or a combination of both). The other is to attempt to portray the section as it actually looked in the ground. The first approach is exemplified by Wheeler's drawings, the second famously by those of Gerhard Bersu.

My own view is that the Bersu-type pictorialism is now better achieved by colour photography with colour-chart control; I have thus gravitated to the Wheeler approach; but where appropriate in two-stage drawings — one of the layers defined with their site coding and names, and the other with the interpretation — 'what it all means' (cf 172 for this applied to elevations of the church walls of Deerhurst; and for the combined illustration of sections).

A further more difficult stage is the pseudo-three-dimensional drawing — projections in isometric or axonometric modes. I had done very little of this until the compilation of Deerhurst, with suggested reconstructions of what the church had looked like in different periods.

I resurrected for this book two battered early reconstructions (**98 & 99**) I had done in the 1950s of the Pagans Hill temple, which perhaps fortunately never got published. They were interesting to dredge up, as they showed that even in those early days I was trying to marry the below-ground evidence with what had been above it, with a deity statue thrown in for good measure, to emphasise scale and function.

True three-dimensional drawings and pictorial 'artists' reconstructions' are rather beyond my talents. They are, however, of great importance in reaching out to a wider public; they have played an important role in *Time Team*.

One of the best of these archaeological artists was the late Alan Sorrell. He produced those for Cheddar (87). He came to the site when we were digging, and walked around to make sketches from several points of view. He talked to me about the archaeology and what I thought the great halls were like, and what life was like in the palace area. His pictures do not often show the sunnier side of life in Roman forts or medieval abbeys. There is usually a dark storm approaching; miserable figures are wondering around bent double under loads of firewood or something. Smoke drifts out of chimneys or kitchens. I asked him why everybody looked so beaten down by the trials of life. 'That's the way I always feel myself' was the reply.

He sent me a sketch (**100**) of the main (tenth-century) palace complex, a first draft for that which he published in *The Illustrated London News* and in my final report (87). It shows

98 My first efforts at archaeological reconstruction drawings (1951) I: the temple as seen from the east

very well his method of working — a tentative attempt with marginal queries which we sorted out. I reproduce this here from the original; in some ways I find it more evocative than the final version. Attractive though such reconstructions are, they do fix an image in people's minds, and in this case become the standard image of what Cheddar looked like, echoing down through textbooks and museum displays. Again, one needs alternative with radical contrasts.

I have over the years adopted a particular relationship between text and illustrations, which has helped to make my reports as reader-friendly as an archaeological report can be (I'm not a Jean Auel!). This is to regard the graphics and photographs as the essential basis of the report, and to write the text (or at least the description and synthesis) as a commentary on the illustrations rather than use the latter to illustrate a dense text. Recent reports (eg. 172, 177) have a high ratio of graphics to text.

I must by now have done thousands of archaeological drawings. I enjoy the process; it satisfies whatever minimal need I have for artistic expression, and my desire to make my

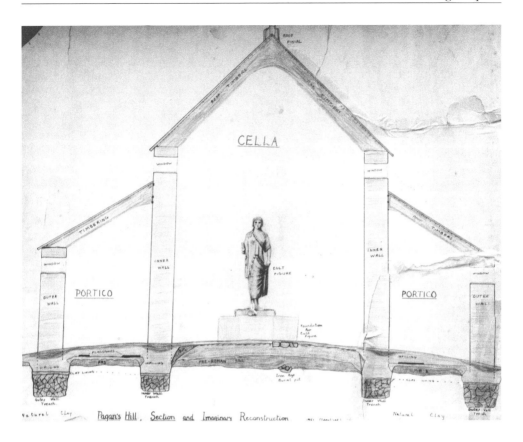

99 My first efforts at archaeological reconstruction drawings (1951) II: a section through the temple, with a cult statue (not Apollo!) and the below ground foundations

findings clear to the reader. So far, eyesight and steadiness of hand have not deserted me; and I have learnt how to master that most intractable instrument — the drawing pen!

It is thus satisfying to have written a report on a dig, or a piece of synthesis, review or comment; and to have persuaded an editor or publisher that it is worth putting into print. The first stage is often a referral of one's piece to an external peer-review; their comments are usually helpful, sometimes discouraging, and may lead to the need for revision.

If all goes well, the text and illustrations arrive at the printers. They vary a great deal in their willingness or ability to design and print a nice-looking page, and to cope adequately with complex line drawings and half-tones. Many of my drawings and photographs have been badly mauled in this way, by poor printing or over-reduction; in one case the printer made blocks from the xeroxes in my mock-up! One must anticipate the worst, and give the most comprehensive and didactic instructions.

In a later stage, the next pleasure is to get a set of proofs, which make one feel things are really moving. Their correction involves very careful proof-reading, and the spelling-out in elementary language of corrections to be made. Rarely does one's work finally appear with no errors; it takes a superb editor to achieve a perfect result.

100 Cheddar palace in the tenth century; preliminary sketch by Alan Sorrell. This served as a basis for discussion, in preparation for the final version published in Illustrated London News

It is another good moment when the published version arrives, followed by offprints of one's piece. This is very good for the ego; the offprints are sent round to one's friends and colleagues, to try (usually unsuccessfully) to impress them.

There the matter rests for a year or two, when (in the case of a book) reviews begin to appear. This can be devastating if they are critical, severely damaging the author's ego and reputation. Or again very uplifting to one's self-esteem if they are good, in direct ratio to *how* good. One's eyes are brightened by such words and phrases as: 'epoch-making', 'major contribution', 'significant advance', 'couldn't put it down', or rather less by 'readable', 'thorough', 'detailed'; or financially promising: 'I shall recommend this to all my students', or 'include it in my reading lists'.

Invitation to Archaeology (150) elicited a varied response: 'archaeologists can make infantile laboured jokes as well as anyone . . .' (*Yorkshire Archaeological Journal*); 'nostalgic, sentimental, garrulous, anecdotal, prejudiced and inaccurate (quoting from my own introduction to the book) — all of these'! (Tom Hassall); 'most honest and unpompous account of what archaeology is all about . . .' (Henry Cleere).

When this phase has passed, the work passes into obscurity. Few people will have read it thoroughly. It periodically becomes a quarry for synthesisers and research students. Its ultimate fate will depend on its intrinsic importance and changing fashion. One may judge how useful a piece is by the number of occasions on which it is cited in other writers' books; and over how many years. A few of my productions have passed this test: *Invitation to Archaeology* (150), *Cheddar* (87), *Tamworth Watermill* (153), *The End of Roman Temples* (88) and *Late Roman Cemeteries* (82).

They do, however, continue to be of interest to the author, especially in a retrospect such as this; sitting in metres of shelfspace as silent witness of a large amount of work.

13 Other archaeologists, countries and institutions

I have mentioned other archaeologists earlier in this book where they have been directly related to my work; and I have indicated in the acknowledgements those to whom I owe a special debt. In my career I have been aware of, or influenced by, many others; it may be of interest to consider how the archaeological establishment has appeared to me at various points in my life.

As a beginner, I was given by Ernest Greenfield a copy of Richard Atkinson's *Field Archaeology*, which became my handbook; I did not realise it at the time that Atkinson was only 24 when he wrote this, and was in fact a near contemporary. We encountered each other at infrequent intervals; I visited his excavation at Stonehenge (where he was working with Stuart Piggott) and was duly impressed by the sight of big machines moving big stones on a world-famous monument. He seemed an important man; his book on Stonehenge appeared to me to be wholly authoritative.

The archaeological world was however rather shocked at his treatment of another world-famous site, the unique mound of Silbury Hill. He used coal-mining machinery and personnel to tunnel in from the side, to locate any central feature which might enlighten us to the function of this remarkable monument. The work was paid for by the BBC, who used it as the basis for some rather good TV programmes which have not since seen the light of the screen. Important data were recovered on such matters as environmental conditions and preservation within the mound, and some understanding of how it was built: but it was not exactly compulsive viewing for the couch potatoes.

The results of the excavations at Stonehenge, Silbury and other places were slow to get into print. The reason he gave was that he had become too heavily involved in university administration to write up his sites; even though in his book he had stressed the absolute duty of doing so: an injunction which I took very much to heart.

Much later, I was a member of a committee chaired by him to further the progress towards publication of Derek Philipps' epic excavations under York Minster (170). It was clear by this time that he was not well, and he died in 1994.

The records of his excavations were passed to others to work up: notably in the case of Stonehenge to English Heritage, resulting in a fine book on this world heritage site.

In the light of my own experience of Atkinson and his status in the archaeological hierarchy, it was a shock to read in the *Archaeological Journal* 153 (1996) what must be one of the most damning review articles ever written by one archaeologist about another, by Professor Anthony Harding. It concerned the English Heritage *Stonehenge* book, and while giving this the highest praise, it opened the lid of a whole can of worms. Atkinson's book on Stonehenge appears retrospectively to have been at least partly fabrication; many records of the work were missing, either never made or lost. Harding even used the adjectives 'criminal' and 'immoral'. How was my mighty exemplar fallen!

In the course of reading I had become too a great admirer of General Pitt-Rivers, the founder of modern scientific archaeology; he seemed to embody all the proper ways of approaching a site with the right questions, of causing it to be dug skilfully with splendid records (though the excavation was not of the quality we'd expect today), and he published at length and promptly. In 1958 I came to even closer grips with him, in re-excavating part of a site where he had mounted a great campaign, Bokerley Dyke. This was to do with a road-widening operation. I dug trenches either side of his, but found that my observations did not agree with his; notably in the depth of a rather important ditch (27); the difference was no mean one — between his 5ft (1.5m) and my 11ft (3.5m). So I actually dug out his spoil, and found he had (or his site recorder) had indeed nodded. Moreover, the spoil was dense in potsherds and bone, which rather made nonsense of the statistics in his famous 'Relic Tables'. More recently, I have had occasion to redraw and reinterpret the very first section he ever drew, at Danes Dyke in East Yorkshire (182); his Neolithic dating for that great earthwork is not now generally accepted, but it is not easy to dismiss his careful recording and percipient observations — he may be right!

Early in my career in Somerset, I met his 'Secretary', Harold St George Gray, then Curator of Taunton Castle Museum. Although he had worked closely with the General, he should have carried on the torch in his series of excavations in Somerset, but didn't. Especially was his work poor (and worsening with time) on the Glastonbury 'Lake Village'; and he was rude to me, as a beginner, when I approached him for advice.

Bokerley Dyke also gave me an introduction to another great scholar of the past generation, Christopher Hawkes. He had reinterpreted this earthwork; he was able to do so wholly on the basis of the General's recording, and on his own surface observation and re-examination of key finds; his was a classic study. Again however I had the temerity to disagree with him on the dating and interpretation of the sequence. I felt nervous about doing so with my limited knowledge; but I did so, and sent him a copy of what I had written. He was at that time acting as finds assistant to his wife, the late Sonia Hawkes, on an Iron Age excavation at Longbridge Deverill Cow Down in Wiltshire. He asked me to go and see him there, a frightening prospect, since he had a reputation for being highly irascible. It was a great relief, and an encouragement to me, when he came running out of the finds shed to welcome me with the words 'That's right, my boy!'.

The giant of that generation was of course Sir Mortimer Wheeler, who laid the foundations of the popularity of archaeology on television. It seems superfluous to add anything to the mass of material written about him, and by him. My first real contact was with him on the Cadbury Castle Committee of which he was the dynamic chairman; though over 80, he was still active at leaping in and out of Leslie Alcock's Land Rover and was still a power in the land, although having the nickname of 'Flash Harry', because of his flamboyant lifestyle. One anecdote will suffice. About 1969 I was met at Euston by Sue Hirst. As we came up the platform to the exit, she pointed to an impressive figure, in a long trenchcoat, standing static, waiting for the same train. 'WHO IS THAT!' she asked. 'That, Sue, is Mortimer Wheeler'. As we watched, a gorgeous girl arrived, and was swept into his arms and into a waiting taxi.

101   Martin Biddle and the late Harold Taylor using a pneumatic drill on concrete at Repton, 1974

It is perhaps not customary to talk about one's contemporaries who are still alive, but (as Wheeler said when asked how he'd cope with the heat in India), 'I propose to ignore it'.

Each generation throws up a few great practitioners of their art, whether in literature, music or archaeology. Are they really far above their fellow archaeologists in the quality of their minds and work? It is currently, in 1998, difficult to assess those in Britain under 40, but I would single out in the generation below mine (there are not many of my generation because of the 1939-45 war) four who seem to me to be quite exceptional, as polymaths who have had a major influence in more than one specialised field of archaeology — Colin Renfrew, Martin Biddle, Barry Cunliffe and Martin Carver.

Of these, Renfrew is the one with whom I have had least personal contact; I can only admire the way in which he has immediately seized on every opportunity (such as the advent of radiocarbon dating) to draw out universal significance; and to promote both research and academic archaeology in a very effective way.

Martin Biddle I know better. I was very impressed by the breadth of his approach to Winchester, Nonsuch Palace, and St Albans. That these remain unpublished is no criticism of his capacity (with his wife Birthe) to work unrelentingly and effectively, but to the enormous scale of his enterprises, and to the lack of vision of those who could have provided him with the resources he deserves and needs.

Biddle is a brilliant lecturer, and it is unfortunate that he had never held the kind of university post where he could have influenced and inspired a whole generation of

102 *PAR at the bottom of the Viking ditch at Repton, 1976; note rope to reach me if sides collapsed*

undergraduates. That he has not done so is due at least partly to his uncompromising insistence in upholding the highest ethical values in the practice and publication of archaeology. This led to a disastrous involvement in American academic life, where he found himself battling with major corruption (or so it appeared to English eyes).

When he decided to dig at Repton (Derbyshire) (**101**), a site central to the Anglo-Saxon history and archaeology of Mercia, I was interested in the project sufficiently to enrol as a volunteer for the first three seasons in the early 1970s. My personal digging technique was not up to Biddle standards, but one episode is worth recounting. The then-young Mark Horton and I had been excavating together in an area where all features seemed to be sinking. We realised it was a ditch we'd encountered. Our part of the dig got so deep that when I was down at the bottom a rope was tied around my waist, so that if the sides collapsed (no shoring!) I could be dug out fast (**102**). When we did hit the

103 Group assembled on occasion of the presentation of Festschrift *to the late Gerald Dunning in 1974; left to right Kenneth Barton, John Hurst, ?, ?, Martin Biddle, Gerald Dunning (in academic robes), Barry Cunliffe, John Musty*

bottom, we could see we had, by great fortune, came down on a terminal, i.e. the end of the ditch ending short of the church. Biddle came to look, and straightaway realised that this was part of a Viking fortress known from history to have been at Repton in 878; the church being turned into a gatehouse. By that evening he had laid out the projected line of the fortress ditch in white tape and gave a public lecture on it to a crowd of visitors. In later years I visited but didn't help; his excavation in the vicarage garden was the most skilful dig I've ever seen.

Barry Cunliffe (**103**), though also an upholder of the highest standards, has been more successful in academic life, not by compromising, but by an extraordinary gift of getting his own way without anybody realising they've been 'persuaded'. Like Biddle, he has dug sites ranging from prehistory to post-medieval, on a large scale and with great skill, but has been better at matching post-excavation funding to that spent in digging. His chairing of committees is legendary, deciding beforehand how the decisions should go, and steering them in that direction — a consummate art. He was chairman of the four-professor academic advisory board set up by Dover District Council to oversee the archaeology of Dover, and especially the creation of the White Cliffs Experience, a £13 million pound 'heritage' project; a board of which I was also a member.

He is a very hard worker. When he was professor at Southampton, he had a large house, with a large upstairs room in which he worked. As one entered, on the left, there were bags of unwashed pottery; further along were washed finds, then marked finds; then

104 The new and the old professors at York; PAR cutting the first sod at Sutton Hoo, 1986, with Martin Carver

drawings in various stages of finalisation; then drafts of the reports; and as one completed the circuit, galley proofs, page proofs and the finished books ready for distribution. This I witnessed myself (though I may have embroidered it a little). I was not however witness to another, perhaps apocryphal tale, told me by another; that while thus engaged, his wife called up the stairs 'Barry, lunch is ready' to which the reply came 'Send it up!'. His output of fine books is quite remarkable.

The final member of my invidious quartet, Martin Carver, is much better-known to me personally. I met him first in the late 1960s when he had forsaken an army career to do a postgraduate course at Durham. We clicked immediately, finding that our minds, tastes and ideas were very much on the same lines, as indeed were our psychological and personal histories. We became close colleagues in the 1970s in the Midlands where he

105   *The Sutton Hoo Research Committee, King's Manor, York, 1997; left to right, Leslie Webster,*
Martin Welch, PAR, Martin Carver, David Attenborough, John Cherry, Keith Wade,
Stanley West, Madeleine Hummler, John Knight, Annette Roe (Photo John Bateman,
Department of Archaeology)

played an important role in the coordination of rescue archaeology, and began to show some of the originality for which he has become well-known since, coupled with a clear and analytical approach to the subject.

When Sutton Hoo was set up (see p126), the final selection committee interviewed six people. We met in the pub afterwards to compare notes, looked at one another and simultaneously (again I am exaggerating) said 'It has got to be Martin Carver', so skilfully had he dazzled us with his rhetoric and his plan for a long campaign. This turned out to be his 'magnum opus' of a dig, an experience of a lifetime for all who worked there (**104**). The results were vastly in excess of what any of us had hoped; they have reached fruition in the volumes now published or now in the press (**105**).

A series of lectures on Sutton Hoo, in several countries, were equally brilliant, and won him many admirers in the archaeological world. When I retired, it was my personal opinion that he was the only person I would be happy to succeed me. Although I was not (as a matter of ethics) on the interviewing board, my opinion was sought, and I gave it. Again his persuasive manner won the day, notably his great enthusiasm for archaeology in all its manifestations (an increasingly rare attribute in time-serving professionals).

Rather to his annoyance, he quite liked the way I had set up the York degree course (see p120), as he would in some ways have enjoyed creating a wholly original framework; but since we thought very much alike, a number of my courses have survived to this day. He has been a great teacher and leader, if sometimes a trial to his colleagues (in his more mercurial moments), and a terror to other York archaeologists. He has become well-known for his books on archaeological strategy, evaluation and especially the archaeology of towns. A major undertaking was the editing of York Minster; I have dwelt on his skills in my review article (170).

Those four are my choice; it would be interesting to know which quartet others would choose. I could do a further league table of at least 50 archaeologists who I have had reason to admire in the last 50 years, for particular reasons connected with the development of theory, skilful synthesis, excavation skills, draughtsmanship or just sheer enthusiasm; but it would be invidious to list them, and some are too close in friendship or affection to be able to give an impartial 'rating'. Suffice to say, there are many who have inspired me and given me enormous enjoyment, and who have furthered the discipline in Britain since the 1939-45 war, and made it the envy of archaeologists in other countries. To them I offer thanks.

Other Institutions

Apart from my contacts with other archaeologists, I have had some contact with other institutions. My links with the CBA I shall describe more fully later. I have had, however, only limited contact with other institutions in Britain, both academic and practical.

As I explained in relation to Birmingham, I knew little about other universities or how they worked. The most I ever saw of them was when I lectured to their undergraduate societies. On taking up the appointment at York, however (see below), I had to have some yardstick to aim for; so in 1978 I made a tour of those that I had some reason to believe were the best models. I was hospitably received as the 'new boy'; impressed by much that I saw, but frightened by what I now realised lay ahead of me in designing a new degree.

My contact with other universities continued spasmodically with visits to colleagues; but my only chance of evaluating our York degree (apart from the opinions given by our own external examiners!) came when I was external examiner to University College, London, and Durham; both useful to me assessing quality and method, and in fact rather reassuring as far as York was concerned! There were also special occasions in being external examiner for postgraduate theses at Nottingham and Cambridge.

Apart from the CBA I have had little involvement with other institutions, not being London-based. I was elected as a Fellow of the Society of Antiquaries in 1965 and qualified as a member of the newly-developing professional association, the Institute of Field Archaeologists (the IFA). I gave the after-dinner speech to their first Annual Conference (Appendix D), and was later made an Honorary Life-Member. This class of membership is rare, numbering only six at present: Henry Cleere (formerly Director of the CBA), Graham Webster (my former mentor — see p81), my old friend Philip Barker, John Coles and Francis Pryor, and myself. The IFA is representative of a professionally-orientated world of archaeology which largely by-passed me.

106 Professor Wim Van Es, formerly Director of the Dutch State Archaeological Service (ROB), at Dorestad 1974

Other Countries

Some archaeologists work extensively abroad, lecture at distant universities, and attend international conferences: they travel a great deal. My own total inability to speak any language other than English has discouraged me from such European participation, and limited me to visits to places where English is spoken or to situations where my contacts spoke English. I have already described in detail my term in Ghana. Other distant contacts have been limited to the USA, Canada, Holland (**106**), Yugoslavia, and Spain.

The USA and Canada

I visited North America and Canada three times (in the 1970s and 1980s). The first two were to Rochester, New York, by invitation of David Walsh, with whom we had been collaborating at Bordesley Abbey (p104). Rochester had a flourishing Medieval Studies Institute, and the purpose of my visit was to persuade the powers that be (i.e. those that were giving money) that Bordesley Abbey, although not a ruin of the kind they were familiar with, was nevertheless at the forefront of British Cistercian studies because of its stratification, its methodology and in its holistic approach to all aspects of a Cistercian Abbey, its estates and granges, its local environment, its range of activities subsidiary to the nucleus of its church, the techniques of its construction, and even its dead; these were matters that had not before received much attention in primarily architectural and art-historical studies.

I was not very good at this, not being very good at hyperbole, but they were impressed by my falsetto rendering of 'O Mistress Mine' at a 'medieval' dinner!

There were, however, useful experiences outside. I went up to Toronto to give a lecture on Cheddar to the Institute of Pontifical Studies, one of the major centres of medieval scholarship in the world. On a quite different tack, I visited Sturbridge Old Village, a remarkable reconstruction of pioneer architecture and life, one of the first and best of its kind. On a very large estate, a complete eighteenth- to nineteenth-century village had been built, with church, houses, workshops, mills, etc. Each morning, the staff arrived and changed into their traditional dress, ready to set about their daily business of ploughing, milling, wood-turning, dress-making, etc., and very willing to talk to visitors about their traditional skills. In the village shop, one could have furnished one's whole house with 'ancient' furniture and equipment, claimed to be made in the village; this gave me my first taste of what in America constitutes 'Historical Archaeology'.

I was also very taken with the gravestones of the early settlers in New England, in classic cemeteries such as Marblehead and Salem. The gravestone makers brought with them pattern books from England; but developed their own vernacular style which has been made much of by American archaeologists and art-historians, such as Deetz and Ludwig.

The modern cemetery of Mount Hope, Rochester is equally famous — a vast array of probably a million or more stones of many immigrant races. Here I learnt how a cemetery can become an 'attraction' by all kinds of guided visits, occasions and exhibitions; a lesson later learnt in the revival of interest and care in British nineteenth century, non-ecclesiastical cemeteries such as York and London's Highgate. News of my interest reached the local press, and I was made a 'Friend of Mount Hope Cemetery' and given an appropriately-printed T-shirt.

In New York State I also saw a little of the rather hidden dark side of white exploitation of the Indians, and the appropriation of their land, which I made something of in *Invitation to Archaeology* (150).

To Calgary, in Western Canada, I went as a visiting lecturer in 1987, at the invitation of Peter Shinnie, who had been the agent of my visit to Ghana (chapter 5). Peter had been professor in Calgary for some years, with his wife Ama, a member of the Ashanti aristocracy. Here I found a very modern and eminent department of archaeology, with widespread interests, adequate finance, and every facility of conservation, etc. I gave half-a-dozen lectures on British archaeology, including a public one in the city on Sutton Hoo; I was made to feel very welcome, and was invited to come again for a term, but I never did.

Yugoslavia (as it was in 1968)

Another stimulating experience was participation in an excavation in Split, in the former Yugoslavia. This was the world-famous palace of Diocletian, built in the late third century. This was at the invitation of a colleague at Birmingham, John Wilkes, a great Romanist (now Professor at the Institute of Archaeology in London).

The dig, in a central area of the place, was actually directed by an American art-historian, Sheila McNally, and was financed by the residues of Marshall Aid; accordingly Yugoslav personnel were also involved, with Albanian workmen, who spoke neither Serbo-Croat or English; so, as a site supervisor, I had to give instructions in sign language.

Diocletian's Palace is a huge walled town. The Emperor set himself up there in great luxury with large service areas and great walls, much of which are still standing to their original height. It is one of a few great European sites which has been occupied (principally because it offered a safe walled refuge) by successive 'dynasties' of people — Slavs, Venetians, etc. — right down to the present, when it is still the nucleus of an extremely crowded and vibrant town, with much tourism (now beginning to revive after the disastrous civil wars).

Its importance as a tourist centre led to its development as an 'ancient monument', so massive 'clearance' was initiated in the 1960s, hardly to be dignified by the name of archaeology (a procedure equivalent to the disastrous decades of 'clearance' of our own castles and abbeys by successive predecessors of English Heritage, so that they could be 'elucidated' for public inspection).

The cavernous cellared basements of the palace complex were emptied of many thousands of cubic metres of rubble and rubbish accumulated over sixteen centuries. This was emptied by shovelling it onto conveyor belts and dumping into the sea. It was cursorily inspected for important finds such as sculptures.

American involvement sought to improve matters; but it was soon clear to me that the primary objective of the dig was to expose fine Diocletianic mosaics, which would then be incorporated into new cafes and restaurants. There were two or three metres of stratification above the mosaics, with structural remains and burials. My attempts to disentangle these were not welcome; nor were my attempts to suggest that the historical sequence of the palace could be best understood through the sequence of ordinary domestic pottery: only the exotic glazed and decorated pottery was being kept. More seriously, the recording was not up to the standards that had been developed elsewhere from the 1930s onwards. Site recording was by daily diary. 'Today we found a wall . . .', (next day) 'today we found a skeleton by the wall we had found yesterday' etc. As the areas of excavation deepened, vertical sections were left, and when they reached the mosaics, they were drawn; not by archaeologists, but by graphic artists sent for from excavation HQ; with no reference to any record of what had been removed to expose them! However, the brief recording I had done in the area assigned to me was duly acknowledged by Professor McNally; and it had also given me a valuable experience in Mediterranean archaeology and its material culture; and to Yugoslavia, where we subsequently had many naturist holidays on this coast and its achipelago.

Spain

Spain, its culture, landscape, and antiquities, has long been of major interest. It began in the late 1960s with a one-week winter break at Mojacar, where the warmth of the winter sun was an enormous tonic. Next was a whistle-stop Cosmos tour of the great cities of the peninsula by coach, visiting Elche, Seville, Granada, Madrid, Toledo, Salamanca, Lisbon, and (across the Straits) to Tangier. This involved great transects across Spain, which we

107   El Balcon, our house on the mountain at Fortuna, in south-east Spain, 1993

later repeated on our own. Taking ship at Plymouth with our motorcaravan, the 24-hour ferry took us to Santander, and from there to the South over two or three days, visiting many sites, including the splendid Arabic centre of Cordoba.

To anticipate my main narrative and retirement, on one of these trips we encountered a spa in the south-east, in the province of Murcia, west of Alicante, called Fortuna, where there were a number of Germans, Dutch and English sitting out the winter.

The attraction of Fortuna, apart from a warm dry semi-desert climate, was a large swimming pool, with a natural hot water supply at *c*.35°C, in which one soaked from 10am until 3pm each day. The name Fortuna of course suggested that the Romans also made use of this. On our way to this place in 1988, I tripped awkwardly over a root in a campsite and broke a bone in my ankle. A Spanish hospital encased my leg in plaster, which rather set us back; but we did get to Fortuna, where I was for a few weeks a familiar sight, body in hot water and leg out of it.

We made friends there, and found that an elderly couple named Andy and Jay had a small house on the mountain above the village, where they spent six months every winter. They wanted to be nearer the hot pool, renting a house, and wanted to sell their mountain house. The upshot was that we bought it, hoping that we might sit out the winters here.

The house (El Balcon) (**107**) had been built in 1978 and had a superb location, looking out onto six lines of sierras. There was only rainwater (though one could buy a tankerful if there was a long drought); nor was there electricity; one had to rely on bottled gas, a petrol generator and 12V batteries. The latter powered lights, radio and TV; we subsequently put up a small wind generator and a solar panel to charge the battery.

Temperature could get up to 25°C or more even in January, and we spent many pleasant weeks there in the next three or four winters. A major part of the Deerhurst book (172) was compiled there, writing and drawing in the sun.

The importance of this was that it gave us an entry into the archaeology of the area which was extremely rich and even more unrealised; extending in date from the Neolithic to the ethnography of recent centuries. We soon located many sites by finds of pottery and structural remains; we had to learn from scratch a totally new archaeological repertoire. The only aspect where we were on familiar ground was the Roman, the range of pottery and other finds being largely similar throughout the Empire.

We realised that there were severe limitations on what we could do without advice. We wrote to the University of Murcia, asking if any work had been done in the Fortuna area. This elicited a very quick response; within a week or two a car drove up to the house. The driver introduced himself as Professor Antonino Gonzales Blanco; an archaeologist and ancient historian, who, it turned out, was the kingpin of Roman and later archaeology in the province of Murcia. He was, surprisingly, very pleased that an English person was taking an interest in the area, which he confirmed was urgently in need of fieldwork, not least because of the rapid degradation by modern agriculture and development. When he found out who we were, he showered us with several books he had written.

We showed him the sites and places we had found; he was especially interested in those of the Roman and Visigothic periods. Of particular interest was a spot in Fortuna itself; a rain washout had exposed a deep stratum with Roman pottery of the first century AD (Augustan) including some quite exotic material, imported from the eastern Mediterranean. This was clearly a pointer to the Roman background to the natural hot water. He filled this in for us by reference to some other material found in the past which hinted at a baths/temple/religious complex here. He then produced his big surprise. Only a few miles along a track from our house was a big cave, the Cueva Negra; the water came from springs here and was much valued by local people, for its purity and therapeutic properties. They came in cars to fill up containers with this precious fluid. We had been there to see it, but so poor were our powers of observation that we had quite failed to notice large Latin inscriptions in red-painted letters, covering a substantial area of the outer edge of the cave roof. Admittedly, although local people had been aware of 'squiggles', it had not been until recent decades that a post-graduate student of Gonzales had realised that they were written in Latin. The latter had in fact been studying them for some time, and had published a major monograph on them, from several interdisciplinary points of view.

The inscriptions are of the greatest interest. It is sad that they have never been published in English. They refer, among other things, to a cult of the waternymphs; and to a visit to the place by a priest of Aesculapius; it also has the earliest known quotation from Virgil.

The cult festival was on the Kalends of April (15th). Here is a splendid example of continuity. Until quite recent years the cave was the resort, on this very day, of young people of both sexes from the surrounding area, who meet (a kind of marriage market) and had a special feast. A party of us revived this on 15 April 1989.

Such continuity was taken for granted by Gonzalez. We took him to see a site in a neighbouring village (Abanilla) where there were a number of Roman architectural fragments, pottery, and other finds scattered around a farm; there had clearly been major Roman buildings here. The farm was now a major olive-oil production centre. Local

108 Professor Antonino Gonzalez Blanco, of the University of Murcia; on our excavation at Fortuna, with an early Roman jar

farmers brought sacks of olives to be turned into olive oil by a process involving large presses and huge revolving conical stones moving around a circular stone trough. This was now powered by diesel, but would formerly have been animal driven.

When we looked round, Gonzales noted a number of special-shaped stones, which he identified as components of a Roman olive-mill: 'Dos mille annos' — 2000 years of milling. When we spoke to the lady of the house, she was not surprised: 'Si, dos mille annos!'. One of Gonzales' major hypotheses was that this part of south-east Spain had never known any real change between Roman times and the Civil War of the 1930s. Roman estates survived here virtually intact, with the same technology, through various changes of master, but no change in peasant life.

We agreed to do an excavation together at Fortuna (**108**), with his post-graduate students, near to where we had found the Augustan material. Here were also two great tanks of built masonry, which we had thought were post-medieval but which he confirmed also as Roman. Our excavations in 1990 showed that all this area had been in

109 Mick Aston as he was in 1978, at Birmingham

the nature of a *mansio*, buildings where people had stayed, while visiting the baths complex. The religious nucleus, a presumed temple, lies (to judge by earlier finds) a few hundred metres away, nearer the present hot pool, and is at present inaccessible.

The two great sites, Fortuna and the Cueva Negra, were, Gonzales believed, part of a large sacred complex, a place visited by the literate aristocracy from Cartagena, a big coastal town in Roman times. They added their contributions to the cave inscriptions, honouring the nymphs and visiting the baths and temple. We published a joint paper on all this (156, see also 165) which, alas, appeared only in Spanish!

Gonzales (who had earlier spent some time in Oxford) came to England to visit us, with his family (who included two Virgil-reciting daughters); and more recently, in 1997, Martin Carver was external examiner in Murcia, for a post-graduate thesis on Heritage Management, a concept just beginning to hit Spain.

Our life however changed in 1992, on 1 January, when Matthew Philip Merlin was born (see chapter 14). I was then 70, and it was a long time since I had last been a father. We took Matthew down to Fortuna the next winter, but the conditions at the house on the mountain were really not very suitable for my wife to look after a baby, especially the lack of running hot water! So we reluctantly sold the house to a family who appreciated it as much as we did; and thus our long association with Spain ceased, except for later airborne holiday trips.

Gonzalez very kindly arranged a collection of essays on the Roman complex of Fortuna; this was published as a *Festschrift* in my honour; he included also a piece by my wife on myself, and I contributed a summary (for Spanish readers) of the archaeology of Dark Age western Britain (165).

I end this chapter with an offering myself to Professor Mick Aston (**109**), with whom I have had a long and fruitful collaboration (see his semi-autobiographical *Mick's Archaeology*, (Tempus 2000)). He has done more to bring archaeology to a wider public in Britain than it has ever had before, of many millions, through the TV medium of *Time Team*. Many years ago I was inspired to write the following by reading the table he had compiled for a paper on the names given to types of roofing slates, and of the slaters.

Stonesfield slaters — old Oxfordshire song

Let us go slating in the merry month of May
With short and long bachelors and Muffity too
We will wippet and wibbett in the nines and elevens
In long and short cuttings in the short and long becks.

Now is the time for cussems and mopes
And undereaves mumfords, even the short 'un
It's a long job, an even job, that we all have to do,
In the long fourteens and fifteens in the middle of May.

Now All Up, lads, short pricks and long 'uns
In-bow and out-bow to set 'em all free
With wivets and short cocks, the beast with two long backs
And middle cock and long cock, and LONG SIXTEENS!

To be sung by James Bumpus, Caleb Oliver, Solomon Oliver, Uncle Mick Aston and all.

PART THREE

Retirement and other lives (1986-?)

14 Retirement (1986-?):
still digging, travelling, writing, drawing and talking

We thought a lot about where to retire to. One is often advised on leaving a university post to move hundreds of miles away, rather than hang about as a 'grey eminence', haunting the department. The Welsh Marches (Hereford/Brecon/Clyro area) was one possibility. We were fond of that area, having married in Hereford, when digging at Kenchester in 1978. Another possibility was Wells, which would have taken me back to the familiar territory of North Somerset, and its archaeology. I could have become honorary curator of Wells Museum, which carried with it a splendid house, looking onto the Cathedral's west front. I realised, however, that to run this museum would tie me down too much, and prevent us travelling freely. So we decided to stay in Yorkshire, risking being a ghostly hanger-on; and I have had nothing but help in continuing a loose association with the department and University. We had also made many friends in Yorkshire and felt at home in the splendid landscape, at Harome near the North Yorkshire Moors National Park.

A substantial part of the 14 years since my retirement has been spent in bringing the results of excavation to final publication. The department's work on the North Manor at Wharram Percy has been written up as far as is possible. We still await the finds reports since there is some delay in these from the relevant specialists. Bordesley Abbey was taken over by Susan Hirst, Susan Wright and Grenville Astill, and Kenchester by my son Sebastian and Tony Wilmot. Other long-standing sites have been published, some going back to the 1950s (142, 149), others rather later, such as Mary-Le-Port (112), Cadbury Congresbury (152), Tamworth (153), Liddington Castle (171), Deerhurst (172), and Cannington (181). Only St Oswalds, Fulford, a church on the outskirts of York, where we watched its conversion to a house, remains to be written up (186).

A major new opportunity was a three-year presidency of the Council for British Archaeology (CBA). This involved chairing a number of committees and Council in London, visiting regional groups, and finally delivering a Presidential Address on 'Ethics in British Archaeology' (144), deploring the decline of standards and behaviour in the last decades.

I also tried my hand at journalism in the CBA's *British Archaeological News* (BAN, now *British Archaeology*). I had some success with my popular book *Invitation to Archaeology* (150), and it was even translated into Portuguese (108); one wonders what they could possibly have made of such an essentially English book. Now I cast my net wider with a series of short articles which I named President's Pieces (a name misunderstood in some quarters). They ranged widely (120-127, 132-141, 145-148) from Japan to the Scilly Islands, Archaeo-Sci-Fi to metal detecting, the archaeology of the dead to Pepys, Philip Barker and

110 *On the Odessa Steps, Russia, 1990; the first Rahtz to visit this town since my grandfather's return there with his bride in 1873*

Raymond Hayes, the scandal of the Bush Barrow gold, and Life Among the Cave Bears: very good exercises in widening my written horizons. I continued to be involved in CBA affairs in more recent years.

In the summer of 1986 we went on a cruise on the P & O Princess to Greece, Turkey and Russia. We could not normally have afforded such a luxury, but all expenses were paid, plus a fee, in exchange for giving six lectures on board. These included 'The Archaeology of Turkey' (using material collected on a tour); Istanbul (again from a visit); the development of Christianity in Asia Minor (very thin ice here!) and a running commentary from the bridge on the passage through the Bosphorus into the Black Sea (my wife compiled this from written sources and a map).

215

111   Matthew aged 2, Harome, 1994

We did not entirely enjoy this trip, though we were glad to get to Varna in Bulgaria and Yalta and Odessa in Russia (**110**); the latter place was where my grandfather had worked, and had taken his English bride to in 1873 (see p22). The passengers were, however, mostly Americans of the worst sort. Only about a hundred came to the lectures out of a company of 750. The rest were interested only in ballroom dancing, bridge and napkin-folding. They over-ate from an over-lavish menu, very shocking to us relatively puritan English; especially when most of the crew were from the Third World, whose families didn't get enough to eat at home.

The next year (1987) we went to Israel to see the marvellous archaeology there, and to feel ourselves very pro-Zionist. An unexpected entree to the synagogue by the western wall in Jerusalem was a major anthropological experience; a boy was being initiated into the Torah; savants were expounding the holy texts; American Jews were flashing cameras and videos; and segregated women, in a gallery, were ululating and throwing sweets down to the lower concourse.

In that year, too, we had another anthropological experience in attending the World Science Fiction Congress in Brighton, in which archaeology played little part at that time, in spite of my President's Piece on *Archaeoscifi* (132), a field I have explored again more recently.

The major event of my retirement was, however, the birth of our son Matthew Philip Merlin (**111**). Lorna had had several miscarriages, but we had some complex treatment at

112 PAR and Lorna, Harome, 1995 (copyright Stockton and Darlington Gazette)

Leeds, involving transferring some of my blood to her; this may well have prevented another rejection, and allowed a fine baby to come to term; he made his wish to come into the world clear at about 00.30 on 1 January 1992, and was born later that day at Leeds. We were both rather advanced in years for parenthood, Lorna being 41 at that time and myself 70 (**112**); there are clearly problems for Matthew, but he is now 9 and doing well at school and elsewhere. Our lives, however, have been radically altered, as always by the advent of a child; there has been a good deal of stress associated with lack of sleep and worry over minor illnesses, etc.; but although our freedom has been drastically restricted, we have continued in the same mode of life. For a brief few weeks in early 1999, I was 77, Lorna 7 x 7, and Matthew 7.

I have continued to write papers other than excavation reports. 'Pagan and Christian by the Severn Sea' (151) took me back to a reconsideration of old haunts and themes in Somerset, in a contribution to a book of essays on Glastonbury to celebrate the 90th birthday of the late C.A. Ralegh Radford. This was followed by yet another book on Glastonbury (158) in the English Heritage/Batsford series; this was shortlisted for the Archaeological Book of the Year Award, and has done well. It would have sold even better if I had included 'Arthur' in the title (as Charles Thomas did in his companion volume on Tintagel) but I resisted the temptation in spite of the financial gain!

I have said nothing about another very enjoyable part of writing, that of reviews. They not only normally gained one a free book, but also ensured that it was read carefully with great personal enlightenment. I have listed but not numbered the 60 odd reviews in my bibliography in this book, except for review articles, in which one takes the opportunity to look at the entire state of knowledge (or as much as one knows about) regarding the particular subject. I was particularly pleased with some of these, such as *Yeavering* (93), the *West Yorkshire Survey* (101) and (since retirement) 'The Onymous Dead' (160), 'The incomparable hallmark of the divine image' (164), and *York Minster* (170).

We have continued to travel, in search of ethnography and archaeology, in Yugoslavia (before it collapsed), the Dodecanese Islands, Malta and (with Matthew) to other islands in Greece; and to Norway, Cyprus, Tunisia, Spain, Madeira and the Canary Islands.

Until recent years, there has not been much excavation. We participated in training exercises at Langton (run by Andrew 'Bone' Jones) and in study tours to Lindisfarne for the University of York.

In retiring to Harome, we had not surprisingly taken an interest in the archaeology of North Yorkshire, and especially Ryedale, the area on the north side of the Vale of Pickering. In the nearby small town of Helmsley we have a flourishing local archaeological society, which organises excavations in the summer, and a lecture programme in the winter; for the lectures we get an average attendance of 60. The Society had also produced in the 1960s a major book on the archaeology of the area, and publishes *The Ryedale Historian* every other year; this combines local history and archaeology and enjoys a high academic reputation. I was its chairman for three years, and was able to use my contacts to get some eminent archaeologists to come and lecture to us. I was later Treasurer from 1997-2000. Two pillars of the Society were the great North Yorkshire archaeologist, the late Raymond Hayes, and Tony Pacitto; the latter had helped me on several excavations in earlier decades.

In 1995, a need for a rescue excavation arose in nearby Appleton-Le-Moors; a substantial medieval communal oven turned up in a new housing development; the excavation involved Society members (169). In 1996 another problem arose in Helmsley itself. The flourishing Arts Centre is located in a former Quaker Meeting House, built in 1812. A new extension was proposed, involving constructions on and into the disused burial ground. The Quakers themselves did not raise any objection to the graves being destroyed, since it was a century and a half since anyone had been buried there. A total of a dozen names were known from their Registers, including some from Harome. The archaeology section of the North Yorkshire County Council made development conditional on archaeologists watching the work; and with the consent of the Home Office, the Society agreed to undertake a watching brief; we expected that a few graves would be disturbed in the digging of foundation trenches but in the event there were nine, mostly in wooden coffins. Residues of these were found, and also a few copper alloy shroud pins. Corrosion from these had preserved some greenish hair.

Excavation of Quaker cemeteries is a fairly recent development in British archaeology, as is indeed the excavation of any post-medieval cemeteries (see 137). They are now

113   At Kirkdale, North Yorkshire, 1995 (John Makepeace)

recognised as having considerable historical interest, not only as illustrating recent burial practices, but also because it is sometimes possible to identify skeletal material with people whose names, occupation, sex and age at death are known. With full cooperation of the builders we were able to draw and photograph those burials which were exposed, to reasonable if not high standards; it was not possible to delay the building work.

The work of conserving coffin residues, hair, etc. was taken on by Andrew 'Bone' Jones (himself a Quaker) as part of his educational programme at the Archaeological Resource Centre (ARC) in York. Bone also arranged for the bones to be studied by Dr Chris Knüsel and his students at the University of Bradford.

The intention in 1996 was that the bones would be re-interred in the garden of the reconstructed Arts Centre in a special occasion of reburial. In 1997, however, Dr Knüsel asked if the bones could be retained at Bradford. It turned out that they were of unusual interest, being those of *very old* people; specimens of great value in teaching. Again the local communities of Quakers raised no objection; nor did the Home Office; or Martin Weyer, the Director of the Arts Centre. In the light of worldwide concerns about disturbance of the dead, and ethics of museum display, scientific study and reburial, this was an enlightened decision (190).

Our major opportunity came, however, in 1994, in relation to the Anglo-Saxon church of St Gregory's Minster, at Kirkdale, only a few miles from our home. After our experiences at Deerhurst (172), we were 'into' Anglo-Saxon churches, as I have described on other pages (p106, 169); there were a number in Ryedale, two of which (nearby Lastingham and Stonegrave) were known to have been monasteries in the eighth century or earlier. Richard Morris (Director of the CBA) had long suggested that all those places which had structural remains and/or sculptures of pre-Norman date had been monasteries; either small secluded eremetical retreats, or playing a more active role in evangelisation and pastoral care. They could be seen as offshoots of the great English/Irish foundations of Christianity in the north-east of England, so graphically described by the great historian Bede, writing in the early eighth century.

The sculptures in Ryedale numbered over 80 pieces, mostly cross fragments of eighth- to eleventh-century date, and several of these (including some very important pieces) were at Kirkdale.

We had of course been familiar with St Gregory's Minster ever since we came to York in 1978; it was one of the places to which we took students; not only to see good examples of Anglo-Saxon architecture and sculpture, but also because of a world-famous inscription in Old English (I say world-famous because there is a cast of it in Australia!).

The inscription is on a long stone sundial slab (originally the side of a sarcophagus) set in the wall above the south doorway of the church. It records how one Orm Gamalson (an Anglo-Scandinavian local magnate) restored St Gregory's Minster 'from the ground', a church which by his day was 'fallen and broken'. This was done, the inscription goes on, 'in the days of Tosti the Earl and Edward the King', dating the inscription neatly to 1055-65, just before the Norman Conquest. In the centre part of the stone are the divisions of the dial into parts of the day, with appropriate further words of a symbolic nature (174) and the names of two people responsible for the work.

Not surprisingly, this inscription, the longest of pre-Norman date in the north, is very famous and much visited by a wide range of people. Whether any part of the present structure is that of Orm is another matter. It provides clear indication, however, that there had been a church on the site before the middle of the eleventh century, which had by then become ruinous. That the church could have considerably older origins was suggested too by two great decorated slabs, now inside the church, one dated on art-historical grounds to the eighth or early ninth century, i.e. before the Scandinavian settlement of the area. These were considered to have been the cover-slabs of box-shrines, hinting at Kirkdale having been a place of prestigious burial.

In 1994, there was concern that the western tower (of 1827) was not perpendicular, but was leaning slightly to the west. The Department at York, through Martin Carver, was consulted over the archaeological implications of an underpinning operation, which were clearly considerable. The query was passed to us as the 'local archaeologists', and we wrote a report. This led us to examine the whole structure more carefully than we had hitherto. In view of its importance, and the number of articles that had been written about it, we

114   The diggers at Kirkdale, 1998; Debbie Haycock, Basil Wharton, Lorna Watts, PAR, Denise Wilcox, Marion Atkinson

did not expect to make any new observations. To our surprise we did (168) and our appetite was whetted for further work.

The first thing was to look at the whole background of the environment, the economy, the prehistoric and Roman finds in the area, and what earlier scholars had said. St Gregory's Minster lies in a secluded dale by a beck; there are now no houses in the vicinity. It has a large churchyard; but there are open fields to north and south. That to the north exhibited the ridges and furrows of medieval cultivation; Richard Morris thought that any earlier monastery might have extended into this area, and traces of it might be found below the ridges.

Firstly, however, there was 'rescue'. A ford at the north end of the field was used by tractors, causing erosion of the strata on either side. So members of the Society cleaned back the section and enlarged it a little, providing a useful and encouraging preview of the sequence of deposits (114). We were able to define here a series of layers extending upwards from the bedrock of the dale, through very ancient riverbed boulders to an old land surface of Roman and Saxon date; all, as we had hoped, well sealed and protected by the deep soil of the headland of the medieval cultivation. This was a promising start. We next turned to the south end of the same field, and made a cutting of 25m^2 by the churchyard wall, our first substantial excavation since Wharram Percy (except that in Spain).

Next, Tony Pacitto carried out a geophysical survey of the field, indicating possible features (177). Here, all expectations were more than fully realised; Richard Morris was right. The earliest features here were 14 graves, probably of eighth- or ninth-century date, and of all ages and both sexes. Above this were post-holes of a substantial timber building, metalling and debris of craft/industrial activity: iron-smelting and smithing, copper-alloy working, and work in other materials; associated pottery dated all this to the ninth and tenth centuries. Finally, later than this, was the churchyard wall, built in the eleventh or twelfth century, separating what had been part of the monastery from its nucleus; and the ensuing arable cultivation.

This sequence would on its own have been very gratifying; but in addition to this, luck brought two finds of the highest importance. The first was a piece of half-melted lead sheet, on which were incised part of a lengthy inscription in eighth- or ninth-century Old English; the decipherment of this has been a lengthy process, resulting in a large publication by five authors (174). It appears to refer to a 'bone chest', some reliquary, chest, or ossuary, in which the bones of someone important had been put, with the lead as an identification plate (unfortunately the name is missing). This provided further evidence for prestigious burial to add to the slabs in the church.

The second find was very tiny, a 6 x 3mm fragment of twisted greenish glass rod, with yellow and white opaque spiral trails (177). Such 'filigree' glass was used as decoration on glass vessels. The little rods are rare in Britain; the largest collection known is that excavated from the church of the great Carolingian monastery of San Vincenzo, in central Southern Italy. Hundreds were found here dated to the early ninth century; they were made there in glass furnaces. Exports from the Mediterranean, or copies, are known; some from Scandinavia, at the famous trading centres of Kaupang, Birka and Ribe; and at Dorestad, in Holland. We do not yet know if the Kirkdale piece is an import, or a copy made elsewhere; but it at once put Kirkdale right in the mainstream of the great European trade/gift/exchange routes; well-known also from the pages of Bede.

We had thus made a major contribution to the archaeology of monasticism in Ryedale, and shown Kirkdale's importance in the development of Early Christianity in the north-east, which we are inclined to link with the better-known monastery at Lastingham — perhaps as elements in a 'twin' monastery, like Wearmouth/Jarrow.

We now planned to work on the church itself. St Gregory's Minster happens to be not only a famous church, but also the home of a very flourishing Christian community, under the leadership of the Reverend John Warden, an eminent priest and scholar. He and his staff gave us every welcome and encouragement, helped by a lecture I gave in the Minster to the Friends of St Gregory's.

As I have explained in chapter 10, digging in and around churches is not so straightforward as digging in an open field. Firstly one has to get not only parochial but also diocesan permission, the latter by a Faculty, which we did get; secondly there are burials, some of quite recent date; and finally (and this was especially true of Kirkdale) one was dealing with unique stratification in an important building; there is a question of archaeological ethics here (see p126 re Sutton Hoo). We did, after only a little heart-searching, go ahead in a cautious way by examining the west end of the church; students from York, under the direction of Jane Grenville, drew the elevation of the west end

115 Anglo-Saxon sarcophagus at Kirkdale, 1997 (Andrew Selkirk)

stone-by-stone, as we had at Deerhurst; and in 1995-7 we examined the below-ground foundations. A fine double-step foundation was we believe attributable to the rebuild of 1055-65.

On the same orientation as those in the north field were other graves at the west end, and a great, almost complete sarcophagus (**115**), weighing over a tonne. This is of tenth- to eleventh-century date; the original inhabitant had long since been displaced; but the sarcophagus is yet more evidence of prestigious burial at Kirkdale. There were also in these cuttings further sculpture of ninth- to eleventh-century date, and a few architectural fragments which give some clues about earlier churches.

One final discovery here was a Roman coin, of Constantine the Great (issue of 332-3) and a melon-bead (also of Roman date) found close together. These may suggest that the history of the site extends back three or more centuries before the days of Bede; a Roman site (villa, temple?) providing a nucleus for the implantation of an English monastic community. We also have ghosts! (176)

In 1998, we excavated a small trench in a field south of the church. Here, extensive geophysical survey by Arnold Aspinall and Tony Pacitto showed many features. During the very cold Easter we made a small trench; there was nothing Anglo-Saxon, but some prehistoric flints and medieval features. We hope to do more extensive work here in later years. In the same year, we excavated all along the exterior of the north aisle, and showed all the foundations here were of medieval and modern date.

During that year, we had become interested in the area on the south side of the Vale of Pickering, and especially in the church of All Saints at Appleton-le-Street. The fine tower had been long recognised as late Anglo-Saxon, but we were able by close examination of the exterior and interior of the tower to show there were three Anglo-Saxon phases, the first probably of tenth-century date (183).

But now *anno domini* became a problem. I was beginning to get tired, and getting breathless in walking, especially up-slope, and with some feeling of restriction in my chest. My excellent doctor sent me to York, and I went through the usual heart tests; these confirmed that I had mild angina. The York heart specialist put me on a regime of medicines for artery dilation, calcium inhibition, cholesterol reduction, aspirin and a diet; these improved my condition gradually, but the warning remained that I am at risk from heart failure — echoing the condition of my father at a similar age.

In the spring of 1999, a quite unrelated crisis came — a serious attack of gastro-enteritis. The normal treatment had no effect, my temperature was up to 104°F, and after several days of severe diarrhoea I was taken to York hospital; I was monitored, but no further treatment was given, and after a few days I was recovering and was able to return home. An uncomfortable episode — the only bright part was that while I was in hospital, I had long phone calls with Philip Barker, also in hospital, in Worcester, about the book Mike Baillie had written about catastrophe (Baillie 1999)!

I was rather weakened, and had lost weight; the cause was never found. The only after-effect has been a slight impediment of speech, fumbling over some words, getting genders and verbs wrong, and this deficiency extended slightly into my writing. In lecturing since I am conscious of a loss of fluency but other people don't notice it, I have been able to overcome the problem.

I had the angina to cope with; the treatment had been successful, and I have had no serious problem since. On a 'belt and braces' basis, I also became a patient of a very successful herbalist and archaeologist, Christine Haughton; and have since taken her seven-ingredient mixture. I don't know whether this or the conventional treatments have been successful; I keep taking both, in case!

In the summer of 1999 we nevertheless had a very successful holiday examining the amazingly well-preserved Bronze Age stone structures in Menorca, and a camping trip (we have a trailer camper) to the Isle of Wight. In the autumn we made another excavation in the field north of the church at Kirkdale. This time we used a mechanical excavator to dig a narrow trench, to test a hypothesis that an anomalous sinuous feature was the monastic boundary. It turned out to be the edge of a huge wash-out area, the result of a major flood about 1000 years ago; the wash-out had mostly silted up, to be suitable for medieval ridge-and-furrow cultivation.

In October there was a memorable occasion, taking me back to the early digging days. This was the conference to celebrate the 150th anniversary of the foundation of the

116 Dominic Powlesland, 1981; he is the director of the largest archaeological landscape project at West Heslerton in North Yorkshire

Somerset Archaeological and Natural History Society. I gave the keynote lecture on '150 Years of Somerset Archaeology' (184), and Matthew was able to use the replica Neolithic bow, based on a well-preserved part found in the Somerset Levels.

We also as 'archaeological consultants' were asked to monitor the work of making an extension to the local nineteenth-century church, St Hilda's at Beadlam. We made a preliminary evaluation to assess whether the work might encounter any archaeology. We then watched the work; there was no archaeology, but we recovered a useful transect through the upper parts of the geology.

Before Christmas and the horrors of the millennium celebrations (a year too soon!), we again headed for naturist sun and sea in Lanzarote; by this time I felt better than I did in 1998. On 29 December, twenty-one of the Rahtz family and their partners together with children, grandchildren and one great-granddaughter all met for a millennium lunch in Helmsley; four generations of us. On the last evening of 1999, I went to the midnight service at Kirkdale; the newly-restored bells brought us in the new year, while campers in the field let off fireworks.

117   Cornwall 1997, PAR with Matthew

In January of the new year, I gave a public lecture in Helmsley on 'Glastonbury, Arthur and Archaeology', which had a large audience; I was not seriously inhibited by speech problems.

In the mild and sunny January and February of 2000, and in September, we were able to dig yet again at St Gregory's Minster, uncovering the foundations of the south side of the nave; we had not hoped to be able to do this, but the architect had recommended the setting of a new French drain, and we offered to dig the trench before a gravel fill was put in. We recovered some useful data on the eleventh-century and earlier churches; this operation will continue. Much remains to be done at Kirkdale, including analysis and drawing of the whole church structure.

A new project is now developing. This is at Blansby Park, near Pickering. Over the last 20-30 years, Richard and Edward Harrison, who farm the land, have collected a very large number of finds from ploughsoil, ranging in date from Neolithic to post-medieval times. By the Pickering Beck (the southern extent of the Park) the plough turned up Roman tile and stone, indicative of a villa here. A geophysical survey showed the presence of a large circular building. In the autumn of 1999, in an unploughed piece of land by the beck, moles began to kick up tesserae. Roman mosaic work always generates excitement — it is so exotic in the British rural landscape. We were invited to do some evaluation excavation; and to take the initiative in setting up a wider landscape examination, and get the find collection catalogued, drawn, photographed, and examined by specialists.

In May 2000, we dug two trenches at Blansby Park. We uncovered part of a hypocaust, probably part of a bathhouse by the riverside. In the destruction levels, we recovered 760 tesserae of several colours, painted wall plaster and many other finds of tile, bronze etc.

In September, I gave the Deerhurst 2000 lecture in St Mary's Church. In spite of being at the time of the petrol crisis, I had a full 'congregation'; the lecture has now been made ready for publication (191). I am also finalising a piece on an interesting group of gravestones there (187).

So far, Blansby and Kirkdale (and the writings listed in 'in press', 'forthcoming' and 'in preparation' in the bibliography) represent the latest phases of my activity in retirement. They will keep me busy for some years, together with seeing other things safely into print, but there are still a number of projects I would like to do if I live long enough.

As this book is going to bed, we have other things to which we can look forward to. There is of course the new Rahtz, Matthew Philip Merlin, now 9, who has already wielded a trowel to devastating effect at Kirkdale . . .

15 Other possible lives in alternative universes

The reader may be thinking by now that I have done nothing in my life but dig, travel, draw, talk and write. They may be curious to know the author as a more rounded individual than the one who has this obsession with archaeology; for external views, see Appendix E. In this chapter we look briefly at other aspects of my life, and other lives I might have led if the balls had tumbled a little differently. Given my genetic, cultural and educational background, could I have been anything else?

The other aspects of my life would be a different autobiography, one which I have partly written, and which I may complete, with a 50-year moratorium. Its title is not yet fixed, but a good one might be 'Girls Grow Up'.

Music has been one of my greatest pleasures, since I abandoned Radio Luxembourg in my teens. Coming from a family whose upper limit was Finlandia, it was easy for me to take an eclectic view of music, from Machaut to Steve Reich, and from Schoenberg to Bach. The advent of the Third Programme (now Radio 3) in 1948 was a major event, providing over the last fifty years an education in many subjects, as well as a familiarity with music which only the rich and privileged would have known a century ago.

I also get a lot of pleasure from playing instruments badly; firstly the viola (**118**). The late Eric Brown persuaded me to play in the school orchestra; later I took up the tenor recorder. I wish I had more time to improve these skills — now it's the amazing electronic keyboard.

I listen to music on radio, tape or CD in virtually all waking hours, when I'm writing, drawing or reading; or perhaps 'listen' isn't quite the right word! Only rarely has it been possible to have music on when I'm digging; it is not conducive to the disciplined atmosphere of a dig, nor to the care needed in digging and recording. As with films on TV, I prefer recorded sound to live performances; the latter are rather embarrassing, sitting with a lot of other people and being passive.

I would also like to have been an artist. I have painted four pictures since 1949, which have remained attractive to my family (**119**). The most recent has an archaeological inspiration, an Iberian pot decoration (**120**). I have also recently completed a piece of sculpture in olive-wood of a sad bird (**121**). As I have explained above, such artistic aspirations as I have have been expressed in archaeological draughtsmanship.

Pleasure in open air, landscape and the countryside has been well catered for by digging and travelling; and so has another great love of 70 years, swimming. When the Wiltshire Archaeological Society visited my excavation of the big field at Downton (p73), a lady asked why I had decided to dig there. 'Because of the excellent swimming in the River Avon' was my truthful reply, which occasioned a stunned silence.

118 PAR
    playing
    viola, 1951

In my first *Festschrift* (Carver ed. 1993), the editor commented 'There can be few people resident in the northern hemisphere quite so fond of undressing'. Indeed, since my teens I have never seen the point of wearing clothes when it was warm enough not to; nor the point of wearing clothes to go into water, except wetsuits in Cornwall (**122**). It has been difficult to combine nakedness with archaeology; that brings us back to Kent Flannery's dictum that 'archaeology is the best thing to do with your trousers on'.

What other lives might I have led? Some are more likely than others. I would like to have become a bishop, and this would clearly have been more viable than being a tightrope walker. Not believing in God was in earlier years more of a drawback to being a bishop than it is nowadays, and I could have been an *antiquarian* bishop.

One profession I might have gone on with was obviously accountancy. Had I been philosophically inclined to capitalism and all the subsidiary activities, ambitious to make money and be respectable, I might have continued with this. I was not wholly useless at it; I just drifted away from it. This was partly because of the unsettling circumstances of war, and the imminence of being drafted.

There there was the Royal Air Force; but five and a half years of being told what to do by morons dissuaded me from staying in it an hour longer than necessary; and I could never see the virtue of human beings marching in step, or other funny walks; quite apart from the problems of killing people.

119   Painting by PAR of a mountain forest, 1950 (poster colour)

Photography I could well have taken up; I do have certain talents here, and did live on it for a while as I explained above (p53); I still take pleasure in it, both for archaeology and other purposes; but with modern cameras and colour processing, it's become rather too easy for even my nine-year-old son to take good pictures. One of the pleasures of becoming a professor, however, was that at last I could afford the king of cameras — the Hasselblad.

Had my background been more scientific, it would have been good to be involved in more 'universal' studies. One of the most absorbing 'spheres' of work in my lifetime has been the brilliant efforts to understand the cosmos: its origins (or non-origins, if its age is infinite), its physical nature, and its future (which seems to me to be certainly infinite).

These vast leaps into understanding have been (like archaeology, but in a very different way) interdisciplinary, with inputs from physics, mathematics, optical and theoretical astronomy, and the manned and unmanned explorations of space. There is a slight family link here in that my father taught Paul Dirac at the Merchant Venturers College in Bristol in the early part of the century, a boy who was the bane of the mathematics master.

I try to keep up with these and other scientific matters by reading *New Scientist* each week, or at least as much as I can understand. As a determinist, I find it difficult to believe in the non-causative aspects of quantum theory, or in the need to abandon common sense. Nor do I believe in the Big Bang, even if 95% of scientists do. It begs the question, which

230

*120   Oil painting by PAR of an animal depicted on an Iberian pot in Murcia Museum, South
East Spain, of the second to third century BC (begun 1989, and still unfinished, 1999)*

the physicists dodge, of what is meant by the 'nothing' that preceded it (unless it is a 'local'
event, in our system of galaxies). I lean towards infinity, and still feel sympathetic towards
the concept of Time as having a linear character, Einstein or no Einstein.

Such heady matters are a useful mental correction to the comparatively blinkered
interests of archaeology, which is by definition anthropocentric. Our interests take us
firmly back only to hominid origins, a few million years at best. Again on a Terran scale,
geology offers a wider scope; and unlike archaeology, its data are at least being steadily
whittled away by natural and anthropogenic agents only very slowly.

I have indicated above what really swung me permanently into archaeology — the fear
of having to be a schoolmaster after all if I failed once again — I have never regretted it.
Being an archaeologist has been a rich and varied life, and an education for me, having
lacked it in earlier years; and I suppose that such talent as I had for teaching and
communication has been well satisfied; but ironically enough at the other end of the
spectrum from my backward boys.

What remains in the rest of my life? At 79, it is difficult to make long-term plans. I shall
do archaeology for as long as my muscles, sight, hearing and brain stay in working order;
and I shall go on travelling, though less adventurously than hitherto. I hope though there

121 Sculpture by PAR in olive-wood, of a rather sad bird, 1990

may be other things to learn: all of science, especially great astronomical advances; how to talk to a computer; more music playing; painting; and writing, and not just technical or factual writing, such as the bulk of my input has been, but fiction — whether the science-fiction at which I've made minor stabs, but something more extended, such as a biography or a novel. I'd quite like to try my hand at the kind of imaginative reconstruction of past life such as the Palaeolithic epics of Jean Auel. I have now plenty of descendants who might take an interest (however voyeuristic it may be) in my 'other' autobiography — would that my grandmother had written about her love affairs! I now have ten grandchildren and two great-grandchildren. (Even my nine-year-old son Matthew is a grand-uncle to this fourth generation.) So let us conclude by hoping that they enjoy at least this autobiography; and perhaps will be led on to my archaeological writings.

122 In a wet-suit at Watergate Bay, Cornwall, 1988

Appendices

Appendix A: Letter to David

My second son David (born 11.8.48) had a troubled adolescence, and led a chequered life all over Europe before arriving in Australia, as a down and out, and in poor health. In Sidney, he was befriended by members of an American evangelist sect; he was 'born again' and married its deaconess and became a minster. Part of their beliefs was an adherence to the literal truth of the Bible, even in translation, God having 'supervised' every version. This extended to a calculation that the world had been created in about 6000 BC. This sat rather uneasily with the scientific estimate of *c.*5 billion; 'creation science' attacked the very basic tenets of all science. It also led to a breach with his family. His siblings had little patience with this irrationality; as his father, I tried to explain how science could not be neatly circumvented without denying the evidence of our senses. In 1986, I wrote him a letter (which I also sent my other children) setting out my general attitude to religion and philosophy; it expresses my views in 1986, which have not changed very much since then. I reproduce it here as the record of my standpoint.

Dear David

I fear I am not a believer in your sense, I am an agnostic insofar as I am open-minded about the possibility of exterior 'controlling agencies', and certain only in other vastly more advanced societies who may be 'keeping an eye on us' in the sense of T.S. Eliot's 'Family Reunion'. I also believe in man's need to have religious beliefs, however rationally unfounded they may be. They manifest themselves in all cultures in the world from earliest times to present (1.5 million years at least). In recent times i.e. 200 years or so, some major religions have been successful in gathering millions of adherents, Islam, Confucianism, Buddhism, Christianity; and the last-named has been obviously the one most familiar to us, and remarkably successful in the light of its beginnings (historical reasons can be addressed for its success). All these religions have many points in common, though also some essential differences. Comparative religion is a very interesting study. In all anthropological work, it is seen there are certain common origin myths, notably the Flood and the Genesis account is a complex and interesting one. The Great Dreaming, of the background of what is now known to be 40,000 + years of Aboriginal settlement in Australia, is an oral and pictorial one.

Now all this is the rationalist stance in which I as a scientist share. One can only go beyond this into a supernatural explanation if one has an 'experience' as you have - either a sudden flash or as a result of charismatic influences. When that happens, you are able or willing to step over the frontier of rationalism into faith, in which rational, intellectual arguments or evidence cease to be relevant. I've known many people who have either always had such faith or have acquired it, people of considerable intellectual powers (eg. Harold Taylor, the doyen of Anglo-Saxon church archaeology). Doubtless if an 'experience' happened to me, I would also go over the frontier. With my respect for rational explanations, I cannot do so; nor do I feel any need to. Human life and experience on earth, good or bad (and here I've been lucky) is quite enough for one existence, without risking immortality (except through descendants or one's published works: this is my own form of immortality with over 200 to my credit now — publications, not children!).

As an archaeologist, conversant with world culture and history over 5 million years, I take, not surprisingly a broad view. Although we are far from understanding the origins of life (these are early days — modern scientific thinking is only a hundred or two years old) an enormous amount has been learnt and especially so concerning the evolution of species. Whether this proceeds in a steady Darwinian way or in neo-Darwinian 'sudden jumps' is a matter for continuing debate. The fossil record is sparse and discontinuous. What is clear however is the basic descent through mammals, primates and precursors of man (e.g. *homo habilis* etc.) to a point relatively recently (1-5 million years BC) when we can discern *homo sapiens sapiens*, very like ourselves, though *homo neanderthalis* is for instance, burying his dead earlier. The debate on the 'missing link' is dead — forget it! — it's a non-concept. The entire sequence of fossil man is incomplete since the conditions for survival are rare.

At some point in this sequence, at present uncertain, there are changes which result in self-consciousness and rapid intellectual and technological growth. Reasons are uncertain — ? climate, ? upright stance, ? food-sharing — there is much debate. But no supernatural intervention need be postulated — remarkable though these changes are. You can, if a believer, postulate a 'divine spark' at this point, 'injected', and still believe in the basic evolutionary sequence; or believe that man is suddenly created, in which case you have to explain the overwhelming biological similarity to other advanced primates. If you believe in God you can believe in anything since by definition, he/she is all powerful, able to create the whole fossil and evolutionary and geological record at one go, with everything in position to fool us poor rationalists. Read Leakey's *The Making of Mankind* to see my perspective - if you want to understand the opposition. Don't rest on ignorance like out-dated stuff about missing links. If you seriously want to counter scientific rationalism, you'll have to master the arguments on both sides.

As to Christianity, one can separate what is clearly by and large a humane and socialist life conduct from belief in Jesus Christ as the son of God. It has unfortunately been responsible also for dreadful crimes and massacre, including (in its name) Christian Falangists in Beirut. It has shown (as most deeply-held religions do) an appalling intolerance to other faiths which is counter to humanistic values. There is a note of such intolerance in your letter which I find sad, in saying you can't marry Janey because she's an unbeliever (of Christ). Christianity is also rather sadly as much on the side of capitalist exploitation of the workers (i.e. the stations of life) as on the admirable 3rd world work done by Christians. If Christians followed the words of Christ, they'd be unbeatable as a humane force, but faith leads to bigotry and intolerance, however much someone like Cardinal Hume (who we gave a honorary degree to this year) a near-saintly man.

Another facet of my personal belief which makes it impossible for me to believe in sin, wickedness, good, bad, etc is, as you may remember (since it caused a lot of family dissension) my belief in determinism. If you don't remember, or don't know, the principle is that all human behaviour (and all life) and all decision making especially, is determined by genetics (i.e. heredity) and environment, plus all other influences in the external world. If A decides to do B rather than C (say commit a crime or not) his decision is the result of a multitude of complex factors. If it were not so it would be a random decision, which is more difficult to understand than a cause. If any all-knowing, all-seeing being (i.e. God) knew all the factors, he could predict precisely what decisions anyone would take at any moment in time. If predictable, even theoretically, then inescapable. So no logic in praise or punishment; they function only inasmuch as society wouldn't work without them; indeed individuals couldn't function without the illusion of freewill. But deny the logic of freewill, and pride, good and bad become only relative terms. You'll appreciate that this makes sin only a word to me in a social context - what has survival value or otherwise to the human species. Similarly, 'good' and 'bad' tendencies, eg. foodsharing and aggression have in my view both survival value in natural selection, so not surprisingly we are all a mixture of the two. Some people have more of one than the other; but each of us potentially a murderer or a saint if the stimulus arose. Your own life is determined by the combination of mine and Wendy's genes, by the world and school you were brought up in, by your travels, and now finally (or transitionally as the case may be) crucially influenced by experience or a charismatic individual or group.

From my belief in determinism comes alas my political beliefs, leaning heavily to the left in believing that people can no more help being clever, stupid, lazy, incompetent than having red hair (see Samuel Butler's *Erewhon* for a satire on the theme), and any praise, blame, higher or lower income is again a social and economic mechanism. Everyone should have the same standard of living, getting their satisfaction not from a higher standard of living or more money, but from giving more to society or (at worst) the satisfaction of power. This in contrast to right wing attitudes of pulling yourself up by your own bootstraps, anyone can become president. If you're unemployed its your own fault, etc. We've come a long way along my road in my lifetime with no one starving (at least in UK) a minimum standard of living for all, improved prisons where healing a person of (some) crimes is widely believed in, etc. — not to mention the NHS — and surprisingly much of this continued by right wing governments which years ago would see the present one as wildly socialist! So some things move towards a better world, and indeed in terms of Christ's teaching a more Christian one. Indeed much of Christian (and older Greco-Roman ethics) frowns on pride, blame, etc. (if Greek *hubris*) in the feeling that 'pride comes before a fall', etc. etc.

Well that's a few of the things I believe in, and archaeology encompasses all this in its major value of giving to me and others in this field the best broad perspective of human existence and problems that one can get.

Do keep an open mind and analyse the difference between any faith you may have in things that can't be logically proved to an unbeliever, and a rational and scientific approach to facts, evidence, and ideas. If you wish me to, which is unlikely perhaps, I will enlarge on any of above points, or issue further manifestos on other aspects of my life and beliefs (it strikes me I should circulate copies of this to all my children in case they don't understand what makes their dad tick!)

love

Philip

Appendix B: Imperator Sexualis

This essay is not meant to be particularly autobiographical, but rather a reflection on how sex seems to me at the present time (1997).

Sexual dimorphism is a common feature in the evolution of life-forms, but by no means universal. I agree with Richard Dawkins, in his Neo-Darwinian interpretation of life, that the primary purpose of life is the passing on of genes to the next generation. 'Purpose' is perhaps the wrong word — it implies a conscious design on the part of someone or something. Rather it may be seen as the rationale of evolution. By definition, species survive only if their genetic pattern is perpetuated. Where this does not happen, the species will never develop, let alone survive from generation to generation.

Self-reproductivity, as in cloning, may assure perpetuation of species, but does not appear to allow for change by the introduction into the genetic make-up of new features, by mutation. Such changes may be detrimental to the species, in which case they will be discouraging to adaptability or 'improvement' in the process of natural selection, tending towards extinction of that strain or pattern in the course of time. Some such detrimental mutations have however, survived to give rise to deficiencies, 'diseases' which modern gene therapy attempts to define and alter.

Other mutations have proved beneficial to adaptability or survival; it is these, over the last three billion years, which have led, by natural selection, to the complex and adaptable life-forms of the last billion years; successful inasmuch that certain species, such as those of the great reptiles and bees, can (or could in the former) look back on hundreds of millions of years of success in passing on their genetic pattern.

Sexual dimorphism allows for a continual mix of genes from male and female, which ensure the occurrence of mutations at regular intervals (or concentrated at certain epochs in 'punctuated equilibrium').

For the system to work, it is clearly essential for male and female to get together in some way to produce a member of the next generation, with its appropriate mixture of genes. Failure to do so would result in a dead end for the genetic package in male or female. There is clearly an advantage if the union is made attractive to both parties. Over millions of years, a sexual imperative developed: the more the sexual drive, the better chances there was of union. The less there was, the greater the risk of not passing on the genetic package.

In many species, reproduction and the resultant genetic survival was achieved by the male creating sperm, and the female preparing ova which were capable of being fertilised by the sperm. In some species the female laid eggs, often in large numbers, which were either fertilised by sexual union or deposited where they could be fertilised by the male. In a minority of species, the male guarded the young until they were independent, but more usually the female took on this task, with the male providing sustenance and protection.

In more complex species, those of mammals, sexual union was by the male depositing sperm in the interior of the female, where it fertilised an ovum and a foetus developed, growing inside the female until it was ready to be born. We are familiar with this mechanism in the wider family of mammals and especially in the primates.

Desire to effect this bodily union in mammals is strong in both mature male and female. It manifests itself as bodily changes, notably erection and the release of lubricating fluid in the male, to effect penetration; and in enlargement and dilation, and other bodily symptoms, together with a similar release of lubricating fluids.

In less complex mammals, the female is only periodically fertile, and when this time is ripe, bodily odours and other symptoms alert males to female receptivity, which in turn excites strong desire in the male. While the processes are by and large capable of analysis as chemical changes, they also appear to dominate the mind, to the partial or temporary exclusion of other appetites. In less complex species such as dogs, felines, or apes, there does not seem to be much picking and choosing. A female bitch in oestrus is attractive to every male dog within signalling distance. The exceptions are animals of which the female will reject weaker males, but choose the strongest available, made manifest by battles, displays or shows of strength. Clearly in these cases she is anxious that her genetic package has the best possible union to strengthen its chances of being passed on.

The sexual imperative is equally strong in *homo* species, and has doubtless been so since the time of our splitting off from our ape ancestors at *c.*7 million BC, relatively recently in the history of life. We may speculate that early hominid females gradually became selective of the available males, choosing those which offered the strongest protection while she was pregnant and nursing, herself vulnerable to predators. Protection was a desirable thing to look for, and was often allied to a capability of acquiring the best and most regular food supply, by fair means or foul.

We may also speculate that during the last few million years, as hominids developed the ability to make more efficient tools, hunt effectively, use fire, and build shelters, so too the sexual imperative, while still dominant, and an attractive proposition to say the least, was accompanied by an increasing consciousness that it was enjoyable to a high degree.

Again we may speculate that, as group societies become more complex, and with the use of ever more useful language, brute strength was no longer the *sine qua non* of female choice. More subtle qualities may have been increasingly attractive - a kindly disposition, a fondness for offspring, or a tendency to stay with the same female and family, or even to show talent in art, story-telling or music. Here we may envisage the origins of love and affection.

In the upper Palaeolithic, *c.*35-40,000 years ago, *homo sapiens* began the most far-reaching changes that led to modern society. We now see the first evidence that sex, *inter alia*, was no longer mechanistic, but was a matter for consideration and expression in art - the depiction of sexual activity and attributes of fertility and of certain types of women. The very plump females with prominent sexual attributes depicted in the figurines used to be taken as evidence not so much that such fuller figures were the norm in Palaeolithic society, but that they were desirable attributes, providing for men evidence that such women were not only sexually attractive, but were move likely to survive harsh conditions and food shortages, increasing the chances of the male's genetic package being passed on to a further generation and beyond. Anthropologists are no longer so confident of this interpretation, thinking it equally possible that we are seeing depictions not of women who were desirable but were symbolic of something else allied to religion.

In historical times, from *c*.10,000 BC, there is ample pictorial and written evidence for sexual union and love being important, indeed basic. While we may speculate on developed societies of thousands of years earlier having 'trouble with sex', it is now made manifest. Women being taken captive, sexual jealousy, appropriation of a woman or man by someone other than their regular partner, rape, perversion, etc: they are all there and probably had been for a long time.

There had doubtless long been a conflict between the naked sexual imperative, the strong bodily and mental urges without which we would not be here, and the increasing need for society to be stable and secure, and especially for women to be able to bear and nurse a family without anxiety.

Early societies could be polygamous or polyandrous. Polygamy is comparable to the well-known phenomenon of the monopoly exercised by a bull over his females; this ensured the widest dissemination of the genetic package of the bull, and benefited the herd by ensuring that all offspring were half those of the strongest male, temporarily holding power.

Human polygamy had the same end: apart from sexual variety one man could have dozens or hundreds of children by diverse women, ensuring both his genetic survival directly and a good mix for beneficial mixing of the gene pool.

Polyandry, while less common, could similarly be the prerogative of a queen or other powerful female, who wished to ensure the best dependants. Obviously the number of offspring were limited; but this may have been secondary to satisfaction of the sexual imperative. In similar cases, a *menage a trois* could offer some safeguards against the problems of losing one's partner by death.

Monogamy has also been a sought-after way of regulating the sexual urge for the benefit of society. A successful monogamous partnership could and does offer not only a potentially wholly satisfactory way of achieving love and sexual satisfaction, but also a stable unit in which offspring can prosper and live to be parents themselves, taking two and more genetic packages into future generations.

In our own western society, Biblical teaching and Christian precepts recommend monogamy as the most desirable form of sexual union, avoiding the twin sins of fornication and adultery. Unfortunately (as it seems to much modern opinion) the 'evils' of irregular sexual union, and the dire results of such, as graphically depicted, led to the concepts of sexual desire, far from being the very root of life, as something inherently shameful; something to be avoided if possible: but if not, then regulated by marriage.

It seems likely that this horror of sex was related to the religious belief that humans were something special, divinely created, not just another animal (since animals obviously enjoyed sex, however unconsciously). This was the same kind of horror of humans not being special that led to such passionate outbursts against the conclusions of Darwin in the last century, continuing with the mistrust of Dawkins and his 'selfish gene' theory in our own day.

More tragically, these largely male-derived attitudes tried to reduce the status of women as something inferior, if not actually vehicles of sin - suitable only for our own base natures and for the continuance of the race. The best thing of all was to renounce sex altogether, as many priests and monks tried to do; treating sex as a snare of Satan, an enemy to be fought, either by sheer will-power or with the aid of scourges, or immersion in cold water (a recommended cure for schoolboy sexuality!).

Women too could feel the horror of sex, and (in their case) of the base demands of men. At worst they could put up with it to become mothers ('think of Britain'!). At best they could abjure it and become nuns. The female sexual imperative, as in monks, had to be sublimated, or transmuted into religious fervour as the 'brides of Christ'.

While most people in the world enjoy heterosexual sex, there are many who don't. Homosexuality is rather puzzling, since it should lead to a dead end for the individuals concerned; one might think that natural selection would have doomed it millennia since. Yet our biological make-up is not wholly male or female. Even the heterosexuals among us have some element of the opposite sex in their biological or psychological make-up. Others seem capable of heterosexual and homosexual activity. There is no doubt, however, that many males and females have an innate tendency to be attracted to their own sex from birth, and seek to change their sex. Perhaps more, however, become homosexuals for other reasons: being at public school or other sexually segregated societies such as prison, or (for males) the Navy; or (in a tolerant modern age) as a fashionable trait.

The sexual imperative is powerful. When frustrated, or sublimated, or otherwise diverted from its natural outlet, it can lead to murder, rape, or an astonishing variety of perversions, involved the planting of semen in orifices wholly unsuitable for procreation (or even ones of the wrong species!). More commonly it is one of the major factors in the breakdown of monogamous relationships, causing males and females to seek sexual satisfaction beyond their partners, and leading not only to broken partnerships but to major problems for offspring deprived of their natural mother or father.

Why do so many relationships break down? Are their reasons other than sexual jealousy, or just plain bad behaviour such as wife-beating, or crime, or poverty, or stress. Do women or men change, so that they cease to be as compatible as they appeared to be in the early stages of their relationship? Or do they simply choose an unsuitable person, paying over-much attention to sexual attraction?

Men and women are more selective in their choice of partners than other animals. Men, if at an uncynical stage in their lives, and if asked what sort of a female would make a suitable life companion and mutual parent might list sexual attractiveness, beauty, suitability to be a successful mother, (big breasts, or wide hips as in the American ideal), health, caring, loving, intelligence, mutual interests, sense of humour, good cook and housekeeper (but not in that order). A wise advice is 'see what her mother is like'!

A women may select a man who is sexually attractive, handsome, intelligent, rich (or likely to become so), good with children, caring, loving, clean, non-violent, etc. Oddly, women sometimes choose men who are not of these (usually with dire results). In marrying what may seem a thoroughly nasty, violent, brutal male, she may be harking back to an undeveloped stage of society, where to be unpleasant had as much survival value as to be kind, gentle, cooperative, etc.

From the beginnings of history and probably long before, the sexual imperative in the human species is very commonly associated with an affection which often seems far removed from sexual desire: and that is love. Love raises the spiritual level of sexual desire and congress, and can often be the prelude to it; so that sex becomes apparently the expression of love rather than its root cause. Love often survives sex, and is a strong element in permanent relationships, heterosexual and homosexual alike. It can also lead to a great sense of loss, when one or other partner responds to the sexual attractions of a third party.

Sexual jealousy is thus also a formidable force and a major factor in destroying relationships; there are few partners who can accept sexual infidelity with equanimity; those who can often save their marriages in the long run.

The sexual imperative may be viewed as a major source of both happiness in modern society, and also as a major cause of unhappiness. A rational approach to modern life may recognise this and seek yet again to regulate it into channels where human happiness is not threatened. This seems as unobtainable as attempts to regulate armed conflict. The power of the sexual imperative as a biological urge is able to, and often does overcome, any rational urge to be prudent, sensible, just, honourable, faithful or caring; we would be wise to recognise this and seek ways in which we can cope with its power, as we must try to deal with the problems of world government; and not to continue to pretend that we are in control of it, and only will-power is needed. As Wilde pointed out, 'he who controls desire does so because his is weak enough to be controlled'.

From an early stage (some say from infancy), children exhibit a sexuality, more consciously in some cases than others. Boys show off in front of girls and each other. Girls learn to behave appealingly and adopt ornaments from an early age (thought it is claimed that this divergence is largely the result of social conditioning, and there are many exceptions apart from homosexuals).

As pubescence develops, these traits may become more marked. Both sexes use gender signals (hair styles, body ornament, clothing) to attract the opposite sex, often without realising the powerful sexual reaction that can occur (and being surprised or even horrified when it does). Females especially use make-up and clothing to emphasise secondary sexual characteristics and attract attention. The sexual feelings can be relieved by masturbation (with 'wet dreams' as an added bonus for boys!), but is increasingly likely to lead to sexual union, often with the disastrous result of infection by sexually transmitted diseases (STD), some (such as AIDS) being life-threatening; or premature pregnancy.

These attempts to secure the sexual attentions of the opposite sex are often disguised as 'making oneself look smart', 'increasing self-confidence', or as a means to being popular and sought after in a more general way. The habit of maximising one's sexual attractiveness is carried on into adulthood, as a means to secure the best partner; or to hold his or her attention through the problems of getting older and having children. These are the dangerous years (the 7-year itch, etc) when the sexual imperative is not satisfied and seeks alternative outlets.

Unfortunately all these attempts to look sexually attractive, lead on not only those that are welcome, but also those that are not. This applies especially to females, who are often unable to cope with unwelcome advances, including (at the extreme) violent rape. While the latter is universally condemned, its incidence might decrease if females made themselves less attractive! They underestimate their power.

One thing that does worry me, is the isolation of sexual desire from its function. This has been brought about partly by contraception, but it is a more general malaise of greater antiquity. If the essential element of the sexual imperative were more widely understood, it might not only add to the intensity of the experience, but help people, and especially adolescents, to understand the processes developing in their bodies and minds, and take desire rather more seriously, together with the human relationships it generates.

Appendix C:
How likely is likely?
and
How to get an excavation finished

How likely is likely?

(originally published in *Antiquity* (65); and again in *Invitation to Archaeology* (150))

This was written in half an hour as a fringe item at a local conference, but, because it expressed some fundamental truths and was quite funny, it was published. This short piece has been quoted more often than the major reports I've written, which is rather galling!

Modern archaeologists are constantly urging the necessity for a stricter and more scientific use of language and logic in archaeology. Some archaeological interpretations are based on such poor evidence in the ground that one can only say that the conclusion is 'possible, though very unlikely'; others are so positive as to be 'very probable, amounting almost to certainty'. Between these two extremes lies a range of quality of evidence which is infinite in its diversity both in kind and degree. Can the range be quantified? Windstrengths are given a ten-point (Beaufort) scale based on measurable characteristics. While archaeological evidence has more diversity than windstrengths, is it possible to erect a ten-point scale ranging from quality 1 (very unlikely) to 10 (certain), which can be linked with written equivalents?

We set it out thus:

Probability Scale	Literary Equivalent
1	Very unlikely
2	Unlikely
3	Possible
4	Very possible
5	Likely
6	More than likely
7	Probable
8	Very probable
9	Virtually certain
10	Certain

The more 'elegant' archaeological reports are littered with dozens of such phrases used to express subtle nuances of degrees of probability. Are they used as sober assessments of the evidence; or as elements of rhetoric to persuade the reader to one subjective opinion on what the evidence can bear? The use of a scale might force archaeologists to think more carefully about what weight the evidence will bear. Too often, the choice of the elegant phrase covers up a vague and woolly approach to the evidence; in the best of hands it will of course express half-tones of delicate balance between this and that which simply cannot be quantified. This is a valid technique if its object is to direct the reader's attention to the evidence itself, a challenging invitation to decide for him or herself just how likely the claim made is.

Unfortunately, few writers of archaeological reports are skilful in the use of words, even if they do in fact fully appreciate what can and what cannot be deduced from the evidence in the ground. If they do not have the gift of words, they might do better to use a number scale; their readers would then at least know how likely they thought was likely!

Even worse, some writers are more concerned with converting readers to their point of view than with expounding a balanced estimate of the validity of the evidence. To do this, they use literary techniques which are misleading or even dishonest in a 'scientific' report. They do in fact create an inverse scale of probability. Discerning readers will see through this, and apply a reversal factor; others will be persuaded. Examples of such an inverse scale might run thus (the 'modesty' of the first example is as misleading as the persuasiveness of the rest):

Phrase	Actual Meaning
'Just possible'	I'm pretty certain but I can't actually prove it; the reader will see how cautious and clever I'm being
'There is some evidence pointing towards . . .'	There isn't any but it would be nice if there were
'The evidence suggests that . . .'	If it were twisted beyond recognition
'It is reasonable to suggest that . . .'	It is unreasonable but I may persuade my readers to believe it by an appeal to their reasonableness
'Virtually certain'	I'm on very shaky ground here
'There can be no doubt that . . .' (or more commonly) 'doubtless'	Anybody who disagrees will feel a fool
'Plausible'	Well, ever so interesting if it were true
'It would be premature to suggest'	But wouldn't it be fun

'All the evidence taken together points to . . .' It all points in different directions

'Obviously', 'indisputably', or 'presumably' There is no actual evidence

'No right-thinking scholar can doubt' These are my final trump cards
or 'the discerning reader will observe . . .'

These dubious phrases about the quality of evidence should put the discerning reader on guard, but an ability to 'translate' other statements found in archaeological reports is also needed. For example:

Phrase	Actual meaning
'Further research may indicate . . .'	Mine certainly doesn't
'Adverse excavation conditions . . .'	The recording was terrible
'There is no evidence of . . .'	If there was, we didn't see it
'The object crumbled into dust on exposure to the air . . .'	Joe sat on it
'The relationship between these layers was uncertain . . .'	Joe dug it away when we weren't looking
'The date of the end of the occupation of the villa was shown by the latest coins, which were of Honorious . . .'	I don't believe in all this Dark Age nonsense
'A scatter of small stones associated with two handmade sherds . . .'	I do
'It was not possible . . .'	We didn't think of it till afterwards
'A flimsy structure . . .'	Moira planned the post-holes

How to get an excavation finished (after reading Philip Barker)

(reproduced from *Current Archaeology* 63, 127)

No one is a greater admirer of Philip Barker's work than I am. But since few of us are going to live to be 200, as he clearly is, we need a textbook on how to dispose of a site fast, as an antidote to the increasing number of excavations which look as if the diggers were rehearsing for a slow-motion film. Until such a book appears, I offer a few pointers for those who like to see spoil-heaps grow visibly, day by day.

Concepts
1. A layer is a load of dirt of no importance whatsoever until proved otherwise.
2. Excavation strategy is an expression of the director's interpretation.

Excavation
3. If you can remove several layers at once, do so — it's much quicker.
4. Always overdig everything; underdigging is dangerous and misleading i.e. always take off at least 2cm of the layer below or the edge of a feature.
5. Dig sites photographically, not stratigraphically.
6. If you remove human skeletons fast enough, they look like animal bones and can be thrown away.
7. If a feature does not survive being forked over, it's not much of a feature — worry it away.
8. If in doubt, have it out.
9. If still in doubt, put it back.
10. If you still don't understand it, get rid of it fast before tedious discussion is generated.
11. Metalling is only metalling if it takes a pick to shift it, ditto a wall.
12. All ditches have straight 45° sides — you use a spade for this.

Recording
13. If a layer does not appear in a drawn section, and has no important finds in it, forget it.
14. Don't record anything unless it merits a sentence in the interim report.

Finds
15. Soils are for scientists — to archaeologists they are different kinds of dirt.
16. Environmental evidence is terribly dreary (except at York).
17. Don't look for anything you can't see clearly with the naked eye.
18. If a find is not immediately identifiable and in good condition, throw it away; objects should be cleaned with a wire brush and dipped in acid — if they don't survive this, throw them away.

(If by chance you don't agree with these maxims, then Barker is the book for you!)

NB: Sadly, Phil did not live to be 200; he died on 8 January 2001, while this book was in the proof stage.

Appendix D: IFA lecture

(Although there is repetition here of some material that is in the body of the book, this lecture text gives some idea of my public lecturing style (as it was in 1987) and contains some anecdotes and other material that is not in the book. The reader has to imagine the slides that accompanied this lecture!)

The first after-dinner lecture at the first annual conference of the IFA
(The Institute of Field Archaeologists — April 1987)

40 years of field archaeology — a view from the Old School

The foundation of the IFA is a logical stage in the development of archaeology from its origins as an amateur/gentlemanly/scholarly pursuit to its present status: still scholarly, but mostly not amateur and not, if one may so say, gentlemanly. It is not the case here if it ever was (as it is in Canada where I've just been) that the qualification to undertake contract archaeology was a relevant master's degree.

This conference has had a very big response, and I believe may prove to be a decisive landmark in the IFA's gaining wide acceptance in British archaeology. It's reassuring to see that while we have themes reflecting the professional aspects of archaeology — Professional and Public Archaeology and Regional Archaeology — we also have more academic aspects of the discipline: method, theory and syntheses by period.

What strikes me about the programme is that this is the new world of archaeology — the new men and women : notably absent are all the stale old war horses that would have been speaking 10 years ago.

My own address this evening will have things to say about some of the conference's themes, but will be principally about field archaeology as I've seen it in my own times.

I could of course have given you a lecture to open your conference based entirely on my own reminiscences, but I have confined myself to those relevant to the particular themes I want to explore. My viewpoint over the last 40 years has not been that of an academic — I was mainly in it for the money — but as an amateur turned professional my view of the last 40 years is of some relevance. I am obviously bound to be personal and idiosyncratic; and I hope to be provocative and generate a few hisses; the last time I was hissed was when my towel slipped in a Turkish bath in Eastern Turkey.

When I began archaeology in 1946, there wasn't much archaeology around — everything had to start again rather from scratch — anyone who knew one end of the trowel from the other could get on fast in the amateur world and become professional; as I did in 1953, followed by 10 years as a field archaeologist and 24 as an academic. My 40 year retrospective is of a post-war archaeology which has I think seen most of the important developments in the history of the discipline.

Fieldwork, in the non-excavational sense, has never been my scene. Whenever I saw some new bump or hollow, my reaction was if it doesn't move, dig it — I have nevertheless been impressed by my colleagues' systematic mapping of surface features and exposed finds, and admired their capacity for indulging in such excruciatingly boring work. Nor have I personally found it very easy to read about — it's not very romantic. Cumulative fieldwork leads to important conclusions — fine, as long as someone else does it.

To me, as I've said elsewhere, the surface of the ground is like a crumpled duvet — what I'm interested in is what goes on in the bed. Developments in remote sensing I have therefore found more exciting — it does to some extent tell us what's going on in the bed, and I like the SF aspects of being able to know in the future everything that's in the ground; excavation will only be needed to recover objects or to expose structures for public display or further study.

Metal-detecting is another skill, like air photography, which owed much to war-time development. In skilled hands, the modern sophisticated detector is a powerful tool; in responsible hands it can materially enhance fieldwork and can be a useful monitoring tool in the excavation process. It is unfortunate that it has been the cause of one of the bitterest wars that archaeology has been involved in; this has also been a class conflict, the roots of which lie much deeper than the threat to the archaeological heritage. This topic will be explored in a day conference at Keele next month, organised by the CBA and the NCMD.

The excavation process has been of central concern to me and to many of us present here. Expertise in digging and post-dig analysis has after all — to the dismay of some — been one of the principal criteria for membership of the IFA. We have seen the change from a primarily vertical perception of strata seen in section to a horizontal perception of spatial relationships; the latter has now been refined to a more formal 3-D approach which I shall say more about. The *planum* method, of horizontal slices of fixed depth, which has been so successful in Germany and Holland (on such sites as Dorestad and Feddersen Wierde) has not caught on in Britain. It is efficient in enabling large excavations to be done and precisely planned to a fixed budget, with a largely unskilled labour force. It may be that conditions of soil are rarely appropriate here; and that the social structure of British archaeology has increasingly militated against the sharp trichotomy of academic director / skilled technician / unskilled labour force that seems inescapable in this system. What is perhaps surprising is that it has never been tried on an experimental basis, rather than just fulminated against by Martin Biddle.

The Wheeler grid system was still *de rigeur* in the 1940s for a big area excavation, together with the trench, also then fashionable. My first dig was a trench through a mound which I thought was a barrow, but which turned out to be a windmill. My second dig employed another variation of the vertical approach — the quadrant method. This was another mound I thought might be a barrow, but turned out to be a temple. I seem to have made a habit of getting these things wrong; but my quadrants were actually quite appropriate here. I tried the grid system in 1953 on a villa, and quickly found the snags — one never saw all of one context at one time, features remained hidden in baulks for weeks or months, as did the total finds assemblage from any context. Worst of all, the task of correlating contexts through grid squares and baulks, and reassembling finds groups was a fearsome task. The attractions were clear; one could separate the work force into discrete groups, spoil removal was easy, there were lots of sections etc — we all know the pros and cons. It was said that Wheeler invented and used the system for several good reasons. He liked striding up and down the baulks looking handsome and barking comments or orders down to those in each hole, rather like a general inspecting his troops; he could look down into the cleavages of female volunteers and approve their potential; and that it was the only way he could keep his female supervisors apart from each other. Such sexist approaches are of course quite unthinkable today; especially since the foundation in September of the International Forum for Women in Archaeology.

The grid system may have worked for Wheeler — and it has remained popular in many parts of the world, being still taught as standard practice in America and elsewhere. Phil Barker and I saw both the ultimate *reductio ad absurdum* of the grid system at Knowth. The same day I saw Brian O'Kelly's meticulous open excavation at New Grange. I expressed my surprise at what I'd seen at Knowth — there was a pause — we went into his site hut — the door was shut, a bottle of whisky was produced from under a table — and O'Kelly said 'I thoroughly agree with you'.

I was therefore in the 1950s only too ready to change to open area. John Hurst was a junior inspector fresh from Cambridge in 1954. He wanted me to try open area on the Chew Valley medieval sites. I said, 'I'll do anything for money, John' and became known as a stripper. The great advantage to me was that as there were no standing baulks or sections, no one could check on my fantasies; for the same reason I liked to dig sites that were subsequently destroyed completely.

We all know the subsequent history of open excavation. All over the country you can see keen young chaps cleaning up hugh areas of meaningless gravel spreads, and what was worse, drawing and photographing them.

Again, like Wheeler and grids, these techniques were fine when in the hands of the master, in the case of Barker, but led to a colossal waste of resources and excruciating boredom in the hands of lesser mortals and caused an even greater bottle neck in post-excavation.

The new techniques did lead to the defining of more subtle kinds of data, enhanced by the increasing application of scientific techniques. It was now possible to determine wear patterns caused by a flock of sheep crossing the site, the difference between rain dripping off roofs and the local urination place. What has increasingly worried me over the years has been that the extra time and expense spent in recovering even more subtle data has been out of proportion to the information recovered about the past. It's worth it when a whole set of massive buildings is revealed at Wroxeter, where none had been suspected before; but too often the extra data were mundane. 'It all depends what you're interested in'. One is interested in one's own dig and the clever way one has found a dog's footprint; other archaeologists may be interested mildly; but who else? This is one of the reasons why we have had difficulty in getting real archaeology across to the public: most real archaeology is pretty boring. The more subtle and ephemeral the evidence is, the less positive appeal to outsiders such as historians and anthropologists. Years ago, I suggested that we should make an equation between the resource expenditure and results, measured in units of historical interest — history with a capital H — HISTS, and I still think there's a lot in this. But everyone vies to recover higher and higher proportions of the archaeological residue, while at the same time evaluating what that residue is a residue of, by a study of SFP (site formation process to you). This is I suppose theoretically defensible and a necessary adjunct of technical development, especially in prehistory. Meanwhile many sites are being destroyed through lack of resources. Would we do better to emulate the Dutch and Germans and suggest that 50% of the data from 100 sites is more useful than 90% from 25 sites — as long as we know what we're throwing away — and that's the problem. Sheppard Frere knew what he was proposing should be thrown away when after a visit to York in the early 1970s, he reported with horror: 'They are drawing nineteenth-century drains IN COLOUR!'

Now we are involved in a new revolution which threatens to produce even more boring and unselective data — single context planning. This deceptively simple title sounded like just a new trick of recording, but masked proposed major changes in the way digs were planned, run, analysed and published. Philosophical, political and social issues are involved apart from merely technical ones. The system was invented by Steve Roskams and Henry Hurst to cope with the problems of data-analysis at Carthage. It was then introduced to London, and later to York and even into the fastnesses of Wharram Percy.

Its adherents and exponents were quite evangelical, and adopted the rather shining confident and superior look of those who know they are right, when talking to other old-fashioned archaeologists. The saved or the unsaved — as my born-again son says to me, 'Where do you stand with Jesus, Dad?'. In a recent seminar Roskams defined the political aspects of SCP. This is seen as a manifestation in the field of the more general tendency for archaeology to be socially relevant and therefore overtly political, a question which came to a dramatic climax in the events surrounding the World Archaeological Congress at Southampton in September.

To Steve, traditional site management was seen as hierarchical, with a project director, specialists, and subordinate workers, all being paid according to worth; the new system allows work on site to be done by a team, with defined areas of responsibility, and being paid according to need.

The trend to automatic recording on context forms or into hand-held computer has of course, as SPR points out, already undermined the central role of the director as the maker of records. Specialised languages have been developed in recent years, but have tended to be restricted in their use to elite recorders and computer experts. In the new system all would be systematically trained in the new languages, so that there is communication between all workers, and everybody feels part of the excavation enterprise.

The technical aspects are fine, the 3-D definition of contexts in sequence, and their separation in plan, rather than being grouped together on successive plans of stages of excavation, provided that one had an unlimited budget for Permatrace and didn't mind a pile of 5000 plans, it was dandy (or neat as they used to say across the Atlantic) and represented a real advance in ordering data for post-excavation analysis. The other aspects are however rather more disturbing. One of these is the insistence of the purity of the primary record. There must be no overt site interpretation — a regularly-aligned arrangement of stones held together with mortar must on no account be called a wall. A pattern of bones in an elongated pit, which reminded one vaguely of one's own body, must not be called a grave. The purpose of this is to avoid colouring the primary record. In relation to post-excavation analysis, the on-site inspiration of the individual director is replaced by detailed analysis by a post-excavation team, some of whom may never have been involved in data production.

I can see the point of this; but it does rather cut the ground from the traditional way of running a dig where the director strides around being frightfully clever and telling each digger what it is they are uncovering or have dug, what its significance is in the site sequence, and how it fits into the general pattern of the history of Western civilisation. This of course was the point — the political point. Everyone was fed up with the pyramid of direction, and the star role of the director. Charisma was out, site discipline was in. A democratic system now ruled. With suitable training, anyone could define the latest pancake in the heap, a patch of yellow-brown gritty clay, could clean it up, smell it, describe it on a form, take a picture of it, level it, make a plan of it, enter it on the site matrix, and then — joy-of-joy — remove it and define the next pancake in the heap. The heap of plans in the site hut grows. The director's job (he or she is dressed the same as everyone else, of course) is to go round quietly, unobtrusively and uncharismatically, and check that all is going well and no one has gone to sleep on the job or in the hut. All this seems rather dreary to my generation compared with the old days when we used to prance up and down in white shorts and sunburned torso and shiny trowel providing instant interpretation and encouragement. But it must be said that diggers seem to enjoy the new system, and are content to wait a few months to the time when the director gives a public lecture and they find out they had been digging an Anglo-Saxon ship burial of the seventh century AD.

You will see from this lengthy discussion what I mean by SCP being far more than a merely technical development; it is a major and important trend. Not everyone is in favour of it; Martin Biddle has expressed strong disapproval; and a public debate is badly needed.

One feature of archaeology which has actually declined in quality in my time is draughtsmanship. There have always been archaeologists who did their own drawings, and those who delegated this task to others. Where the former was true, individual archaeologists developed an individual style — extreme in some cases, like Heywood Sumner whose beautiful drawings have been given a new lease of life by Barry Cunliffe's eulogistic volume. Pitt-Rivers delegated and the illustrations to his great blue and gold volumes are mostly rather sombre and functional. Wheeler was an artist, and so is Hope-Taylor, and between them they published, in Maiden Castle and Yeavering, some of the finest drawings that archaeology has ever known; beautiful to look at and evocative in plan, section and reconstruction of what they were trying to express.

While we can all recognise a Barker, a Cunliffe or Hobley drawing, it is becoming more difficult to see any distinctive style in modern drawings; and archaeological reports are often less interesting to look at, there are several reasons for this:

1   Increasing pressure of work has led to more delegation.

2   There has been increasing specialisation in units.

3   More fundamentally, some modern archaeologists regard skill in draughtsmanship as being more suitable for an artist-technician to do, something rather mundane and functional, not a proper part of intellectual activity. So more and more we find field drawings of varying quality being passed to a technician to prepare for publication — as has always been the case in geography — the result is hundreds of drawings that look rather alike and require close inspection and reading of titles to see if it's a Neolithic henge, a Roman villa, or a medieval castle that is being portrayed.

There is also perhaps growing a feeling that somehow an 'artistic' drawing is rather improper. On analogy with what I have said of the social and political overtones of single context planning, to do a drawing distinctive of a particular person is another form of élitism, a rather indecent showing off; and indeed also that any drawing that enhances the interpretation it is putting over is suspect; it is the antithesis of an objective presentation; a plain and functional plan or section is nearer to the purity of the primary unbiased record.

My next theme is the relationship between theoretical archaeology and professional archaeology. Since the early 1970s there have been major changes in the theoretical basis of archaeology which have had worldwide repercussions. We have seen the evangelical attempts to persuade archaeologists to a more hypthetico-deductive approach; we have been through systems theory and out the other side; social anthropology has made an appearance; there have been neo-Marxist and neo-structuralist approaches, and in our own day psychological, symbolic, and cognitive avenues. There is a good, though loaded, review of all this in one of Hodder's latest crop of books, *Reading the Past*. He has now brought theory full circle with a reaction back to cultural-historical and narrowly anthropocentric approaches. Indeed to him archaeology is no longer about the past — it is the study of the relationship of material culture to human behaviour; when we use this to explore the past, this is history.

These weighty and important matters which seek to define the very nature of our discipline find extensive expression in books and papers published in most parts of the world. They are debated at conferences and discussed when 2 or 3 academics are gathered together. Responsible departments of archaeology keep their students abreast of current debate, so that they can understand what they read in books and hear at conferences, and can form their own theoretical stance to archaeology.

The relationship of all this however to what goes on in professional field archaeology is very varied. In Canada, where I've just been, there is quite a close integration between theory and fieldwork. In Japan, as I recently recounted, rejection of theory is total. In Britain reaction is mixed; there are some people working in units today who are interested in theory and who also attempt to apply it to their day-to-day work, in the field, in excavation, in interpretation and in publication. But mostly there is a notable lack of interest and often downright hostility and an expressed desire to go on recovering data regardless of the theoretical framework within which it is perceived or published. Especially is this true in Roman and medieval archaeology, less true of those working in prehistory. It is possible that this is only a passing phase, and as more student graduates move into field archaeology, there will be greater integration. This is certainly a matter on which the IFA should have a stance. I'm not aware that their entry form ask the extent of the candidate's awareness of theoretical studies.

Where theory has made some inroads, it is its more practical aspects that archaeologists in the field have found most attractive — they have found it easier to relate to relatively mundane theory concerned with environment and resources, spatial patterning, and subsistence; rather than with more psychological matters in cognitive studies with behaviour rather than beliefs. Here there appears to be a sharper divide between academic archaeological projects and the day-to-day work of units.

The units themselves had their origins principally in the period of expansion of rescue archaeology in the 1970s. One of the few occasions when British archaeologists got together with a unanimous voice was the famous Barford think tank which resulted in the foundation of RESCUE. Philip Barker was very gratified at the response to his *cri de coeur* about the crisis in British archaeology and the three day mid-week seminar was one of the most stimulating times in the life of all those who took part. Here was sketched the blue print of the structure of British archaeology we all wanted to see. Martin Biddle set out on a blackboard a hierarchical structure with, at the top, a single person. Biddle said, 'I'm not quite sure what this person will be called — perhaps Queen's Antiquary?' A voice from the back was that of Ken Barton, 'Why not just call him Martin Biddle?' — and perhaps things would have been very different if this had happened.

The interesting thing about those days was that the MOPBW, as it was then called, was set up as the Aunt Sally — the reluctant bureaucracy who were not facing up to their responsibilities as a central government agency responsible for recording the nation's cultural heritage. In vain did the inspectors — and some were present at Barford — disclaim such a statutory obligation. Their mandate was really to look after monuments — big upstanding things like castles, abbeys and huge earthworks — certainly not sites where there was nothing for the public to see. Even preservation of known but invisible sites was difficult to achieve; let alone any excavation. The rescue excavations during the war on airfield and other areas of military destruction were very much a by-product, not a perceived duty. Digs that were done in those early years were the result of personal interests within the Ministry. This did not mean that the Ministry did not excavate — it did so on a considerable scale on its own monuments — not to preserve threatened data, but to assist in the historical understanding and exposition of monuments to a fairly elitist public. These excavations were of course often rather unfortunate; these were safe sites; at kindest one could say that the methods used and skills deployed would now be regarded as archaic, and can now be seen to have been moderately destructive; at worst it can be said (as I think John Hunter did) that the stratification of our monuments was being removed so that they could be used for some other purpose.

Excavation on monuments is of course now of much higher quality, such as the brilliant work of Glyn Coppack on our Yorkshire monasteries; and presentation of monuments by English Heritage is now deliberately aimed at a much wider public — at least those who can read: though not as wide as the appeal of the Jorvik Viking Centre, where you don't really have to do much reading to get the message.

During the 1950s the DOE did try to expand the rescue work (fortunately for me), but it must be stressed that this was wholly on their own initiative and not as a result of pressure by archaeologists. It was only when their resources were clearly not sufficient to cope with increasing destruction that they changed from being the beneficent provider of funds to the hopeless bureaucracy who were not spending enough. But RESCUE was formed and the budget was spectacularly raised. MOW/DOE/HBMC/English Heritage have never however admitted publicly that the rise was the result of RESCUE's pressure — they have always said they would have raised the money anyway. The truth about this is one of the great unsolved mysteries of British Archaeology.

But the pressure is now on, and in the early years of RESCUE much was done to take the initiative and force the apparently reluctant DOE to set up the kind of regional organisation that Biddle had suggested at Barford. Ten Regional Units were proposed, costing £100,000 p.a. each — a total of 1 million in 1972, equivalent to perhaps £5 million today — which is in fact about the current HBMC budget for rescue archaeology, so we haven't done too badly. These regional units were talked about in the early 1970s and I wrote a detailed piece for *Rescue News* in 1974 'What kind of Regional units do we need?'. The aim was to impose on DOE a framework not of their designing — which they didn't take very kindly to — hardly surprising. regional units never happened, but Regional committees were set up, again by local initiative; I remember the excitement that surrounded the formation of WEMRAC and the rosy visions we had of a vast programme of excavations all to be financed by DOE, but decided on by us; there was in the West Midlands some precedent for this in the earlier formation of the Severn and Avon Gravels Research Committee — a local group concerned with a specific area and type of site, whose activities were during the 1960s funded by DOE in an amicable way. Indeed it was out of such local groups that the regional organisations were born — together with of course the crucial regional organisations that had existence for many years already — the 14 CBA regional groups. Now these were largely amateur organisations, founded on the long tradition of local archaeological societies and strongly supported by adult education tutors — notably in this area Graham Webster and Philip Barker.

In the 1970s it wasn't only DOE who were slightly reluctant to join the circus; it was also the universities and their archaeologists. They were and are shy about supporting CBA groups, with notable exceptions; and they were in the 1970s very largely against rescue archaeology as such, regarding it as contrary to research-orientated archaeology of an academic kind. Here in Birmingham Lawrence Barfield and I were the only intra-mural archaeologists to give time to rescue, and I incurred the considerable displeasure of the Archaeology Department when I published a map showing the wide geographical scope of their activities — almost anywhere indeed except the West Midlands; and drew attention to the destruction of a Roman fort on this campus (no one from Birmingham at this conference?).

The regional committees were useful in co-ordinating regional excavation strategies, where DOE were willing to give financial backing.

These locally-inspired regional committees were later superseded by the Area Advisory Committees set up by DOE with paid expenses — these could be seen as a serious attempt to set up regional archaeological strategies; but the advice of these committees was not always taken (advice from period bodies?); they were financially killed off in the anti-quango movements.

The original proposals for regional units carried the implication that available finance should be spread evenly geographically over the country, irrespective of the density of archaeology or rate of destruction. That may seem unrealistic today, but we still hear a lot of 'regional presence' and there is no doubt that by Parkinson's Law any regional unit will soon find enough regional archaeology to keep it busy — a point to which I shall return.

In those days, units were formed — in cities, in regions, in rural areas, in areas of special interest; and many if not most survive today, albeit with difficulty and depleted staff. They have had to cope with a competitive situation in which the better-devised schemes — which also met current ideas of what was archaeologically important — got the central government money. Projects could be site-specific, or area-based, or even regionally based. The most remarkable of the latter was the grand strategy for Wessex constructed by Dr Ann Ellison (now Woodward), then director of the Wessex Unit. This gave a priority-rating to a wide range of site types within the region; so that when an opportunity arose through impending destruction, decisions could be taken about resource-expenditure. Such a ranking was bound to be subjective, but it represented the best then available. DOE approved, and it looked as though Wessex at least could have an academically-related research strategy which could be carried through into the 1980s and 1990s. That it was never implemented was not the fault of Ann Ellison. Local and partisan interests intervened. Subsidiary organisations — units, local authorities or museums which were notionally components of Wessex archaeology, if not actually under the direct control of Ann Ellison, didn't altogether relish being told what to do, or what they couldn't do; and moreover they felt some responsibility to parochial interests. If these didn't fall into a high-ranked category, they felt deprived. If a Roman villa was threatened in Little Bagshot, that's what Little Bagshot wanted dug, even if it came bottom of the ranked pile of Ann Ellison's devising. So there were problems with collaboration, and an unwillingness of DOE to force the issue; so this attempt at regional policy was not fully implemented.

Parochial archaeology was often made possible too by local sponsorship, independent of DOE; and since there was and is a growing trend away from central government funding to private or local sponsorship, the trend away from academically-based research strategies was accelerated. The archaeology of Greater Manchester would never have been part of anyone's research strategy in British archaeology — indeed it was doubtful if it actually existed. But it was created, and provided a lot of jobs. The dreaming-up of non-academic archaeology was also multiplied by the huge involvement of MSC-sponsored labour who had to be found something to dig. It was reported, with what truth I'm not sure, that an MSC team was set to dig in a field at Wigan where there was no reason to suspect that there was any archaeology, and indeed nothing was found. Perhaps it was hoped that buried deep here might have been Wigan Pier, with the road leading to it.

The units that were created in the 1970s or later have in some cases had a tough time keeping their staff, and in some cases, like CRAAGS/Western Archaeological Trust, went under. Those that have survived or flourished have done some by an agglomeration of astute and imaginative management, ability to attract good staff, support of local authorities, museums and universities, skill in attracting money from commercial or tycoon sponsors, ingenuity in getting and deploying MSC schemes, and to some extent the creation of local public interest; and of course the ability to invent excavation or post-excavation projects that would appeal to the *eminences grises* in HBMC who decide funding.

A further threat to the units was perceived when the Central Excavation Unit was formed, an extension of large rescue excavation done by central government on their own initiative. I remember suggesting such a thing to the then Ministry of PBW in the 1950s — a flying squad with well-equipped Land Rovers and caravans who would go anywhere and dig anything. It was hardly surprising that DOE/HBMC decided to have their own unit, which could operate quite independently of local units and was directly under the control of the inspectors. There was a good deal of disquiet about the way the CEU was set up — a certain feeling of jobs for the boys, including some boys who didn't have too high a reputation. A lot of good work has in the event been done by the CEU, though there have continued to be murmurings about CEU teams failing to make contact with local archaeologists or units, of resources wasted because of lack of local knowledge and contact, of slowness in publication, and of general lack of accountability to the archaeological public at large. The CEU did not have to go through the laborious process of designing and costing projects, nor did the work done form any part of an agreed academic research framework. This disquiet culminated of course in the decision to dig at Maiden Castle, when it became clear that English Heritage intended to do what it liked with its own money, and a 'them and us' situation was explicit in Lord Montague's words. All attempts to build up a national framework of research, let alone regional ones, have not been successful in our own day. Advice is sometimes sought, but not often taken. An exception is Wales — the trusts *and* CADW.

We need not go into the well-worn problems of project funding or post-excavation backlog funding, but it has become clear that units cannot rely on being kept going by HBMC, even to the extent of retaining core staff; while some units are starved of resources and have to cut back; new ones, like the Fenland Archaeological Trust, are created with HBMC encouragement. In the current year York put in large excavation bids for millions and were given nothing for digging. York has of course diversified, so that this did not lead to wholesale sackings, or indeed any. The units have thus had to be very entrepreneurial in keeping going, and mostly diversified within their own sphere of influence.

We have however seen recently a big change. There had been at least a notional idea of territories and boundaries, within which each should operate. These are now crumbling, and this is presumably currently a problem for the IFA management. We have seen the moving out of urban units into the countryside, where money was available. York is steadily encroaching into North and West Yorkshire, and so far this has not led to any guerrilla warfare or fights with ranging poles. Other units have become even more ambitious, seeking financial support from agencies in Italy, France or elsewhere; and there have of course been gaps in Britain, where there were no units, in which colonisation might be attempted, either by establishing temporary branches of units, or having a flying squad. A good example of this is the territory left vacant for exploitation by the Western Archaeological Trust. This is fair enough as long as there is mutual discussion. There is however latent even in that situation an element of competition, which could lead to cut-price archaeology and lowering of standards. What is more serious is the possibility of units seeking opportunities not only in empty areas, but poaching into the territories of neighbouring units, by foul means, rather than mutual agreement. A few instances of this have been darkly hinted at, but no names, no backfill! It would really have been simpler if we had had our ten regional units as suggested in 1974, each with its own staff and defined territory.

An interesting parallel development has been the involvement of universities in contract archaeology. I have already discussed the gap between academically-generated theory and professional field archaeology. Quite separate from this however has been the struggle of university departments of archaeology themselves to survive. Leeds and St Andrews have gone, and there is a strong pressure group to reduce the number of departments teaching first-degree archaeology from 21 to 9. There has of course been a reaction to this in academic terms, arguing for the special qualities of small departments like York in purely education terms; and the outcome of this war is still in the balance. But all departments have been caught up in the general move towards academic entrepreneurial action to bring not only research funds into departments, but also contract funds. Thus we find university departments have sought funds from diverse sources for rescue and research excavation on a contract basis, for evaluation and fieldwork projects, for post-excavation and publication teams, and even direct involvement in units. Funds coming in this way are welcome to university administrators, boosting the university's paper research revenue and bolstering it against threats of financial cut-back or closure. Individual departments of archaeology can thus safeguard themselves against their own colleagues in other disciplines who want to get rid of archaeology, but are also able to buy hardware like computers, get more space and facilities, and expand staff. They thus appear to be more influential, larger, research-active and socially relevant, which helps to safeguard them against the UGC and Mrs Thatcher. So we may see university departments increasingly in competition with units to secure available money and contracts, in this country and abroad.

We have heard a lot about the need for all archaeologists to communicate with the public; to increase public awareness and interest; to secure public support in local situations, and ultimately in legislation to promote archaeology and preserve its data. A bright spot here is English Heritage's latest membership figure of 89,000 — a great achievement in 2 or 3 years; but we should look very carefully at why so many people want to visit monuments, and so few are interested in archaeology. It should be the other way round — the monuments are dead and sterile, archaeology is alive, but we are failing to make our postholes and pits appeal, though I think things are improving here.

Finally I would like to review the topic of professionalism and career structures in archaeology, which is what the IFA is all about. We need not look again at the traditional jobs available to archaeology — the inspectors in the Office of Works/Ministry of Works/Department of the Environment/HBMC/English Heritage — you name it, it's all the same; the Commissioners; the university academics, etc. What I am looking at here is the hard core of archaeologists working in the field, independently or in units, local government, or in short-term contracts, and the whole business of careers and security.

For some perspective on this we should go back to the late 1950s when people like myself were hired to be directors of digs. There was Brian Hope-Taylor, Ernest Greenfield, John Wacher, Guy Knocker, Faith Vatcher, Charles Greene and others. We were paid 2 gns a day, equivalent to perhaps £20 a day in today's money or for a 5-day week, 46 weeks, about the equivalent of £5000 p.a. Additionally there was a subsistence payment, claimable if one stayed in hotels or lodgings, up to 6 weeks. We freelance diggers were referred to by Paul Ashbee in a book in 1960 as 'soi-disant archaeologists, sort of archaeological tramps, who were ignorant of the nation's prehistory'. Of course, no payment was made for writing-up — this had to be done in one's own time out of the 2 guineas a day.

I still managed to survive and bring up five children; but I had to work mostly seven days a week to do it. I only reminisce in this way to show that being an archaeologist then was tougher than today, and the need for a professional institution greater.

There was also the first digging units, long before the days of the early 1970s and the talk of regional units. There was Brian Philp and his devoted gang, rushing all over Kent doing rescue digs. That was the beginning of one of the surest signs today of a macho archaeologist — the hard hat. I visited Reculver, where Philp and his gang were working, and I was puzzled that everyone had hard hats and each had REG written on them. I wondered why Philp only recruited people called REG; only much later did I find this stood for Reculver Excavation Group.

In the 1970s jobs multiplied, and there were high expectations of jobs in archaeology. I always told my students that I knew of no good archaeologist who was out of a job, but I knew of many second-rate archaeologists who were in jobs — and many of them were appointed in the 1970s. From then on there was not only an expectation — quite unwarranted in my view — that there should be jobs for all archaeologists, but that there should be security in those jobs, and also a secure career structure. This appeared to mean that once you were appointed to an archaeological job, you not only could not be fired, but at regular intervals you were promoted, or got a raise, no matter what you had done, or had not done — the same trend has been observed among university academics. The gradual decline of jobs and opportunities in more recent years has led to more anxiety about security and career structure; and the general feeling that (a) archaeologists were being exploited and (b) we needed a professional qualification to say who was qualified and who was not; why shouldn't archaeology (it was said) be like any other job where you go at 9 and come home at 5, with suitable breaks for coffee, lunch, tea. Well, to me and some of my generation, archaeology is not a job, it's a vocation, a way of life — as Flannery said, the best thing to do with your trousers on. To be involved in archaeology especially in its modern aspects, is a privilege; other people's lives seem on the whole pretty dreary, unless one is a musician, an artist or a writer — Beethoven didn't have a career structure. So if you want holidays and time to devote to your wife and children, don't go into archaeology — go and work in a museum.

What I have said about the last forty years of field archaeology is perhaps another example of the British muddling through — we are after all still top people in world archaeology — and we see the many problems which face the young IFA in its attempts to put our profession on a proper basis.

Appendix E:
Two quotations about PAR written for his *Festschrift* (Carver ed. 1993)

A. Martin Carver (in his Introduction)

It must be pointed out that none of the authors knew they were writing for such a book as this. What brought us all together was the wish to honour an extraordinary friend and colleague, Philip Rahtz, a brilliant excavator, who throughout his career in the field and the classroom has been fascinated, and has fascinated others, on site and off it, with the great mysteries of life itself: birth, love, cult practices and death. Philip, with his lust for life, his passion for music and his dreadful jokes, is by way of being something of a cult himself; and his contribution to the subject of past beliefs has not been small. While others were thinking their way through the jungles of sophistry which have given us a new sense of liberal adventure, Philip, in an equally liberated and adventurous way, was digging his way through a series of ritual conundrums which began with the Roman Temple at Pagans Hill and culminated in the great Dark Age discoveries of Cadbury Congresbury and Cannington.

Through practice, rather than theory, he has greatly advanced the study of Roman temples, late Roman Christianity, the late Celtic West, Dark Age burial and ceremonial, Anglo-Saxon settlement, religion and industry and medieval monasticism, and pioneered the study of modern cemeteries — which he showed to be a rich resource for information on society and its interior ideology right up to the present day. In his years at York he promoted all these fields of study, showing an awareness of the levels of enquiry necessary in the complex arena of cult. Using his incorrigible sense of humour, he showed how ritual interpretations feed on each other, comparing, for example, Bordesley Abbey with the St Gall plan and the Minoan Palace at Mallia, and then re-interpreting it with a 'cult-free' model, where the cloister has become a bowling green and the chancel a (somewhat open-plan) bedroom (94, figs 10, 11). With a similar lightness of touch, he was among the first to emphasise the ethical and intellectual questions inherent in digging up bodies. In 1989 he was still calling for a code of conduct to help resolve the problems of investigating the cults of others (144, 88). Behind this call for ethical standards was a realisation that archaeologists are not themselves neutral, that curiosity and the search for new knowledge must be powered by a particular motor in the mind. Philip, involved often (but by no means exclusively) in Medieval Archaeology, was most aware of this trend in archaeologists of a Christian persuasion, those most susceptible of seeing the foot-print of an itinerant cleric in the dust of an abandoned chicken run. 'It has taken two decades of hints', he announced proudly in his CBA Presidential Address (144, p79), 'to ensure the secularisation of Tintagel . . . as the rocky stronghold of an early state module, rather than the sea-girt retreat of Celtic ascetics.'

His propensity to detect and unsettle rigid positions, political or religious, is a valuable asset in an archaeologist, especially one concerned from time to time with the interpretation of ritual. If the emperor is not wearing clothes, Philip is delighted to point this out; and even if the emperor is wearing clothes he is quick to suggest he take them off anyway. There can be few people resident in the northern hemisphere quite so fond of undressing.

At York, we not only cherish the Department he established, but the highly original undergraduate degree he created. He has also been a sturdy and unselfish supporter, and constructive critic, of the Sutton Hoo project since it began. Putting this book together has been a small gesture of celebration for all he has done for Sutton Hoo, for York, and for a handful of his many friends, gathered here to salute him.

B. Lawrence Butler (his chapter 25)

In many of our cathedrals and at the great parish churches in the county towns of Britain will be found chapels devoted to the memory of local regiments. From their vaulting hang many embroidered flags, some still new and colourful, others tattered, thread-bare and windswept on which the battle honours of the Crimean and Peninsular Wars can scarcely be discerned. The career of a field archaeologist has many parallels to the travels and conquests of a regiment. He conducts his work in many fields, both literally and metaphorically. He gathers campaign honours: some are the colourful dust-jackets of his latest book, while others are the faded yellowing pages of a long-forgotten offprint. However, all contribute to the corpus of published work that marks the most visible facet of a life spent on the battlefields of archaeology.

When presenting an appreciation of Philip Rahtz, it is important to stress that a mere commentary on published papers, extensive though that assemblage is, would give a biased and unrepresentative view of his contribution to and impact upon archaeology, particularly in the medieval field. Secondly, it is not an entire life spent in archaeology, but rather, like Sir Cyril Fox and Gordon Childe, it is a half-life entered upon in full maturity; in Philip's case after service in wartime RAF, in the schoolroom and as a professional photographer.

A medieval craftsman passed through three stages of development; as apprentice, journeyman and master, and in Philip's own career, we can observe similar stages. The early years in Bristol following in the footsteps of Professor Tratman were the apprentice period. In the show cases at Wookey Hole Cavern are Tratman's trowel, hand-brush and knee pads indicative of the tools of the archaeologist and speleologist. Perhaps a notebook of Philip's should be there too, because it was under the Mendips, and upon the hills as at Butcombe's medieval windmill mound that the formative years were spent. Sharing with Philip in field visits on the deserted medieval farmsteads near Draycott and Cheddar, watching the moon rise over Dundry Hill, staying spartanly at Cotham Road with the 'Studio Rahtz' photo-display board outside gave me an insight into some of the delights and deprivations of an embryonic archaeological career.

The campaign of excavation at Chew Valley Lake with its wide range of settlement sites was the turning-point in Philip's career. With the encouragement of John Hurst he and Ernest Greenfield became in 1953 full-time itinerant archaeologists. The variety of periods encountered at Chew Valley, and the scale of the earth-moving operations to create the reservoir, meant that this was excavation on a heroic scale but the circumstances also provided an excellent training in field method and recording. At a period when multi-period regional archaeology had scarcely been invented, this microscopic examination of a valley floor in totality (not as a variety of isolated sites) was to play a significant part in the development of landscape archaeology. The gap between the completion of the report and its publication in 1979 may well have served to diminish the novelty of the approach, but the urge to publish promptly has been another prominent feature in Philip's career. For him, as for Sir Mortimer Wheeler, the date of discovery stems not from its first excavation but from its first publication. Indeed Philip's continual encouragement of British Archaeological Reports stemmed from his frequent experience of frustrating delays in county journals and government publications.

After Chew Valley, dug from his base in Bristol, the journeyman phase really began with campaigns of excavation short or long throughout southern England mainly for the Ministry of Works and its successive re-incarnations. The site hut, the tools (stamped G VI R), the brown 'shoe-boxes' meticulously tied together with fraying white string, the strawboard tubes, the gummed Official Paid labels and all the other paraphernalia of government excavation might be deposited anywhere, perhaps beside a rutted track on the chalk downland or at the edge of a suburban housing estate. Some sites were prosaic, such as the moated homestead at Humberston near Leicester or the cliff-top fringe of the Saxon monastery at Whitby; others were inspirational, such as the enclosed hut-group at Shearplace Hill or the deserted village at Holworth. In all of these sites, one can discern in the published report the methodical approach to a job — capably tackled, briskly analysed and presented without frills. His photographic flair shows through in the illustrations which conveyed a highly-developed visual sense for the essential character of the excavated surfaces. However, there were two sites which seem to be prophetic of future developments: Cannington heralded Philip's later concern with sub-Roman and Saxon Somerset; the field-courses at the deserted Anglo-Saxon town of Torksey marked a period of collaboration with Maurice Barley which had arisen from adult education teaching and which foreshadowed a change in career direction.

In October 1963 Philip moved to Birmingham as Lecturer in Medieval Archaeology, only the second such appointment in a major university. The skills learnt in adult education at the village halls and in the evening classes were put to good account. Philip is essentially a lecturer to listen to, to be provoked by and be stimulated to new insights, because his material is always the fruit of first-hand experience and not the dull derivative knowledge trawled only from books. In one sense this was a fallow period : the teaching load was not excessive, the students were seldom committed to the subject matter of Archaeology but came as historians wishing to extend their methods of enquiry. Yet those who chose to study The Medieval Village relished the contrast with other lecturers and often met the challenge. This was also a time for consolidation: the treadmill of excavation, analysis and publication had left little time for wider reading or for contact with an academic atmosphere. Now there was opportunity to embark on valuable collaboration between the green field approach and the ivory tower (or at least red-brick) approach; this is best illustrated by the excavations at Upton with Rodney Hilton and those at Deerhurst with Harold Taylor and myself. This was also a period for exploring the limits of the evidence and for testing hypotheses in a more leisurely fashion. At both Upton and Deerhurst there were initiated area surveys to provide an integrated landscape study and a broader context in which to perceive a major field monument or settlement.

With the move to Birmingham the journeyman years were over and the stage of mastership had been reached. This was marked by the award of an M.A. by Bristol University for his work on the palaces at Cheddar, another major contribution to the archaeology of the Bristol region. In a more general sense the master's role was worthily assumed because his supervision of a generation of post-graduates influenced their careers and encouraged their publications. The magisterial view was also expressed in his teaching on the techniques of excavation, in his publication on how to publish archaeological reports (59) and in his strong advocacy of the 'RESCUE' cause. The Barford conference in 1970 ushered in a decade of change in archaeological opportunities; the past was under threat and the challenge was met by more cash, more jobs, more field units and more publications. Philip was characteristically at the forefront of this campaign, and his editorship of the Penguin paperback (61) indicated the respect in which he was held by his fellow professionals. He seldom sat on the routine and repetitive university committees, but preferred the committees with an identifiable objective and a sense of dynamic urgency such as those spawned by the RESCUE initiative. Yet these Birmingham years also marked an extension of his horizons and a crystallisation of his academic purpose. Lectures in the United States, a medieval excavation in Yugoslavia and an academic exchange with Ghana brought tangible returns.

The crystallisation of academic direction was the fruit of two excavations thrust upon Philip (Cheddar and Cannington) and of two excavations undertaken by choice (Glastonbury 1962-8 and Cadbury Congresbury 1968-73). All were located in that area of grassy knolls around the Somerset Levels; all were focused on the early Christian period — that dark age of slow penetration by Saxon settlers anxious to utilise the summer marshlands. Ony the highest standards of excavation could wrest a coherent story from the thin soil cover. At Glastonbury the sites available for excavation were Chalice Well, The Tor and Beckery Chapel. These could be regarded as peripheral to a proper understanding of the main monastic ritual centre, but paradoxically this was a great virtue, affording an ideal opportunity to apply purely archaeological criteria and to strip these three sites away from the accumulated legend and to refute its modern romantic purveyors. This characteristic directness is to be valued highly: the absence of pretentiousness, the readiness to take each site and each person at face value, the honesty of personal approach and the desire to adopt the pragmatic experience were the fruit of experience. The readiness to collaborate with fellow academics and to achieve excellent working relationships with so many, both young and old, has been another distinctive facet of his work. Excavating at 'Cadcong' with Peter Fowler was another fruitful partnership and both contributed to the influential Archaeology of Anglo-Saxon England (68).

The move as Professor to York brought his career to a fitting climax but also carried the responsibility to put his archaeological field experience and philosophy into practice for the benefit of the next generation. He faced squarely the challenge of conveying the subject as a branch of proto-history but also as an integrated subject in its own right capable of being presented thematically. Some of this argument has been expressed as the intellectual partnership of the female academic (Tania Dickinson) and 'a hairy digger' (Philip Rahtz). The need to underpin the York courses as something more than practical and vocational field-training led to two new directions.

One direction was the emphasis upon ethnography and modern material culture. This had been foreshadowed in his study of well ritual at Chalice Well and in Donegal, in his concern with primitive mill machinery at Tamworth and in Crete, and in his encouragement of churchyard studies at Deerhurst and Wharram Percy.

The other fresh academic direction was an examination of the theoretical basis of archaeology, developed in the work of Binford, Clarke, Renfrew and Hodder. Neither academic approach had previously been applied seriously to archaeology of the historically documented periods in Britain. It was worth making the attempt, if only because it challenged the historians' denigrating attitudes to archaeology. Only time will tell whether this approach has a lasting validity, whether it is a temporary academic fashion or whether it is a necessary staging point in the development of medieval material culture studies.

The search for a more rigorous approach to the formulation of research strategies and site interpretations has been applied to Wharram Percy in the recent years of York University's involvement there. This stems from Philip's desire to involve both under-graduates and post-graduates in the decision-making process implicit in excavation and the use of archaeologically-derived material. Such an exploration of new evidence and new perceptions is always a worthwhile challenge and one in which Philip excels.

Another aspect which the next generation of archaeologists will be better capable of judging is the use of video material in lectures. Archaeology is essentially a discipline to be experienced visually; it has far less claim to be deliberately cerebral and literary than the Humanities. It is based on learning through seeing, feeling and doing. The ploughed field is the archaeologist's laboratory; he takes pleasure in what lies exposed on its surface and delights in what can be revealed when the blanket of turf is removed. This is where the accumulation of photographic and video material will not date; Philip has had the percipience to appreciate this as only a few others have.

The lack of pretension, the facility for close collaboration and his intellectual honesty are the principal characteristics of Philip's work. His ready use of humour, often at his own expense, always makes co-operation a pleasurable experience and provided a relaxed atmosphere on excavations and at seminars. My own copy of a 'pin-up' Bokerly Venus with Philip's characteristic comment on her charms illustrates this attitude most succinctly. For those colleagues able to share in his other pleasures, an eclectic love of music and an enthusiastic pursuit of foreign travel, they were privileged to enter a more private and personal world. His whole-hearted approach to life has gained him many friends and disarmed a few opponents. This collection of essays has been inspired by the belief that the practice of Archaeology is a rigorous discipline: one that has public responsibilities and yet provides many compensatory private pleasures. Philip has expressed these views in his words and actions.

List of publications

Lorna Watts has compiled this list of my principal publications (i.e. excluding ephemera); an earlier version was originally published in the *Festschrift* offered to me by Martin Carver and other colleagues in 1992 (Carver ed. 1993); she gave a serial number to each, arranging them in order of publication. These are not the numbers given below; the new numbering is that referred to in the text.

To her list, I have added a few other reports; of excavations which I directed, but which were published by others, in pursuance of higher degrees.

1951
[1]   'The Roman Temple at Pagans Hill, Chew Stoke, Somerset', *Proceedings of the Somerset Archaeological & Natural History Society*, 96: 112-142

1957
[2]   (with L.G. Harris) 'The Temple Well and Other Buildings at Pagans Hill, Chew Stoke, North Somerset', *Proceedings of the Somerset Archaeological & Natural History Society*, 101/102 [volume for 1956-7]: 15-51

[3]   'Kings Weston Down Camp, Bristol, 1956', *Proceedings of the University of Bristol Spelaeological Society*, 8 (1) [volume for 1956-7]: 30-38

1958
[4]   (with M.H. Rahtz) 'T40: Barrow and Windmill at Butcombe, North Somerset', *Proceedings of the University of Bristol Spelaeological Society*, 8 (2) [volume for 1957-58]: 89-96

[5]   'Dover: Stembrook and St Martin-le-Grand, 1956', *Archaeologia Cantiana*, 72: 111-137

[6]   (with A.M. ApSimon and L.G. Harris) 'The Iron Age A Ditch and Pottery at Pagans Hill, Chew Stoke', *Proceedings of the University of Bristol Spelaeological Society*, 8 (2) [volume for 1957-8]: 97-105

[7]   (with D.B. Harden, G.C. Dunning and C.A. Ralegh Radford) 'Three Post-Roman Finds from the Temple Well at Pagans Hill, Somerset', *Medieval Archaeology*, 2: 104-111

1959
[8]   'Humberstone Earthwork, Leicester', *Transactions of the Leicestershire Archaeological and Historical Society*, 35: 1-32

[9] 'Holworth, Medieval Village Excavation, 1958', *Proceedings of the Dorset Natural History and Archaeological Society*, 81: 127-147

[10] (with C. Green) 'Excavations of Ermine Street in Lincolnshire', *Antiquaries Journal*, 39: 77-86

[11] (with J.C. Brown) 'Blaise Castle Hill, Bristol: 1957', *Proceedings of the University of Bristol Spelaeological Society*, 8 (3): 147-171

1960
[12] (with H.M. Colvin) 'King John's Palace, Clipstone, Notts', *Transactions of the Thoroton Society of Nottinghamshire*, 64: 21-43

[13] (with J.W.G. Musty) 'Excavations at Old Sarum, 1957', *Wiltshire Archaeological and Natural History Magazine*, 57 [volume for 1958-60]: 353-370

[14] 'Two Mounds on Row Down, Lambourn, Berks', *Berkshire Archaeological Journal*, 58: 20-32

[15] *Pleshey Castle, First Interim Report, 1960*, Essex Archaeological Society, 35pp

[16] 'Caistor, Lincolnshire, 1959', *Antiquaries Journal*, 40: 175-187

[17] 'Excavations by the Town Wall, Baldwin Street, Bristol, 1957', *Transactions of the Bristol and Gloucestershire Archaeological Society*, 79: 221-250

1961
[18] 'Barrow Mead, Bath, Somerset', *Proceedings of the Somerset Archaeological & Natural History Society*, 105: 61-76

Appendix B, 'The Pottery' (in C.M. Sykes and G.A. Brown, 'The Wraxall Villa') *Proceedings of the Somerset Archaeological and Natural History Society*, 105: 37-51

1962
[19] (with L.V. Grinsell and A. Warhurst) *The Preparation of Archaeological Reports*, Bristol Archaeological Research Group. 33pp

[20] 'Excavations at Shearplace Hill, Sydling St Nicholas, Dorset, England', *Proceedings of the Prehistoric Society*, 28: 289-328

[21] 'Neolithic and Beaker Sites at Downton, Near Salisbury, Wiltshire', *Wiltshire Archaeological and Natural History Magazine*, 58. [volume for 1961-63]: 116-141

[22] 'Farncombe Down Barrow, Berkshire', *Berkshire Archaeological Journal*, 60: 1-24

[23] 'Whitby 1958', *Yorkshire Archaeological Journal*, 40 (160): 604-618

1963

[24]   'A Roman Villa at Downton', *Wiltshire Archaeological and Natural History Magazine*, 58: 303-341

[25]   'The Saxon and Medieval Palaces at Cheddar, Somerset — An Interim Report of Excavations 1960-62', *Medieval Archaeology*, 6-7 [Volume for 1962-63]: 53-66

[26]   (with K.J. Barton) 'Maes Knoll Camp, Dundry, Somerset', *Proceedings of the University of Bristol Spelaeological Society*, 10 (1) [volume for 1962-63]: 9-15

[27]   'An Excavation on Bokerly Dyke, 1958', *Archaeological Journal*, 118: 65-99

[28]   (with L.V. Grinsell and A. Warhurst) *The Preparation of Archaeological Reports*, Bristol Archaeological Research Group (2nd ed). 35pp

1964

[29]   'Saxon and Medieval Features at Downton, Salisbury', *Wiltshire Archaeological and Natural History Magazine*, 59: 124-129

[30]   (with J. Musty) 'The Suburbs of Old Sarum', *Wiltshire Archaeological and Natural History Magazine*, 59: 130-154

[31]   'Excavations at Chalice Well, Glastonbury', *Proceedings of the Somerset Archaeological and Natural History Society*, 108: 143-163

        'The Saxon and Medieval Palaces at Cheddar, Somerset — An Interim Report of Excavations in 1960-62', *Proceedings of the Somerset Archaeological & Natural History Society*, 108: 99-112. Reprint of [25]

        'Review: *Practical Archaeology*, by G. Webster (1963)', *Bulletin of the Bristol Archaeological Research Group*, 1 (8): 106-107

        'Review: *Archaeology and the Microscope*, by L. Biek (1963)', *Bulletin of the Bristol Archaeological Research Group*, 1(8): 107-108

1965

        'The Post Medieval Period - Field Antiquities', in L.V. Grinsell (ed.), *A Survey and Policy concerning the Archaeology of the Bristol Region, Part II, from 1066*, 16-18. Bristol Archaeological Research Group

1966

[32]   (with A. Warhurst and L.V. Grinsell) *The Preparation of Archaeological Reports*. John Baker (Revised ed.) 71pp

[33]   (with R.H. Hilton) 'Upton, Gloucestershire, 1959-1964', *Transactions of the Bristol and Gloucestershire Archaeological Society*, 85: 70-146

[34]   (with G.C. Boon) 'Third Century Counterfeiting at Whitchurch, Somerset', *Archaeological Journal*, 122: 13-51

[35]   'Kenilworth Castle, 1960', *Transactions of the Birmingham and Warwickshire Archaeological Society*, 81: 55-73

[36]   'Cheddar Vicarage 1965', *Proceedings of the Somerset Archaeological & Natural History Society*, 110: 52-84

'Medieval Sites South of Bath', in *A North Somerset Miscellany*, 25-26. Bath and Camerton Archaeological Society

1967

'Sub-Roman Cemeteries in Somerset', *Bulletin of the Bristol Archaeological Research Group*, 2 (8): 103-106

1968

[37]   'Sub-Roman Cemeteries in Somerset', in M.W. Barley & R.P.C. Hanson (eds), *Christianity in Britain 300-700*, 193-195. Leicester University Press

[38]   'Glastonbury Tor', in G. Ashe (ed.), *The Quest for Arthur's Britain*, 139-153. London

[39]   (with P.J. Fowler) 'Somerset Dark Age Problems', *Bulletin of the Bristol Archaeological Research Group*, 3 (3): 57-61

[39A]   'Hereford', *Current Archaeology* 9 (July 1968), 242-46

(with P.J. Fowler and K. Gardner) 'An Introduction to Cadcong', *Current Archaeology*, 11: 291-295

1969

[40]   *Excavations at King John's Hunting Lodge, Writtle, Essex, 1955-57*, Monograph 3. Society for Medieval Archaeology. 118pp

[41]   'Upton, Gloucestershire, 1964-1968', *Transactions of the Bristol and Gloucestershire Archaeological Society*, 88: 74-126

[42]   'Cannington Hillfort 1963', *Proceedings of the Somerset Archaeological & Natural History Society*, 113: 56-68

(with others) *Medieval Sites in the Mendip, Cotswold Wye Valley and Bristol Region*. Bristol Archaeological Research Group. 32 pp

'Review: *The Sutton-Hoo Ship Burial, A Handbook*, by R.L.S. Bruce-Mitford (1968)', *History*, 54: 252

1970

[43]   'Whitby 1958, Site Two', *Yorkshire Archaeological Journal*, 42: 72-73

[44]   'Medieval and Later Archaeology in England and Wales', *Kwartalnik Historii Kultury Materialnej*, 18 (4): 587-615

[45]   'Archaeology in the University of Birmingham', *Alta*, 11: 261-267. Reprinted in
the *West Midlands Archaeological News Sheet*, 13 (1970), 14-24

[46]   (with P.J. Fowler and K.S. Gardner) *Cadbury Congresbury, Somerset, 1968*. Dept of
Extramural Studies, University of Bristol. 48pp

[47]   'Excavations on Knighton Hill, Broad Chalke, 1959', *Wiltshire Archaeological and
Natural History Magazine*, 65: 74-88

[48]   'A Possible Saxon Palace near Stratford-upon-Avon', *Antiquity*,44 (174): 137-143

    (with P.J. Fowler) 'Cadcong 1970', *Current Archaeology*, 23: 337-342

    (with S. Hirst) 'Hatton Rock, nr. Stratford-upon-Avon', *West Midlands
Archaeological News Sheet*, 13: 40
    'Review: *Archaeological Photography*, by H.C. Simmons (1969)', *Post Medieval
Archaeology*, 4: 197-198

    'Review: *Anglo-Saxon Pottery and the Settlement of England*, by J.N.L. Myres (1969)',
History, 55: 231-232

1971
[49]   'Excavations on Glastonbury Tor, Somerset, 1964-6', *Archaeological Journal*, 127: 1-81

[50]   'Castle Dore — A Reappraisal of the Post-Roman Structures', *Cornish Archaeology*,
10: 49-54

    'Review: *Deserted Medieval Villages*, by M. Beresford and J.G. Hurst (1971)',
Archaeological Journal, 128: 281-283. Reprinted in *MVRG Report*, 19 (1971), 16-18.

1972
[51]   (with P.J. Fowler) 'Somerset AD 400-700', in P.J. Fowler (ed.), *Archaeology and the
Landscape*, 187-221. John Baker

[52]   (with S. Hirst) 'Hatton Rock 1970', *Transactions of the Birmingham and Warwickshire
Archaeological Society*, 85: 170-177

    (with K. Sheridan) 'Fifth Report of Excavations at Tamworth, Staffs, 1971 — A
Saxon Water-Mill in Bolebridge Street. An Interim Note', *Transactions of the South
Staffordshire Archaeological and Historical Society*, 13 [volume for 1971-72]: 9-16

    'Review: *Hand-List of Anglo-Saxon Non-Runic Inscriptions*, by E. Okasha (1971)',
History, 57: 412-413

1973
[53]   'Monasteries as Settlements', *Scottish Archaeological Forum*, 5: 125-135

[54]   (with S. Hirst) 'Cheddar Vicarage 1970', *Proceedings of the Somerset Archaeological &
Natural History Society*, 117: 65-96

[55]   'The Crisis in Church Archaeology', *Research Bulletin of the Institute for the Study of Worship and Religious Architecture, University of Birmingham*, 28-43

[56]   '"RESCUE" and Archaeology in the West Midlands', *Midland History*, 2 (1): 1-10

[57]   'What kind of Regional Units do we need?', *Rescue News*, 4: 2-5

[58]   'Grave Recording', *West Midlands Archaeological News Sheet*, 16: 6, 7

'Review: *The Early Christian Archaeology of North Britain* (1971) and *Britain and Ireland in Early Christian Times A.D. 400-800* (1972)', by C. Thomas, *History*, 58: 75-76

'Review: *"By South Cadbury is that Camelot"*, by L. Alcock (1972)', *History*, 58: 423

1974
[59]   (with J. Price-Williams and L.V. Grinsell) *The Preparation of Archaeological Reports*. John Baker (2nd ed.). 105pp

[60]   (with S. Hirst) *Beckery Chapel, Glastonbury*. Glastonbury Antiquarian Society. 93pp

[61]   (editor) *Rescue Archaeology*. Pelican. 299pp

'Rescue Digging Past and Present', in P. Rahtz (ed.), *Rescue Archaeology*, 53-72. Pelican

'Volunteers', in P. Rahtz (ed.), *Rescue Archaeology*, 274-279. Pelican

[62]   'Pottery in Somerset, A.D. 400-1066', in V.I. Evison et al (eds.), *Medieval Pottery from excavations*. Studies Presented to G.C. Dunning, 95-126, London

[63]   (with C. Flight) 'A Quern Factory near Kintampo, Ghana', *West African Journal of Archaeology*, 4: 1-31

[64]   E.C. Klingelhofer, *The Deserted Medieval Village of Broadfield, Herts*, British Archaeological Reports, 2. Oxford

'Rahtz on Standards', *Rescue News*, 7: 7

1975
[65]   'How Likely is Likely?', *Antiquity*, 49 (193): 59-61

[66]   (with J. Graham-Campbell) 'British Antiquity, 1974-5. Western British, Irish and Later Anglo-Saxon', *Archaeological Journal*, 132: 349-361

[67]   (with L.A.S. Butler and H.M. Taylor) 'Deerhurst 1971-1974. The Society's Research Report on the Archaeology of the English Church', *Antiquaries Journal*, 55: 346-365

'Atcham Timber Halls, Salop', *West Midlands Archaeological News Sheet*, 18: 58-60

'Review: [1] *Landscape Archaeology* (1974) and [2] *Fieldwork in Medieval Archaeology* (1974), by [1] M. Aston and T. Rowley and [2] C. Taylor, *Medieval Archaeology*, 19: 276-277

'Review: *Landscape Archaeology*, by M. Aston and T. Rowley (1974)', *Rescue News*, 15: 8-9

1976

[68] 'Buildings and Rural Settlement', in D.M. Wilson (ed.), *The Archaeology of Anglo-Saxon England*, 49-98. London

[69] 'Appendix A: Gazetteer of Anglo-Saxon Domestic Sites', in D.M. Wilson (ed.), *The Archaeology of Anglo-Saxon England*, 405-452. London

[70] 'Appendix C: The Building Plan of the Anglo-Saxon Monastery of Whitby Abbey' in D.M. Wilson (ed.), *The Archaeology of Anglo-Saxon England*, 459-462. London

[71] 'The Archaeology of the Churchyard', in P.V. Addyman & R. Morris (eds.), *The Archaeological Study of Churches*, Research Report 13, 41-45. Council for British Archaeology

[72] 'Research Directions at Deerhurst', in P.V. Addyman & R. Morris (eds.), *The Archaeological Study of Churches*, Research Report 13, 60-63. Council for British Archaeology

[73] *Excavations at St Mary's Church, Deerhurst, 1971-73*. Research Report 15. Council for British Archaeology. 59pp

[74] (with S. Hirst) *Bordesley Abbey, Redditch, Hereford-Worcestershire, First Report on Excavations 1969-1973*, British Archaeological Reports, 23. 277pp. Oxford

[75] (with S. Hirst) *Bordesley Abbey, Redditch. An Introductory Booklet*. School of History, University of Birmingham. 25pp

[76] 'Irish Settlement in Somerset', *Proceedings of the Royal Irish Academy*, 76: 223-230

[77] 'Stonefield Slaters — Old Oxfordshire Song', *Oxford Archaeological Unit News Letter*, 1: 2

[78] J. Woodhouse, *Barrow Mead, Bath 1964: Excavation of a Medieval Peasant House*, British Archaeological Reports, 28. Oxford
'Atcham Timber Halls', *West Midlands Archaeological News Sheet*, 19: 53-54

'Review: [1] *The Mystery of Arthur* (1975) and [2] *Arthurian Sites in the West* (1975), by [1] E. Jenkins and [2] C.A. Ralegh Radford and M.J. Swanton, *Antiquity*, 50 (198): 161-163

'Review: *The Written Record*, by S. Hirst (1976)', *West Midlands Archaeological News Sheet*, 19: 76-77

1977

[79]   (with E. Greenfield) *Excavations at Chew Valley Lake*. Archaeological Report 8. Department of the Environment. Dated 1977 but actually published 1979. 392pp

[80]   'The Archaeology of West Mercian Towns', in A. Dornier (ed.), *Mercian Studies*, 107-129. Leicester University Press

[81]   (with D. Bullough) 'The Parts of an Anglo-Saxon Mill', *Anglo-Saxon England*, 6: 15-37

[82]   'Late Roman Cemeteries and Beyond', in R. Reece (ed.), *Burial in the Roman World*, Research Report 22, 53-66. Council for British Archaeology

[83]   F. Williams, *Pleshey Castle, Essex (XII-XVI Century)*, British Archaeological Reports 42. Oxford

          'Levels in Publication [= WEMORANDA]', *Rescue News*, 14: 2-3

          'Graveyard Recording — A Reply to Dr White', *Bulletin of the Council for British Archaeology Churches Committee*, 6: 9-11

          'Review: *Monuments and Their Inscriptions. A Practical Guide*, by H.L. White (1977)', *Rescue News*, 14: 13

          'Review: *Excavations at Portchester Castle II: Saxon*, by B. Cunliffe (1976)', *Medieval Archaeology*, 21: 266-268

1978

[84]   'Grave Orientation', *Archaeological Journal*, 135: 1-14

[85]   'The New Department at York', *Antiquity*, 52 (206): 241-242

[86]   'How To Get An Excavation Finished; Or Night-Thoughts After Reading P.A. Barker *Techniques of Archaeological Excavation*' (1978), *Current Archaeology*, 63: 127

          'The Concept of Continuity in Settlement Studies', *MVRG Annual Report*, 26: 35-36

1979

[87]   *The Saxon and Medieval Palaces at Cheddar; Excavations, 1960-1962*. British Series 65. British Archaeological Reports. 411pp

[88]   (with L. Watts) 'The End of Roman Temples in the West of Britain [with appendices on 'Lydney' and 'A Modern Shrine in Donegal']', in P.J. Casey (ed.), *The End of Roman Britain*. British Archaeological Reports, 71, 183-210

[89]   'Thirty-Three Years' Digging in Somerset', Presidential Address, *Proceedings of the Somerset Archaeological & Natural History Society*, 123: 19-26

'Sunken-featured Buildings', *MVRG Annual Report*, 27: 32-33

1980

[90] (edited with T.M. Dickinson and L. Watts) *Anglo-Saxon Cemeteries 1979*. British Archaeological Reports 82, 389pp. Oxford

[91] *Wharram Data Sheets*. Department of Archaeology, University of York. 23pp

[92] 'Dilemma of Rescue Versus Research' *The Times Higher Education Supplement*, 376 (4.1.80): 9. [re Sutton Hoo]

'Dilemma of Rescue Versus Research', *Rescue News*, 21: 8 [re Sutton Hoo] (shortened version of 92)

[93] 'Review: *Yeavering, An Anglo-British Centre of Early Northumbria*, by B. Hope-Taylor (1977)', *Medieval Archaeology*, 24: 265-270

(with T.M. Dickinson) 'Editorial Preface', in P.A. Rahtz, T.M. Dickinson, & L. Watts (eds.), *Anglo-Saxon Cemeteries 1979*, British Series 82, 3-7. British Archaeological Reports

'Sutton Hoo Opinions — Forty Years After', in P.A. Rahtz, T.M. Dickinson & L. Watts (eds.), *Anglo-Saxon Cemeteries 1979*, British Series 82, 313-326. British Archaeological Reports

'Motivation in Archaeology', *Popular Archaeology*, 1 (10): 42-44

'Review: *Anglo-Saxon England*, by L. Laing and J. Laing (1979), *History*, 65: 101-102

'Review: *A Guide to the Dark Age Remains in Britain*, by L. Laing and J. Laing (1979)', *History*, 65: 102

'Review: *Rescue Archaeology in the Bristol Area I* (1979)', *Bristol Archaeological Research Group Review*, I: 57-58

'Review: *Medieval Worcester - An Archaeological Framework*, by M.O.H. Carver (1980)', *West Midlands Archaeology*, 23: 137-139

'Review: *Whitbourne — A Bishop's Manor*, by P. Williams (1979)', *West Midlands Archaeology*, 23: 140-141

1981

[94] *The New Medieval Archaeology or 'King Arthur and his Random Number Table'* (Inaugural lecture delivered 1980). University of York. 34 pp

[95] 'Artefacts of Christian Death', in S.C. Humphries & H. King (eds.), *Mortality and Immortality: The Anthropology of Death*, 117-136. Academic Press

[96]   'Medieval Milling (with appendices on 'Horizontal-wheeled watermills on Crete' (with L. Watts) and on 'The Origins of Horizontal-wheeled Watermills . . .')', in D.W. Crossley (ed.), *Medieval Industry*, Research Report 40, 1-15, Council for British Archaeology

[97]   *Wharram Data Sheets*. Medieval Village Research Group. (2nd ed.). 33pp

        'Tamworth Staffs', in J. Schofield and D. Palliser, with C. Harding (ed.), *Recent Archaeological Research in English Towns*, 97-98. Council for British Archaeology

        'Review: *Earlier Medieval Sites (410-1066) in and around Bristol and Bath, the South Cotswold and Mendip*, by E. Fowler and others (1980)', *Medieval Archaeology*, 25: 231-232

        'Review: [1] *The Church of St Helen-on-the-Walls, Aldwark* (1980) and [2] *The Cemetery of St Helen-on-the-Walls, Aldwark* (1980), by [1] J.R. Magilton and [2] J.D. Dawes and J.R. Magilton', *Yorkshire Archaeological Journal*, 53: 157-158

1982

[98]   'Celtic Society in Somerset AD 400-700', *Bulletin of the Board of Celtic Studies*, 30: 176-200

[99]   'The Dark Ages AD 400-700', in M. Aston & I. Burrow (eds.), *The Archaeology of Somerset*, 99-108. Somerset County Council

[100]   'Architectural Reconstruction of Timber Buildings from Archaeological Evidence: Comments on F.W.B. Charles "Post-Construction and the Rafter Roof"', *Vernacular Architecture*, 13: 39-41

[101]   'Review: Archaeology, History and Planning: A Review Article on "West Yorkshire: An Archaeological Survey to AD 1500", by M. Faull and S. Moorhouse, eds. (1981)', *Yorkshire Archaeological Journal*, 54: 153-157

        (with P.J. Fowler) 'Introduction', in M. Aston & L. Burrow (eds.), *The Archaeology of Somerset*, 1-3. Somerset County Council

        'Review: *Birka IV — The Burial Customs — A Study of the Graves on Björkö*, by A.-S. Graslund (1980)', *Medieval Archaeology*, 26: 234-236

1983

[102]   'New Approaches to Medieval Archaeology, Part I', in D.A. Hinton (ed.), *25 Years of Medieval Archaeology*, 12-23. University of Sheffield and Society for Medieval Archaeology

[103]   (with L. Watts) *Wharram Percy: The Memorial Stones of the Churchyard*. Archaeological Publications 1. York University. 38pp

        'Preface', in S.M. Hirst, D.A. Walsh, and S.M. Wright (eds.), *Bordesley Abbey II*, British Series 111, 1-4, British Archaeological Reports

(with L. Watts) 'The Finds', in S.M Hirst, D.A. Walsh & S.M. Wright (eds.), *Bordesley Abbey II*, British Series 111, 129-206, British Archaeological Reports

'The Archaeologist and the Archaeoscientist', *Rescue News*, 30: 2-3

1984

[104]   (with L. Watts) 'Upton: Deserted Medieval Village, Blockley, Gloucestershire, 1973', *Transactions of the Bristol and Gloucestershire Archaeological Society*, 102: 141-154

[105]   'Archaeologists and Architects: Areas of Communication, Collaboration and Conflict', in P.V. Addyman & V.E. Black (eds.), *Archaeological Papers from York Presented to M.W. Barley*, 152-157. York Archaeological Trust

[106]   'The Nuer Medieval Archaeology: Theory vs. History', *Scottish Archaeological Forum*, 3 (2): 109-112

(with L. Watts (eds.)) *Cowlam Wold Barrows*. Archaeological Publications 3. York University. 32pp

'Review: *Early Anglo-Saxon Sussex*, by M.G. Welch (1983)', *History*, 69: 300-301

'Review: *Danebury: Anatomy of an Iron Age Hillfort*, by B. Cunliffe (1983)', *History*, 69: 443

1985

[107]   *Invitation to Archaeology*. Basil Blackwell. 184pp

[108]   *Convite à Arqueologia*. Rio de Janeiro. Portuguese translation of *Invitation to Archaeology*. Dated 1985, but actually published 1989. 187pp

[109]   'Wharram Research Strategies', in D. Hooke (ed.), *Medieval Villages*, Monograph 5, 205-213. Oxford University Committee for Archaeology

[110]   'Wharram Percy Memorial Stones: An Anthropological View from Mars', in D. Hooke (ed.), *Medieval Villages*, Monograph 5, 215-223. Oxford University Committee for Archaeology. (as Rilip Phahtz)

[111]   S. Hirst, *An Anglo-Saxon Inhumation Cemetery at Sewerby, East Yorkshire*, Archaeological Publication 4, York University

'Archaeology and Christian Death', in J. Dyer (ed.), *Archaeology and Death*, 17-19. Council for British Archaeology

'Review: *Excavations on the Site of the Dominican Friary at Guildford in 1974 and 1978*, by R. Poulton and H. Woods (1984)', *Medieval Archaeology*, 29: 244-245

'Review: *Roman Britain to Saxon England*, by C.J. Arnold (1984), *History*, 70: 276

1986

[112] (with L. Watts) *Mary-Le-Port, Bristol Excavations 1962-1963*. Monograph 7. City of Bristol Museum and Art Gallery. 208pp

[113] (with L. Watts) 'The Archaeologist on the Road to Lourdes and Santiago de Compostela', in L.A.S. Butler & R.K. Morris (eds.). *The Anglo-Saxon Church*, Research Report 60, 51-73. Council for British Archaeology

[114] *Invitation to Archaeology*. Basil Blackwell. (Revised re-print). 184pp

[115] (with C. Hayfield and J. Bateman) *Two Roman Villas at Wharram Le Street*. Archaeological Publications 2. York University. 82pp. (Wharram Vol IV)

'How I Became an Archaeologist', *Young Archaeologist*, October: 2-3

'Review: *Roman Bath Discovered*, by B. Cunliffe (1984)', *Urban History Yearbook*, 189-90

'Review: *Middle Saxon Palaces at Northampton*, by J. Williams, M. Shaw and V. Denham (1985)', *Antiquaries Journal*, 66: 450-451

1987

[116] (with A. Ellison) 'Excavations at Hog Cliff Hill, Maiden Newton, Dorset', *Proceedings of the Prehistoric Society*, 53: 223-269

[117] (with A. Ellison) 'Excavations at Whitsbury Castle Ditches, Hampshire, 1960', *Proceedings of the Hampshire Field Club and Archaeological Society*, 43: 63-81

[118] 'Post-Roman Avon', in M. Aston & R. Iles (eds.), *The Archaeology of Avon*, 72-81. Avon County Council

[119] (with S. Hirst) 'The Chapel of St Columbanus at Cheddar', *Somerset Archaeology & Natural History*, 131: 157-161

[120] 'Japan (The President's Piece)', *British Archaeological News*, 1 (9): 78-79

[121] 'Whithorn (The President's Piece)', *British Archaeological News*, 2 (1): 9

[122] 'A New *Antiquity* (The President's Piece)', *British Archaeological News*, 2 (2): 23

[123] 'Sutton Hoo 1987 (The President's Piece)', *British Archaeological News*, 2 (3): 35

[124] 'The First IFA Conference (The President's Piece)', *British Archaeological News*, 2 (4): 43

[125] 'The Keele Seminar on Metal Detecting (The President's Piece)', *British Archaeological News*, 2 (5): 52

[126] 'Monuments in Portugal (The President's Piece)', *British Archaeological News*, 2 (6): 60

[127] 'St Cuthbert AD 687-1987 (The President's Piece)', *British Archaeological News*, 2 (7): 67

'Philip Rahtz [comment on World Archaeological Congress, 1986]', in P. Ucko, *Archaeological Freedom and Apartheid*, 180-182. Duckworth. [also cf. *World Archaeological Bulletin* 1, 21-22]

'Review: *Celtic Britain*, by Charles Thomas (1986)', *History*, 72 (235): 310-11

'Review: *The Archaeology of York: 2/1, 8/1, 14/5, 15/1, 17/3, 17/4, 18/1*', *Medieval Archaeology*, 31: 197-99

1988

[128] 'Decision-making in the Past', *Archaeological Review from Cambridge*, 7 (2): 210-218

[129] 'From Roman to Saxon at Wharram Percy', in J. Price & P.R. Wilson (eds.), *Recent Research in Roman Yorkshire*, British Series 193, 123-137. British Archaeological Reports

[130] 'The End of Roman Wharram Percy', in R.F.J. Jones et al. (eds.), *First Millennium Papers*, International Series 401, 295-301. British Archaeological Reports

[131] (with W.S. Hanson) 'Video Recording on Excavation', *Antiquity*, 62 (234): 106-111

[132] 'Archaeoscifi (The President's Piece)', *British Archaeological News*, 2 (9): 90

[133] 'Theoretical Archaeology Group (The President's Piece)', *British Archaeological News*, 3 (1): 5

[134] 'Perceptions of Bordesley Abbey (The President's Piece)', *British Archaeological News*, 3 (2): 17

[135] 'Homage to Philip Barker (The President's Piece)', *British Archaeological News*, 3 (3): 25

[136] 'Archaeology and the Dead (The President's Piece)', *British Archaeological News*, 3 (4): 33

[137] 'Archaeology of the Dead — Principles and Guidelines (The President's Piece)', *British Archaeological News*, 3 (5): 48

[138] 'Scilly at the Crossroads (The President's Piece)', *British Archaeological News*, 3 (6): 55

[139] 'Beating about the Bush (The President's Piece)', *British Archaeological News*, 3 (7): 66

[140] 'Pepys and Archaeology (The President's Piece)', *British Archaeological News*, 3 (8): 79

[141] 'Raymond Hayes (The President's Piece)', *British Archaeological News*, 3 (9): 88

'Philip Barker — An Appreciation', in A. Burl (ed.), *From Roman Town to Norman Castle*, 68-73. University of Birmingham

'Centenary Address' in *Annual Report Wells Natural History and Archaeological Society 1987-1988*, 15-17

'Review: *Dowsing in Church Archaeology*, by R.N. Bailey, E. Cambridge and H.D. Briggs (1988)', *Antiquity*, 62 (237): 808-9

'Review: *Academic freedom and Apartheid*, by P. Ucko (1988)', *Archaeological Review from Cambridge*, 7 (2): 249-52

'Review: *Anglo-Saxon Gloucestershire*, by C. Heighway (1987)', *Transactions of the Bristol and Gloucestershire Archaeological Society*, 106: 232-3

'Review: *Aspects of the Medieval Landscape of Somerset*, by M. Aston (1988)', *Somerset Archaeology & Natural History*, 132: 356-7

1989

[142]   *Little Ouseburn Barrow 1958*. Archaeological Publications 7. York University. 51pp

[143]   (with L. Watts) 'Pagans Hill Revisited', *Archaeological Journal*, 146: 330-371

[144]   'Ethics in British Archaeology', Presidential Address, in *Annual Report No 39*, 69-82. Council for British Archaeology

[145]   'Avebury and Perception (The President's Piece)', *British Archaeological News*, 4 (1): 5

[146]   'The Bones of St Edward the Martyr (The President's Piece)', *British Archaeological News*, 4 (2): 17-18

[147]   'Life Among the Cave Bears (The President's Piece)', *British Archaeological News*, 4 (3): 38

[148]   'Research in the CBA (The President's Piece)', *British Archaeological News*, 4 (4): 54-55

'Review: *Buried in Hampstead*, by Camden History Society (1986)', *Bulletin of the CBA Churches Committee*, 26: 25-26

1990

[149]   'Bower Chalke 1959: Excavations at Great Ditch Banks and Middle Chase Ditch', *Wiltshire Archaeological and Natural History Magazine*, 83: 1-49

'Forty Years of Research in a Wolds Parish', *The Ryedale Historian*, 15: 9-11.

'Review: *North East Yorkshire Studies: Archaeological Papers*, by Raymond H. Hayes (ed. P. Wilson) (1988)', *The Ryedale Historian*, 15: 34-5

'Review: *The North York Moors — Landscape Heritage*, by D.A. Spratt and B.J.D. Harrison (1989)', *Yorkshire Archaeological Journal*, 62: 220-1

'Review: *The Mills of Medieval England*, by R. Holt (1988)', *Medieval Archaeology*, 34: 269-70

'Review: *Photography in Archaeology and Conservation*, by P.G. Dorrell (1989), *Archaeological Journal, 147*: 471-472

1991
[150]   *Invitation to Archaeology*. Basil Blackwell (2nd revised edition). 182pp

[151]   'Pagan and Christian by the Severn Sea', in L. Abrams & J.P. Carley (eds.), *The Archaeology and History of Glastonbury Abbey. Essays in Honour of the Ninetieth Birthday of C.A. Ralegh Radford*, 3-37. The Boydell Press

1992
[152]   (with others) (CADREX) *Cadbury Congresbury 1968-73. A Late / Post-Roman hilltop settlement in Somerset*. British Series 223. Tempus Reparatum. 261pp

[153]   (with R. Meeson) *An Anglo-Saxon Watermill at Tamworth*. Research Report 83. Council for British Archaeology

[154]   (with L. Watts) (eds) *The Trinitarian Order in England*, by Margaret Gray, Tempus Reparatum 226. Oxford

[155]   (with I. Burrow) 'Archaeology is too important a subject not to be joked about', *Archaeological Review from Cambridge*, 11.2, 373-83

'Review: *The Origins of Somerset* by M. Costen', *Somerset Archaeology and Natural History*, 136

'Sutton Hoo', *Archaeology in Britain 1992* (Council for British Archaeology, York) 172-5

'Review: *Wharram Percy Deserted Medieval Village* by M.W. Beresford and J.G. Hurst (1990)', *Minerva* 1992

[156]   (with others) 'El Balneario de Fortuna y la Cueva Negra, (Fortuna, Murcia)', *Espacio, Tiempo y Forma*, Revista de la Facultad de Geografiá e Historia, Serie II 5, Historia Antigua, Murcia, 421-4

[157]   'Obituary. Ernest Greenfield', *British Archaeology*, CBA

1993
[158]   *Glastonbury*. English Heritage/Batsford. 144pp

[159]   'Review: *Tintagel: Arthur and Archaeology*, by C. Thomas (1993)', *Cornish Archaeology* 32 (1993), 178-80

1994

[160]   'Review article: *The Onymous Dead*, [re Spitalfields], by J. Reeve and M. Adams (1993)', *Antiquity* 68, 658-60

1995

[161]   'Anglo-Saxon and Later Whitby', in L.R. Hoey (ed), *Yorkshire Monasticism*. British Archaeological Association: 1-11

[162]   'Review: *The Uley Shrines*, by A. Woodward and P. Leach (1993)', *Early Medieval Europe* 4 (2): 246-7

[163]   'Review: *Tintagel: Arthur and Archaeology*, by C. Thomas (1993)', *Antiquaries Journal* book review supplement to vol. 75: 49-50

[164]   'Review article: 'The incomparable hall-mark of the Divine image', [re Jewbury] by J.M. Lilley *et al*, (1994), *Antiquity* 68 (no. 262, March 1995), 196-200

         'Obituary: Memories of Leslie Grinsell', *Retrospect* [Axbridge Archaeological Society], November 1995, 3-5

         'Review: *'Churches Built in Ancient Times'. Recent Studies in Early Christian Archaeology*, K. Painter (ed) (1994), *Medieval Archaeology 39:* 325-7

         'Obituary: Harold Taylor', *British Archaeology,* 10: 13

1996

[165]   'El so de Gran Bretaña en los tiempos que siguieron a la dominación Romana', in A. Gonzalez Blanco *et al*, *El Balneario Romana y La Cueva Negra de Fortuna (Murcia)*. Homenaje al Prof. Ph. Rahtz: 559-65

[166]   'Review: *Cadbury Castle, Somerset: The Early Medieval Europe* by L. Alcock (1995)', *Early Medieval Europe* 1996 5 (1), 84-5

         'Excavation Reports and BAR: A Personal View', in D. Davison and M. Henig (eds.), *British Archaeological Reports: Past, Present and Future*, Tempus Reparatum, 16-18, Oxford

         (with S. Roskams) 'Introduction', *Interpreting Stratigraphy*, 8: 1-8

[167]   'Reconstructing Stratigraphy within Burials: the use of the *planum* method', *Interpreting Stratigraphy*, 8: 36-8

         'Review: *Moorland Monuments*, by B. Vyner (ed) (1995)', *The Ryedale Historian,* 18

[168]   (with L. Watts and J. Grenville) *Archaeology at Kirkdale*, Supplement to *The Ryedale Historian*, 18. 19pp

[169]   (with M. Allison) 'A Medieval oven at Appleton-le-Moors', *The Ryedale Historian*, 18: 6-11

[170]   'Review article: *York Minster*, by M. Carver (ed.)', *Medieval Archaeology*, 40: 319-25

1997

[171]   (with S. Hirst) 'Liddington Castle and the Battle of Badon: Excavation and Research 1976', *Archaeological Journal*, 153 (for 1996), 1-59

[172]   (with L. Watts) *St Mary's Church, Deerhurst, Gloucestershire*, Research Report, Society of Antiquaries, 55, 247pp

'Review: *An Anglo-Saxon church at Raunds, Raunds Furnells: The Anglo-Saxon church and churchyard*, A. Boddington (1996)', *Church Archaeology*, 1, 64

'Review: *Archaeology: An Introduction* by K. Greene', *Antiquaries Journal*, 77 (1997), 413

[173]   (with L. Watts) 'Kirkdale Anglo-Saxon Minster', *Current Archaeology*, 155, 419-422

'Review: *Archeologie du Cimitiere Chrétien*, H. Galinie and E. Zadora-Rio (eds) 1996', *Medieval Archaeology 41:* 356-7

[174]   (with L. Watts, E. Okasha, J. Higgitt and S.A.J. Bradley) 'Kirkdale — the Inscriptions', *Medieval Archaeology*, 41: 51-99

1998

[175]   'Review: *Excavations on the Roman Villa at Beadlam, North Yorkshire*, David S. Neal, 1997', *The Ryedale Historian*, 19, 24-26

[176]   'Ghosts at Kirkdale', *The Ryedale Historian*, 19, 17-20

[177]   (with L. Watts) *Kirkdale Archaeology 1996-1997*, Supplement to *The Ryedale Historian*, 19, 16 pp

'Review: *Saint Patrick's Somerset Birthplace*, H. Jelley', *Retrospect* [Axbridge Archaeological Society], November 1998: 5-7

1999

[178]   'Cemeteries unfurnished', 'Cheddar', 'Glastonbury Abbey', 'Mills', 'Royal sites', in S. Lapidge *et al* (eds), *The Blackwell Encyclopaedia of Anglo-Saxon England*: 91-92, 100-102, 206-207, 313-314, 399-401. Oxford

[179]   'Learning by Doing', in J. Beavis and A. Hunt (eds), *Communicating Archaeology* [*festschrift* for Bill Putnam]: 11-19. Bournemouth University School of Conservation Sciences Occasional Paper 4

[180]   'Review: "Whithorn — urban monastery or monastic town?", *Whithorn and St Ninian,* P. Hill, 1997', *Church Archaeology* 3: 64-7

'150 Years of Somerset Archaeology', *Council for British Archaeology South West* 3: 4-6

2000

[181]   (with S. Hirst and S. Wright) *Cannington Cemetery*, Britannia Research Monograph 17, 516pp, London

[182]   'Anglo-Saxon Yorkshire — current research problems', in H. Geake and J. Kenny (ed.), *Early Deira*, Oxbow, Oxford 1-10

[183]   (with L. Watts) 'Appleton-le-Street: All Saints Church', *The Ryedale Historian* 20 (2000-2001), 24-31

[184]   '150 years of Somerset Archaeology: looking backwards and into the next millennium', in C.J. Webster (ed), *Somerset Archaeology* (Somerset County Council) 1-6

        'Ryedale Archaeology at the Millennium', *The Ryedale Historian* 20 (2000-2001), 4

        'Review: *Exodus to Arthur, Catastrophic Encounters with Comets,* by M. Baillie (1999)', *Council for British Archaeology South West,* 2000

        'Preface' to *Recording and Analysing Graveyards*, by H. Mytum. CBA and English Heritage, 2000

In press, forthcoming, or in preparation

[185]   (with S. Roskams, G. Milne, J.D. Richards and L. Watts) *Wharram Percy, The North Manor Area.* York University, Wharram Percy Monograph Series IX

[186]   (with L. Watts) *St Oswald's, Fulford, York*

[187]   'The Dipper Gravestones at Deerhurst'

[188]   'Glastonbury Tor — lynchets or earth sculpture?'

[189]   (with L. Watts) *Kirkdale excavations 1994-2000*

[190]   (with others) 'The Quaker burial ground at Helmsley'

[191]   *Deerhurst above and below ground.* Deerhurst Lecture 2000

        Review: *Mendip's Past – A Shared Inheritance* by P Stokes (1999), *Somerset Archaeology and Natural History*

Publications by others quoted

Alcock 1963 L. Alcock, *Dinas Powys*, University of Wales Press

Alcock 1971 L. Alcock, *Arthur's Britain*, Allen Lane, Penguin

Alcock 1972 L. Alcock, *'By South Cadbury is that Camelot'*, Thames and Hudson

Alcock 1995 L. Alcock, *Cadbury Castle, Somerset*, University of Wales Press

ApSimon 1964-5
> A.M. ApSimon, 'The Roman Temple on Brean Down, Somerset', *Proceedings of the University of Bristol Spelaeological Society*, 10.3, (1964-1965), 195-258

Baillie 1999   M.G.L. Baillie, *Arthur to Exodus. Catastrophic Encounters with Comets.* Batsford

Barker et al 1997
> Philip Barker et al, *The Baths Basilica, Wroxeter, Excavations 1966-90*; English Heritage Archaeological Reports 8

Bell 1990   M. Bell, *Brean Down Excavations 1983-1987*. Archaeological Reports 15. English Heritage

Blair 1996   J. Blair, 'Palaces or Minsters? Northampton and Cheddar Reconsidered', *Anglo-Saxon England 25:* 97-121

Carver ed. 1993
> M. Carver (ed), *In Search of Cult. Archaeological Investigations in Honour of Philip Rahtz.* Boydell Press

Hill 1997   Peter Hill, *Whithorn and St Ninian*, Sutton Publishing

Leech 1986   R.H. Leech, 'The Excavation of a Romano-Celtic Temple and a Later Cemetery at Lamyatt Beacon, Somerset', *Britannia* 17, 63-81

Millett 1996   M. Millett, *Roman Britain*, Batsford/English Heritage

Renfrew 1979
> C. Renfrew, 'Systems Collapse as Social Transformations: Catastrophe and Anastrophe in Early State Societies' in C. Renfrew and K.L. Cooke (eds), *Transformations – Mathematical Approaches to Cultural Change*, 481-4. London

Thomas 1993
> A.C. Thomas, *Tintagel, Arthur and Archaeology*, Batsford/English Heritage

Turner 1956   E.G. Turner, 'A Roman Writing Tablet from Somerset', *Journal of Roman Studies 46:* 115-118

Watts and Leach 1996
> L.R.J. Watts and P. Leach, *Henley Wood, Temples and Cemetery, Excavations 1962-69*, Research Report 99. Council for British Archaeology

Wedlake 1982
> W.J. Wedlake, *The Excavation of the Shrine of Apollo at Nettleton, Wiltshire 1956-1971*, Research Report 40, Society of Antiquaries

Woodward and Leach 1993
> nn Woodward and Peter Leach, *The Uley Shrines*, Archaeological Report 17. English Heritage

Index

Page numbers in **bold** denote illustrations